The Spokesman

A Ken Coates Reader

Edited by Tony Simpson and Tom Unterrainer

Published by Spokesman for the Bertrand Russell Peace Foundation

Ken Coates: Editor 1970 to 2010

Spokesman 158 **2024**

CONTENTS

Cover: The Avenue Coking Works near Chesterfield was one of the most polluted sites in Britain when it closed in 1992. As their Member of the European Parliament, Ken Coates worked with local residents to enlist the help of the European Environmental Commissioner to clean up the site. She, in turn, pressured the UK government to begin the necessary remediation. Hence, 'We Won!'

ISSN 1367 7748

ISBN 978 0 85124 9384

Subscriptions

Institutions £40.00 (ex UK)
£33.00 (UK)

Individuals £20.00 (UK)
£25.00 (ex UK)

A CIP catalogue record for this book is available from the British Library

Published by

The Bertrand Russell Peace Foundation Ltd,
5 Churchill Park,
Nottingham, NG4 2HF
England
Tel. 0115 9708318
email:
contact@russfound.org
www.spokesmanbooks.org
www.russfound.org

Ken Coates 1930 - 2010

Editorial

Ken Coates edited *The Spokesman* journal for four decades from its inception in 1970. He discussed at length with Bertrand Russell the purposes of *The Spokesman* and the contents of its inaugural issue in the months before Russell's death in early 1970. Russell died while that first issue was with the printers in Nottingham. There was only time to add this 'sad but proud statement: *The Spokesman*, founded by Bertrand Russell, is dedicated to carrying on his work'.

We dedicate this special issue of *The Spokesman* to the memory of Ken Coates and his lifelong activism, commitment and creativity. In large part, Ken continued Russell's work for peace, human right and social justice, but he was always his own man, as this diverse selection reveals. Our normal service, in these exceptionally turbulent times, will resume with the next issue of *The Spokesman*.

* * *

More than a decade ago, orders began arriving at Bertrand Russell House for copies of rather obscure titles by Ken Coates — *The Social Democrats: Those who left and those who stayed*, *Freedom and Fairness, Beyond Wage Slavery* and a succession of others. Each individual order was to be sent to a local school in Nottingham for the attention of Tom Unterrainer. In due course, Ken Fleet and I agreed to invite Tom for a chat. For many years, Ken Fleet worked side by side with Ken Coates in the Bertrand Russell Peace Foundation, the Institute for Workers' Control, European Nuclear Disarmament, in the European Parliament and other endeavours.

Tom came for a chat at Bertrand Russell House in Basford, where we were then based. In due course, he set about cataloguing Ken Coates' extensive political archive and compiling a bibliography of his many published works. These were to prove useful supplements to Ken Coates' substantial archives held at the University of Nottingham Manuscripts and Special Collections. Ken Coates taught at Nottingham University's Adult Education Department from about 1960 until 1989 when he was elected to the European Parliament.

This *Reader* is mainly Tom's selection. It's something of a miscellany mixing different aspects of Ken's life, work and interests. These were broad. We hope they will whet the appetite for further exploration of Ken Coates's rich and varied writings.

Tony Simpson

Introduction

The Canadian activist and scholar Leo Panitch has some responsibility for this selection of writings. “Who here has heard of Ken Coates?” he asked at the very start of his lecture on ‘The Making of Global Capitalism’ at the University of Nottingham in late 2012. Not a hand was raised. Panitch went on to explain that his last visit to Nottingham – in the early 1970s – had been made for the express purpose of visiting and talking to Coates. At the time, Panitch was engaged in doctoral research on the Labour Party and trade unions under the supervision of Ralph Miliband. Miliband – an old friend and associate of Coates – knew what he was doing when he sent Panitch to Nottingham. “I must find out about Ken Coates”, I thought to myself. Shortly after, I placed a book order. Tony Simpson explains in his editorial what happened subsequently.

If that first book order arose from a chance comment at a public lecture, the determination to read everything Coates had written was prompted by that first book. Whether Coates was tackling work and alienation, the possibility of socialism, democracy, the Labour Party, trade union issues or education, the essays in *Beyond Wage Slavery* had a major impact on my thinking. The impact was not simply because Coates was writing about things I was interested in – many people write about these things – but because the writing itself struck me as very different to anything I’d previously encountered. Ken Coates meant what he wrote and because he meant it, felt it, lived it and was determined to change it, the ideas leapt from the page and embedded themselves. I was to learn that the celebrated playwright, Trevor Griffiths, once commented that “nobody writes like Ken Coates”. This much is true. What is also true is that very few people managed to maintain decades of not just writing about politics but also campaigning, organising and agitating to achieve fundamental change. How did Coates manage it? What compelled him to keep at it?

The May 1952 edition of *World Youth*, magazine of the World Federation of Democratic Youth (WFDY), features a statement titled ‘What do the young miners of England aim at?’. It opens: “We young miners of Bilsthorpe in Nottingham, England, welcome the decision ... to call a conference of young workers and students throughout the world in defence of their rights.” The second paragraph of this short article begins: “We think that these problems would get nearer to solution if we could get together to talk them over.” Ken Coates features as one of the signatories to the statement.

By 1952, the 22-year-old Ken Coates was already a 'dissident' within the ranks of the Communist movement, with which the WFDY and their conferences were linked. For instance, Coates sympathised with the Yugoslavs in the wake of the 1948 Tito-Stalin split. Further, the arrest, torture and eventual show-trial and execution in November 1952 of Rudolf Slánský and other Czech communist leaders appalled and disturbed him. He broke with the Communist Party of Great Britain in the aftermath of these and other events, some four years before the Hungarian revolution was crushed in 1956 and the subsequent mass exodus of CP members. He was a pioneer in this respect, as in others.

Coates's politics and his 'dissidence' were forged not only down the pit. "I came from a middle-class background" he informed the *Sunday Telegraph* in May 1970. During the 1945 General Election, Coates stood as the Communist Party candidate in a mock election at his West Sussex grammar school. He won. "We're all communists here" Coates informed a perplexed and troubled school governor in the aftermath of the vote. So how did this precocious, middle-class, grammar-school boy end up in the Derbyshire and Nottinghamshire coalfields? "I didn't want to go to Malaya to kill Communists" he explained. The 18-years-old Coates refused to serve in the armed forces of a waning colonial power in what it named the 'Malayan Emergency'. He was on the side of those engaged in the 'Anti-British National Liberation War', as the Malayans called their struggle. He was on the side of those seeking to liberate themselves. This was an enduring commitment.

A further indication of Coates's admiration for those who struggle to liberate themselves can be found in the concluding paragraph of the article on Algeria, included in this volume. Of those he met in the aftermath of that country's self-liberation from French colonial rule, Coates wrote: "Everywhere we met this: a hard, bright dedication that could be felt, touched, and shared; that could not in any sense be avoided."

Reading Coates's works left me with a similar impression: a hard, bright dedication to human liberation is found on every page. This dedication, together with the impulse to solve problems by getting "people together" are at the centre of the third major – and enduring – element of Coates' politics. 'We haven't long', the first article in this volume, is an argument for young people – students, in the main – to come together to debate and discuss the emerging problems of capitalism in a 'welfare state'. The article ranges over questions related to the Labour Party, the risk of nuclear war, culture and much else. The main theme, however, is identical with the third major element. It is expressed in the following quote: "... democracy is a process: it is either expanding always, or it is over and done with." That the final article in this collection – written some fifty years later – asks whether democracy is "growing or dying", attests to the centrality of this concern.

Ken Coates's commitment to liberation, the centrality of democracy and his repeated efforts at solving problems by getting people together are evidenced in these pages and throughout his life. Coates did not simply write, although doing so is an honourable exercise. Much of his writing was done in the service of his commitments and actions, and to encourage others to adopt at least some of them.

To take one example, it would be possible to fill several volumes with Coates's writings on workers' control. In the pages of these volumes – with articles stretching over a period of decades, from the 1950s onwards – you would encounter basic arguments for workers' control, its history, essays on others who positively considered the matter, articles dealing with specific technical aspects of English Law in relation to the idea, commentaries on parliamentary debates, debates with those who discounted the importance of workers' control and much else. In total, these writings would represent a significant intellectual labour, but they would not tell the whole story. Alongside the thinking and writing came the organising: the years of preparatory seminars, workshops and meetings that eventually resulted in the formation of the Institute for Workers' Control in 1968 and all the subsequent activity and its real-world impact. Much the same could be said for subsequent initiatives, such as European Nuclear Disarmament in the 1980s and the campaign to rehabilitate Nikolai Bukharin, which commenced in the 1970s.

When Ken Coates was first elected to the European Parliament, in 1989, a similar pattern was established. Coates was, of course, a diligent and attentive parliamentarian but these efforts – with the assistance of a team including Ken Fleet and Tony Simpson – were augmented by a series of campaigns, including for full employment in Europe. At the same time, the opportunities opened by the European Parliament were put to work for his constituents around a series of issues including mine safety, environmental pollution and much else. Meanwhile, Coates worked with others to achieve an expansion of European democracy in the face of a series of social, economic and political challenges operating at the transnational level. His eventual expulsion from the Labour Party in 1998 did nothing to diminish these efforts, though it did deprive him of the opportunity to continue parliamentary work after the 1999 election.

Having mentioned the Labour Party, it is necessary to note that this

Reader contains none of Coates' writings directly addressing the history, activities and political eruptions within the Party. As with the other questions and campaigns which he addresses, the articles, pamphlets and essays on the Labour Party could fill several volumes in addition to the numerous books Coates published, starting with *The Crisis of British Socialism* (Spokesman, 1972) and ending with *The Blair Revelation* (co-authored with Michael Barratt Brown, Spokesman, 1996). Readers eager to engage with Coates' writings on the Labour Party and other issues can consult the Spokesman website.

Another aspect worth addressing is that of the 22 articles re-published in this volume, only one of them is a joint effort: 'Towards Self-Management', written together with Tony Topham. Coates and Topham formed a prolific writing team and their joint work ranges from short articles to the 900+ pages of *The Making of the Labour Movement: The Formation of the Transport & General Workers' Union 1870-1922*. Coates also wrote with Michael Barratt Brown and some of others with whom he collaborated.

One major omission from this volume is Ken Coates's writings about Bertrand Russell. These range from the internationalism of Bertrand Russell, to some significant introductions to Russell's books including *Common Sense and Nuclear Warfare*. Ken was invited to give the Peace Lecture on 'Working with Bertrand Russell' at McMaster University in Canada, which holds the Bertrand Russell Archive. It is to be hoped that such a volume may be compiled in due course.

The final essay in this Reader includes the following commitment: "while we have breath left, we shall resist these embodiments of militarism [NATO and the Military Industrial Complex], and continue to devote our energies to laying the foundations of the peaceful commonwealth which will come into existence with the abolition of war." This volume resonates with such commitment, along with the intimately connected endeavour to extend democracy. The Bertrand Russell Peace Foundation, which Ken Coates chaired for four decades, exists to further such commitments.

Tom Unterrainer
www.spokesmanbooks.org

Ken Coates at work, circa 1958

We haven't long

Ken Coates

Published as 'Chance for NALSO' in Clarion *Summer 1958.* Clarion *was a magazine edited by a succession of university students, many of whom went on to play active roles in politics, literature and the arts. In this article, Ken Coates promotes an upcoming 'summer discussion camp' titled: Beyond the Welfare State.*

Organisations are usually boring: even when people in them are interesting, they tend to grow an organisation-face that dominates them, so that they look as if they're all shirt and no stuffing. I agree with Sean O'Casey, who once said that there's no man who has the right to be proud of an organisation, although there are plenty of organisations which ought to be proud of a man. On the other hand, I've been taught, and accept, that man is made in his social environment, of which he is a part; and that his organisations, from the family on, teach him to make himself as good a self as they can. Today, when our organisations are manifestly not making very good selves out of any of us, and bid fair to blow us all up into the bargain, it is of the greatest importance that we not only have a socialist youth and student organisation which is as efficient as possible, but that we understand the real meaning of efficiency. I contend that political efficiency is not a question of string and paper-clips, but of ideas. If NALSO [National Association of Labour Student Organisations] has not been triumphantly successful of late, this is far less to do with whether the secretary answers his letters the day he gets them, than with whether the letters he writes back contain things exciting enough to be worth waiting for. The annual conference of NALSO has clearly recognised the job of this generation as being the disarming of its governments and the fashioning of a society in its own more beautiful image. So what follows is certainly not a digression.

Old Jerry Bentham has been pickled a long time now; but at least he's preserved out of reach of the public nose. The society which has taken his image, even in its fabian-paternalist pyjamas, is an unencased abomination, looking more and more like a character in one of Samuel Beckett's novels. You remember the retching and stinking pilgrim's progress of Molloy, crawling through the forest to his city? Stuck in a ditch in sight of the polis, Molloy may bring tears to our eyes: but unless we develop organisations capable of allowing us to stride on beyond him, we shall unquestionably rot with him. Molloy's society is wrong just because it is divided. A society of organisers and organised invariably is wont to become a society of organisers against organised. Democracy is about overcoming this difficulty: but democracy is a process: it is either expanding always, or it is over and done with. Today's democrats, the socialists, must by their very nature reach out to the organised, lend them their strength, help them to become their own organisers. But in England there is only one road to the organised: and that road is the Labour Party. (A Labour Party which itself is significantly imbued with the Big-Brother Organiser-Mrs Webb mentality.) If you like, Mrs Webb levies toll at the near end of the road, so that many of us, from Declarationeers to ordinary rebels, feel disinclined to walk thereon. It is this situation which has so long rendered immobile the young Left: for the only other little alleyway which has presented itself has similarly been fronted with a bureaucratic toll-house: Mr Pollitt, not Mrs W clipping its tickets. Both sets of tickets are marked: 'The Vocation of Leadership'. This vocation, we feel, is a racket: many of us have ground out a place for ourselves at universities although we originate from the working class: and we know that we are just the lucky ones. They can't sell the 'leader' business to us: we've been on the other side of the counter. We have learnt the vital lesson that the only kind of leading that is tolerable is teaching, in which the leader holds before himself the objective of making himself redundant. And so in universities the radicals moan, or pay reluctant homage to the petty figures at the tollgates, through the Student Labour Federation and NALSO. In such circumstances there is little wonder that neither body is particularly effective. NALSO, we discovered at our last conference, has fallen down in that it has failed to find literature, speakers, and other amenities for its constituent clubs. Angry, some of them switch paths, affiliate to SLF, sample the superior philistinism of the straight gate.

What to do? Of course, the new NALSO EC must provide efficient services: pamphlets, speakers, schools. But it is no use questing after abstract efficiency, for if we see this as our solution, our more efficient machine will go efficiently nowhere. Unless our Labour Party can be made to draw back from blindly plodding on to 1984, we're all lost. We must make a coffin for Molloy, and the only thing to hand for boards is the tollgate of Mrs W. NALSO then must provide demolition equipment, because since the end of the war, the incantation of the formula 'socialism' has not proved enough. The chanting, loud as you like, has not so far even raised a blister on the bureaucratic paint. But the appearance of *The Insiders* has. When we begin to use our heads as well as our larynxes, the moral is we can invest our formulae with meaning, strength, consuming fire. Your ticket-man has invented no machine to punch holes in ideas: only better ideas can do that. What *Universities and Left Review* has begun, NALSO must help to grow deeper, to spread, to flourish. For me, if we fail in this and succeed in everything else, we shall still be sterile. So, we must run not one, but many schools – effective schools in which the most articulate partisans of the left put their viewpoint and are cross-examined by us. *Industry and Society* must defend itself against *The Insiders*, and both against all comers. The unilateralists must meet Strachey's arguments, battle must be done between the most powerful expressions of contending opinions. Our debates must be more informed, more thorough, more strenuous, that the ideas formed in them may usefully grow into actions.

And why not begin on the grand scale? Why not, this Autumn, a week's camp, a giant intervarsity presessional conference, in which together, in meetings and seminars, we not only examine the logic of disarmament, the merits of 'new thinking', the rival schemes for workers' control of industry, and all the other questions which preoccupy our annual conferences; but also examine the Osbornes, the Tynans, the Lessings, the Lindsay Andersons, the thought-formers of the radical young, and consider the culture we want to see arise among us? We could go over the Hoggart thesis with its proponents, and ask the *Daily Mirror* to defend itself in open court among us. If we mix together all the struggling counter-proposals, let loose a real and wild debate at the very beginning of the academic year, who knows what may come from the mixing as it continues? The decisions of such a contest are the property of those who make them. But if we can show that socialism means thirst for truth, means keen inquiry, as well as a vote against the rent act, then we may even multiply the votes against the rent act. We will also multiply our numbers.

Thinking alone will pull up no trees. But thoughtful tree-pulling is easier than the other kind. And what begins in universities never stays there unless it is barren. The first among fabians, who saw the world rounder than most of his colleagues, wisely said, apropos of the special breed of cultural paternalists:

> ' – what we want is not music for the people, but bread for the people, rest for the people, immunity from robbery and scorn for the people, hope for them, enjoyment, equal respect and consideration, life and aspiration, instead of

> drudgery and despair. When we get that I imagine that the people will make a tolerable music for themselves, even if all Beethoven's scores perish in the interim,'

Any man who thinks this want has been met in the welfare state is as morally blind as he is aesthetically deaf. The culture of the *Daily Mirror* is the culture of people locked all day in monotony, living in smog, 'educated' forty in a class by harassed teachers, reared to recognise Man's Holy Grail in Her Majesty's Mint. How can their politics rise higher? We must find out: the need to do so weighs heavy on us, for 'if we do not, we shall all blow to hell …' Of one thing, though, I would throw out a guess: that we shall discover, even if all Beethoven's scores perish in the interim, that when the people can make a tolerable music for themselves, they will make for themselves a tolerable polity.

But we haven't got all that long.

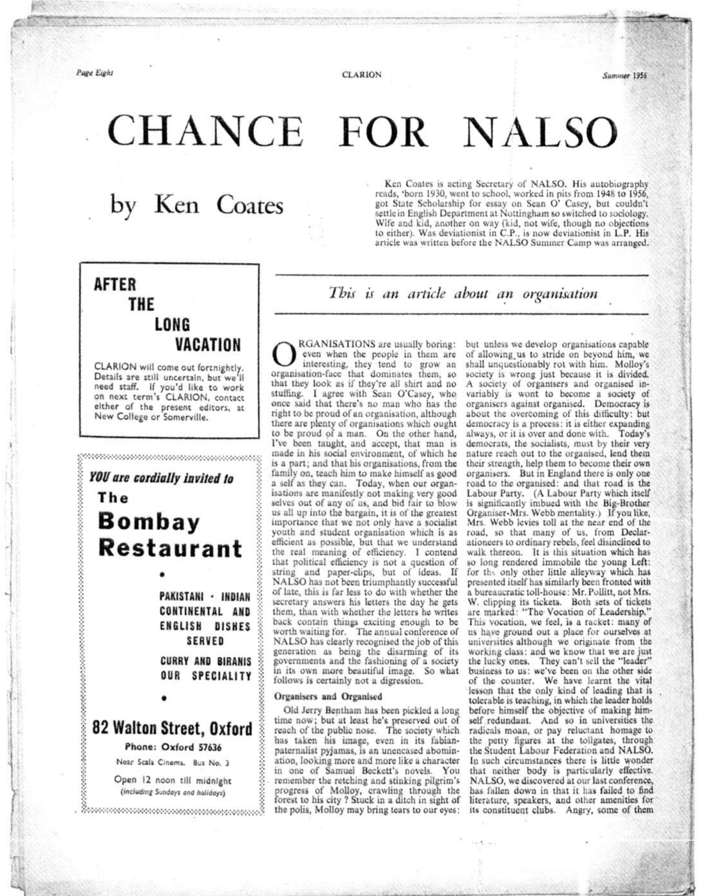

Page Eight CLARION Summer 1958

CHANCE FOR NALSO

by Ken Coates

Ken Coates is acting Secretary of NALSO. His autobiography reads, 'born 1930, went to school, worked in pits from 1948 to 1956, got State Scholarship for essay on Sean O' Casey, but couldn't settle in English Department at Nottingham so switched to sociology. Wife and kid, another on way (kid, not wife, though no objections to either). Was deviationist in C.P., is now deviationist in L.P. His article was written before the NALSO Summer Camp was arranged.

This is an article about an organisation

ORGANISATIONS are usually boring: even when the people in them are interesting, they tend to grow an organisation-face that dominates them, so that they look as if they're all shirt and no stuffing. I agree with Sean O'Casey, who once said that there's no man who has the right to be proud of an organisation, although there are plenty of organisations which ought to be proud of a man. On the other hand, I've been taught, and accept, that man is made in his social environment, of which he is a part; and that his organisations, from the family on, teach him to make himself as good a self as they can. Today, when our organisations are manifestly not making very good selves out of any of us, and bid fair to blow us all up into the bargain, it is of the greatest importance that we not only have a socialist youth and student organisation which is as efficient as possible, but that we understand the real meaning of efficiency. I contend that political efficiency is not a question of string and paper-clips, but of ideas. If NALSO has not been triumphantly successful of late, this is far less to do with whether the secretary answers his letters the day he gets them, than with whether the letters he writes back contain things exciting enough to be worth waiting for. The annual conference of NALSO has clearly recognised the job of this generation as being the disarming of its governments and the fashioning of a society in its own more beautiful image. So what follows is certainly not a digression.

Organisers and Organised

Old Jerry Bentham has been pickled a long time now; but at least he's preserved out of reach of the public nose. The society which has taken his image, even in its fabian-paternalist pyjamas, is an unencased abomination, looking more and more like a character in one of Samuel Beckett's novels. You remember the retching and stinking pilgrim's progress of Molloy, crawling through the forest to his city? Stuck in a ditch in sight of the polis, Molloy may bring tears to our eyes: but unless we develop organisations capable of allowing us to stride on beyond him, we shall unquestionably rot with him. Molloy's society is wrong just because it is divided. A society of organisers and organised invariably is wont to become a society of organisers against organised. Democracy is about the overcoming of this difficulty: but democracy is a process: it is either expanding always, or it is over and done with. Today's democrats, the socialists, must by their very nature reach out to the organised, lend them their strength, help them to become their own organisers. But in England there is only one road to the organised: and that road is the Labour Party. (A Labour Party which itself is significantly imbued with the Big-Brother Organiser-Mrs. Webb mentality.) If you like, Mrs. Webb levies toll at the near end of the road, so that many of us, from Declarationeers to ordinary rebels, feel disinclined to walk thereon. It is this situation which has so long rendered immobile the young Left: for the only other little alleyway which has presented itself has similarly been fronted with a bureaucratic toll-house: Mr. Pollitt, not Mrs. W. clipping its tickets. Both sets of tickets are marked: "The Vocation of Leadership." This vocation, we feel, is a racket: many of us have ground out a place for ourselves at universities although we originate from the working class: and we know that we are just the lucky ones. They can't sell the "leader" business to us: we've been on the other side of the counter. We have learnt the vital lesson that the only kind of leading that is tolerable is teaching, in which the leader holds before himself the objective of making himself redundant. And so in universities the radicals moan, or pay reluctant homage to the petty figures at the tollgates, through the Student Labour Federation and NALSO. In such circumstances there is little wonder that neither body is particularly effective. NALSO, we discovered at our last conference, has fallen down in that it has failed to find literature, speakers, and other amenities for its constituent clubs. Angry, some of them

AFTER THE LONG VACATION

CLARION will come out fortnightly. Details are still uncertain, but we'll need staff. If you'd like to work on next term's CLARION, contact either of the present editors, at New College or Somerville.

Algeria

Ken Coates

A common sight in Algiers not so long ago—French soldiers stop a veiled woman and ask for her pass at the entry to the Casbah. Now all is peaceful, but the new Algeria faces many problems.

First published as 'They Help Algeria to Face the Future' in the Nottingham Evening Post and News, *3 July 1963 and subsequently in* News of NALSO, *October 1963.*

When our party arrived in Algiers we expected chaos. We had been forewarned that there was a lack of skilled people, and that since the majority of the French administrators and technicians had rushed back to France as soon as independence was declared there had been disorganisation on a grand scale.

To our surprise, on the surface these warnings were much exaggerated. Cars and buses crowded the main streets almost as they do in a European city: the driving was a bit rough, but that was all. Shops were open and seemed well stocked. The children running along the pavements looked well dressed and adequately fed.

Only an occasional ruined building, bombed by OAS terrorists, and the strident political slogans daubed on every wall, reminded us that the place had really been at war for seven years, that more than a million people had been killed, that if we looked deeper we could expect to find tens of thousands of young widows and hundreds of thousands of orphans.

We had come to a European conference to organise non-governmental aid to Algeria, and within half an hour of leaving the airport we found ourselves being unloaded at the new University City, a handsome complex of modern buildings left behind by the French. Besides about twenty English people, editors, MPs, teachers, technicians, we discovered big contingents of people from France, Italy, Belgium, Holland, Denmark, Austria and Germany. There was a smaller group from Ireland, a number of Spanish and Portuguese exiles, and a handful of Russian trade union leaders. Our joint purpose was to hear from the Algerians what technical help they needed: how many technicians were wanted by the different ministries, what vital equipment and staff were lacked by the health services, what subjects could not be taught in the schools and technical colleges for want of teachers: in a word, how best we could use our energies at home in an effort to help Algeria to reorganise her battered economy and society.

For the next few days we were kept very busy, cross-questioning the ministers of the Government in a whole series of commissions, drawing up a balance-sheet of needs, and working out a division of labour. The British could train 200 Algerian nurses, the Belgians would fit out a mobile clinic for the rural areas, the Portuguese could recruit so many qualified doctors, and so on. We met the President, Ben Bella, three times in those days, and questioned him in detail about the policies of his administration and his ideas about the help needed from Europe. We argued and finally agreed the texts of our joint appeals to the peoples of our different countries.

During this time we formed a very clear picture, a terrible picture, of the problems of New Algeria. Thousands of villages had been destroyed, agricultural machines had been wrecked, millions of people were unemployed or under-employed, there is a vacuum in supplies of capital, a tremendous rate of illiteracy. The list was long and heart-breaking. But all this was an abstract picture, a catalogue on paper. It was only after the conference was over and we were free to wander about and to visit the countryside, that the figures came to life and the abstractions coalesced into the many miseries of real, living people.

As we went about the incredibly beautiful city of Algiers, stopping to look at the view at each corner of the hairpin bends which coil around down into the centre of the town, built as it is on a huge cliffside, with more steps than people, and as we gazed at the lush hotels and chic Parisian shops of the best streets, we met the beggars.

Boys and girls of three and four, barefoot, perhaps urged on by an experienced and crafty Fagin every day of eight years old, would clutch at us, hold out their cupped hands, tilt their heads to one side, and wait. An hour introduced us to a dozen or more of them, and all our change had gone. We wanted to bring them home; to look after them, but always there were more of them. Perhaps they were orphans. Perhaps their fathers were out of work. We didn't know: what we did know was that there is no National Assistance Board in Algiers, no dole, and no chance of jobs and schools for everyone until huge and unselfish technical and monetary help has flowed into Algeria. Some more enterprising, or richer, children peddled chewing gum and trinkets around the cafes. A few sat at shoe-shine stands. Most of the shoeshine boys had already been gathered into an orphan school which the Government had opened a few weeks ago, and which some of our people saw. They were deeply moved.

We walked through the casbah, seeing the scars of bombing, of OAS raids, looking at the thousands of slogans for independence, and the flies. Many inhabitants of this warren have already been rehoused in the smart flats abandoned by the French. Many remain, and new flats will be needed in thousands if they are ever to live decently, in a way which measures up to their extreme dignity and heroism, so amply called upon throughout the war and the subsequent OAS terror.

We also visited farms outside the city, saw the hovels, which the RSPCA in England would not permit a sow to live in, in which the farmworkers had lived until a month or two before we came. Of wattle and mud, with mud floors; without chimneys or windows, these hutments belonged to the Bronze Age; but their occupants had worked behind powerful tractors and elaborate harvesters, had kept up with mechanical spinners and been ordered about from Landrovers; and they lived a few hundred yards from a palace, with one hundred and fifty elegant rooms, which belonged to the then owner, a famous political figure in France. If he ever grows a conscience, he will cut his own throat.

It was against this background, of shanty-towns and homeless street dwellers, of soul-grinding squalor and poverty, that we formed our judgment of the new nation we were visiting. But the Algerians have one immeasurable asset which I have not described. This is their truly astonishing community spirit, their idealism and unselfishness. Everywhere we met this: a hard, bright dedication that could be felt, touched, and shared; that could not in any sense be avoided. About this I should like to write again.

EVENING POST AND NEWS, WEDNESDAY, JULY 3, 1963

THEY HELP ALGERIA TO FACE THE FUTURE

by KEN COATES

WHEN our party arrived in Algiers we expected chaos. We had been forewarned that there was a critical lack of skilled people, and that since the majority of the French administrators and technicians had rushed back to France as soon as independence was declared, there had been disorganisation on a grand scale. To our surprise, on the surface these warnings were much exaggerated.

Ken Coates, a lecturer at Nottingham University, wrote this article on his return from a recent visit to Algeria, where he attended an international conference called to discuss aid for the new republic.

British help

University City

Come to life

No dole

Bronze-Age huts

A common sight in Algiers not so long ago—French soldiers stop a veiled woman and ask for her pass at the entry to the Casbah. Now all is peaceful, but the new Algeria faces many problems.

The Dirty War in Mr. Wilson

Or How He Stopped Worrying About Vietnam and Learned to Love the Dollar

by Ken Coates

Vietnam Solidarity Campaign 1/-

The Dirty War in Mr. Wilson

Ken Coates

This was the first pamphlet published by the Vietnam Solidarity Campaign in 1966. Ken Coates had been writing and campaigning on Vietnam for some years before the launch of the VSC, of which he was an original National Council member. As Ken recalled in 1970, Labour "kicked me out in 1965, after I raised hell at the party conference over the policy on Vietnam. I was president of the Nottingham City Labour Party, but they expelled me. Unconstitutionally, mind you. Some of the key people at the top of the Labour Party were happy to quieten me." (Sunday Telegraph, 31/5/1970)

Vietnam is a poor country. If you live in the predominantly rural south, you can expect to live for 35 years, provided you are not killed by a lazy dog or 'non-toxic chemicals'. Before the Americans invaded, before the French had been driven out, even before the Japanese had been defeated, the Vietnamese peasants knew Death very intimately. They lived in hunger. They knew their powerful enemies: the absentee landlords who switched their backers with the fluctuations of the international balance of power, but who never for one moment bridled their appetites or let up on their carnivorous extortion; the usurers who swallowed well over half the harvest either as rent or interest; the imperial entrepreneurs who laid down millions of rubber trees across vast plantations and across the bodies and the sweated labour of thousands of conscribed coolies: these they knew well, but even better they knew their police and their soldiers, who had all the mangling arsenal of civilised disciplinary force at their disposal.[1]

But the peasants of Indo-China were not the only people to live in privation: and even today they are by no means the most hungry, or the most nakedly oppressed, peoples of the world. Throughout South-East Asia, over half the peasants' income goes to buy his food, and even then he consumes an average of 2,000 calories a day against our 3,500. While we are eating 40 or 50 grams of animal protein a day, the Asian peasant gets 5 to 10. While we burn 10,000 pounds of fuels each, every year, he burns two or three hundred, much of which is animal dung that could be vitally useful to him in fertilising his land. Fifteen per cent of Indian babies die before they are one year old. In England, two per cent die. In Burma, Pakistan, Indonesia, and India, the income per head of the population, in 1958, was sixty dollars or less. Formosa and Thailand had a per capita income of between sixty and one hundred dollars.[2] Yet in the West, every educated adolescent knows that Vietnam is a desperately poor country, and that its social problems demand solution. The American President and the British Prime Minister find it expedient to talk of extensive programmes of economic aid to Vietnam, after the war. Much less is heard of the affairs of even poorer countries in the same region. Why should this be so?

The answer is a dismal one. Western states are not interested in hungry people, except when Christmas brings the season for free publicity on famine relief advertisements. Hunger, in the rich countries, has a claim for attention only when it presents a political problem.

This is not entirely a strange condition to British political experience. Aneurin Bevan, in his most interesting tract, *In Place of Fear*, recounts a strong parallel case:

> "One experience remains vividly in my memory. While the miners were striking in 1926 a great many people were moved to listen to their case. Certain high ecclesiastical dignitaries even went so far as to offer to mediate between the mine-owners and the miners. They were convinced that the terms the coal-owners were attempting to impose on the miners were unreasonable, and would entail much suffering and poverty for hundreds of thousands of miners' homes. Their efforts failed. The miners were beaten and driven back to work under disgraceful conditions.
>
> For years these conditions continued. But were those high Church dignitaries moved to intervene then? Not at all. For them the problem was solved. It had never consisted in the suffering of the miners, but in the fact that the miners were still able to struggle and therefore to create a problem for the rest of the community. The problem was not their suffering but their struggle. Silent pain evokes no response."[3]

In South East Asia, now, as in South Wales before the Second World War, silent pain evokes no response. The suffering of the poor, in Bevan's compelling words, is ignored "while they lack the power and status to insist on alleviation."[4]

The electric fact about Vietnam is that the people of that country have found power and status, in the organs which they have created in a most ferocious and desperate struggle. The National Liberation Front, like the South Wales Miners' Federation, has taught a whole generation of brutally oppressed people to stand up, to demand and begin to create a society in which they can begin to become persons, and cease to be chattels. The Front takes among the people ideas of direct democracy and economic reform. In the words of an American reporter, who asked a Mekong Delta peasant why so many people support the "Vietcong": "They seize the rice fields from the absent owner's and divide the land among the working farmers."[5]

It is understandable that the American Government, which has vast imperial interests in every continent, which defends the ownership by American corporations of approximately 60% of the world's economic resources, and which depends for its influence upon the most abject and corrupt politicians drawn from the most capricious and backward-looking social milieu of the countries over which it holds sway, should react with fierce apprehension against movements of land reform and national independence. It is far less understandable that the British Labour Movement, which has a long history of opposition to imperialism, based upon the clear realisation that British Imperial exploitation centred on the same elite corps of financiers and businessmen which has inflicted such pain on British trade unions, should find itself today hoist with a leadership prepared to endorse almost every action of President Johnson.

Up to October 1965, 170,000 Vietnamese civilians had been slaughtered in the President's war. 800,000 had been tortured; 5,000 had been burnt alive; 100,000 had suffered poisoning by chemical weapons; while unknown numbers had been disembowelled, castrated, raped, eviscerated.[6] Ears, strung in a grisly necklace, swung across the walls of an installation of the Southern puppet Government which was visited by the *New York Herald Tribune* correspondent last year.[7] The troops which are responsible for these intrepid and valorous assaults on Vietnamese peasants are paid out of U.S. military appropriations.[8] If the peasants kill back, when they can, this is hardly surprising: but when the tally of carnage in this unholy American crusade is carefully elaborated, on the one side will be found discriminate casualties, victims of a war of resistance: on the other will be piled, in an abysmal hecatomb, the legions of those genocidally exterminated by the most advanced and civilised techniques available to a race which is totally, devilishly skilled in mechanical killing.[9] In order not to see this, anyone even slightly acquainted with the news from Vietnam would need to be steeped in the vulgar, philistine bigotry of a Michael Stewart, or morally null, a dollar-neuter like the capricious, ego-centred moral eunuch upon whom he fawns.[10]

For those who are interested in understanding the astonishing abdication of the British Labour Government from the most elementary pretension to a humane polity, it is important to distinguish between the four-square stupidity of the Foreign Secretary, which is a characteristically honest response shared by a fairly numerous body of the more narrow-minded functionaries of the Labour Party, and which could not be less cunning and guileful than it is; and the truly gargantuan duplicity of the Prime Minister, for whom a straight line is the shortest breach between two promises. Mr Stewart is as incapable of telling a lie as he is of seeing the plain truth before his nose. Mr. Wilson, on the contrary, does not tell lies: he lives them, he balances one against another, he juxtaposes, juggles and transfigures them, he banks them and transcends them with more perfect lies. Lies are meat and drink to him: or any moment they maybe also raiment, and all that England will await is that childish voice from the crowd to whisper that the emperor is naked.

It may seem that these are fairly strong words. By analysing the record of the premier, however, it can quickly be seen that they are valid. And nowhere does this become more starkly apparent than on the record in respect of Vietnam.

Mr. Wilson first became apparent as a man of the left when he resigned from the Attlee administration, in 1951, together with Nye Bevan and John Freeman. In a pamphlet entitled *One Way Only* which was published by *Tribune*, the three introduced a five-point programme for the Labour Party. This demanded a "supreme effort to negotiate a settlement with Russia in the next two years"; asserted the right of the "underprivileged colonial people" to complete "their social revolutions" and the duty of British socialists to assist these; insisted that the rearmament of the Atlantic powers should "be subordinate to a World Plan for Mutual Aid"; urged the financing of rearmament in Britain not by inflation "but under a system of socialist controls"; and stood firm on the principle that it was "not only possible, but desirable and necessary, to embark upon a series of measures designed to carry us forward towards the establishment of a Socialist society in Britain." Although this programme was conceived in the heart of the cold war, when Stalin's rule in Russia struck not only loathing, but also fear and irrational suspicion into the calculations of western liberals and socialists, so that it was predicated on the assumption of a possible Russian attack,[11] which retrospectively can be easily seen to have been absurd: nonetheless: it maintained one very clear commitment which today seems entirely subversive, honest and commendable. The colonial revolution, for the co-authors of this pamphlet, required unstinting support and solidarity.

"Is the aim", they asked the western politicians, "to fight poverty, or a plan to purchase mercenaries in another kind of war? Is the aim to destroy malaria and provide tractors or to protect the landlords and prop up feudal regimes? Chiang Kai Shek on Formosa, saved by American guns and subsidies, is a symbol of all Asia. His mere presence there could destroy the effectiveness of America's aid plans even if they were ten times larger."[12]

"Against the background of world poverty" Mr. Wilson and his co-thinkers continued,

> "and the surging discontent which it is now producing among more than half the peoples of the world, the Western nations have so far produced no policy to match the magnitude of events. That discontent, and the revolt or revolution which it brings in its train, are as natural as the revolt of Englishmen in the seventeenth century against the claims of Charles I, or the revolt of Frenchmen in the eighteenth century against the luxury of King Louis' court, or the revolt of the American colonists against the blind tyranny of George III. It is born of the same spirit which inspired the Chartists and the early Socialist Movement in Britain. It will not be put down."[13]

"The only reputable policy for socialists", they concluded, "is to ally ourselves with the forces of social revolution, and to prove by our deeds that our aim is not dominion but honourable partnership."[14]

It is not difficult for socialists to endorse these words. They are both realistic and morally sound. They represent, in the Prime Ministers' words, "the spirit of the imperishable philosophy of Nye Bevan."[15] Alas, they also represent the letter of the rather more transient philosophy of Harold Wilson.

What was Bevan's philosophy, to which the British Premier finds it expedient to defer? It was above all a socialist philosophy. Bevan was not a utopian, and he could compromise in order to make what he considered to be worthwhile gains for his viewpoint. Some of his compromises caused apprehension on the left: but his basic commitment can easily be shown to have separated him by a gulf of lightyears from the totally unscrupulous opportunism of his epigone in Downing Street. Here, for instance, is his assessment of the overall background to the Cold War, spoken at the Labour Party Conference immediately after his resignation:

> "I am now 53 years, of age. I was coming to adult life at the end of the 1914-18 war. I remember so well what happened when the Russian Revolution occurred. I remember the miners, when they read that the Czarist tyranny had been overthrown, rushing to meet each other with tears streaming down their cheeks, shaking hands and saying: 'At last it has happened.' Let us remember

> in 1951 that the revolution of 1917 came to the working class of Great Britain, not as a social disaster, but as one of the most emancipating events in the history of mankind. Let us also remember that the Soviet revolution would not have been so distorted, would not have ended in a tyranny, would not have resulted in a dictatorship, would not now be threatening the peace of mankind, had it not been for the behaviour of Churchill and the Tories of that time. Do not forget that in the early days when that great mass of backward people were trying to find their way to the light, were trying to lift themself from age-long penury and oppression, they were diverted from their objectives and thrown back into the darkness, not by the malignancy of Stalin at first, but the action and the malignancy of Churchill, the City of London, New York and all the rest of the capitalist world.
>
> The reasons for fear in the world at the moment have never come from the poor people, whenever they are trying to improve their lot. They have always come from those who are trying to hold them down ... That is why, now that the Orient is in the same kind of ferment, we do not want China, we do not want Indonesia and we do not want the middle east to be driven into the same kind of totalitarian tyranny that the Tories drove the Soviet revolution into 1917."[16]

Bevan was mistaken about the predatory nature of Stalin's government,[17] but even this mistake did not bind him to the essential truth about the colonial upheaval which is the major social fact of our time: where hungry people found 'the power and the status' to resist the anti-social groupings whose control of their resources engendered hunger, Bevan knew only one impulse, which was that of the South Wales Miners who rushed out on to the grey street in tears of joy at the news of the great Russian Revolution. In his morality, this was a primary response. For this reason, he embraced as his own the cause of the Chinese Revolution, in words which today sound as sharp as they were when he uttered them.

"Everyone here knows" he told the House of Commons –

> "at least every miner, railwayman and agricultural worker knows very well that if he were in China he would be a communist peasant. He would not be a Chiang Kai Shek, he would be a communist. Anyone who had lived under the regime of Chiang Kai Shek would become a communist. He would not be forced to be a communist, because everybody knows that when the People's Armies marched, they occupied a country where people received them willingly."[18]

It is probably fair to say that as a result of his clear and completely unequivocal response to the Chinese revolution, the whole Labour

Movement in Britain was pulled back from its evolution into more and more aggravated Cold War positions. The pressure generated by Bevan helped to persuade Attlee and the rest of the leadership that it was expedient, in 1954, to dispatch a delegation to China to discuss with the Chinese leaders. With these words Bevan broke the news to his constituents:

> "If you South Wates Miners were in China, you would be communists, of course you would, I know you would. The Labour Party delegation is going to China, because they have been bottom dogs for a long time. We are going because we believe that the only people who can talk the language of the peasants and workers of China are the representatives of the peasants and workers of Great Britain."[19]

It was in the debate which arose during the events leading up to this delegation that the problem of Indo-China began to find students in British Leftwing politics. By the time he returned from Peking, Mr Attlee had been converted to at least a part of the Bevanite case. He reported to the Labour Party:

> "The Chinese Revolution is essentially part of that rising of the Asiatic people that has been going on intensely for more than fifty years ... you can see that same spirit in Indo-China. You can see it throughout the East, but I think it came through particularly strongly in China."[20]

In spite of his conviction that the Chinese "have for the first time got an honest government" Mr. Attlee still found it expedient to support the creation of SEATO, the Pacific version of the Atlantic alliance. A great row on the matter took place at the Party Conference, after Bevan had resigned from the Shadow Cabinet in protest. The Bevanites took every opportunity to oppose this policy. In a motion by Harold Davies against SEATO[21] Jennie Lee, seconding uttered a torrential indictment:

> "I say a vote for SEATO is a vote to exclude China; a vote to exclude China is a vote that cuts us off from our own best comrades in India, in Indonesia, in Burma and elsewhere ... I hope this great conference will be true to our own international socialist principles, that we will not play small politics, that we are not going to fight ideologies on the battlefield, we are going to make a stand against aggression ..."[22]

James Callaghan joined in the condemnation:

> "no-one can effectively offer a guarantee to anyone in South-East Asia unless you have both India and China concuring in an agreement. I must say if it is a question of who is frightened of whom, I think on the whole the Chinese have most to be frightened of at the present time. There are, as far as I know, not any Chinese attacking Los Angeles or even an island off the border there ..."[23]

Among other red faces which might be provoked by a re-reading, today, of that Conference Report, would be that of Anthony Greenwood, who sturdily paraphrased the sentiments of 'One Way Only',

> "In the Labour Movement we rose to power because we were on the side of the 'have-nots' of this country. We must never lose our community of interest and our identity with the 'have-nots' of the world ... we have got to convince the masses of Asia that we are on their side in their struggle, and that their struggle against exploitation and foreign domination is exactly the same struggle that we have carried on in this country."[24]

These speeches all reflect, directly, Bevan's influence. It is, as Mr. Wilson rightly indicates, 'imperishable'. However, this spirit can be detached from the earthly clay through which, from time to time, it speaks. If one wishes to discover it again in 1965 or 1966, one may find many echoes of Bevan's words in the British socialist press. One cannot find even the slightest memory of them among the ministerial team which includes the Right Honorable Anthony Greenwood. After grafting minority rule on British Guiana, this spokesman of the masses of Asia convinced them of his unlimited goodwill by gassing their children in the colony of Bahrain.[25] He is still, of course, on the side of the have-nots. Formerly, he embraced those who have not wealth: today, less immoderately, he aligns with those who have-not conscience.

On the broad issues of foreign policy and opposition to Imperialism, the philosophy of Nye Bevan can obviously not in any degree suffer reconciliation with the actions of the Wilson administration. But even on the immediate issue of Vietnam the Prime Minister has no more right to the mantle he is so concerned to flaunt.

The whole British left approached the struggle of the Vietnamese against French rule with a sharply critical eye for French colonialism. In 1953 there was a debate on Foreign Affairs in the Commons, in which this attitude was not only clearly expressed, but in which the impact of the growing sympathy with the Chinese Revolution became very plain. The Labour team led off with a statement by Mr. Attlee, in a similar vein to the later one already quoted:

> "It would be quite contrary to the whole history of that part of the world to assume that the Indo-Chinese want to be satellites of the Chinese. I cannot help thinking that there was a possibility at one time, that this business might have been settled and that Ho Chi Minh might have been Prime Minister in a part of Indo-China, Vietnam, just as some other people with whom we have disagreed in the past are now Prime Ministers in the British Commonwealth. It is essential that the French understand the logic of events ... Colonialism belongs to a past age. It undoubtedly does in Asia."[26]

Through this breach fanned out other attackers. Mr Crossman, in strong form, echoed:

> "I was delighted to hear Mr. Attlee say what we all know is true, that Ho Chi Minh leads the real national movement in Indo-China. Do not let us be hypocritical about it. It is time to tell the French and the Americans that they are fighting an unjust war in Indo-China. If the French had done the right thing, Indo-China today would stand alongside Indonesia and Burma. Ho Chi Minh and his rebels are not communists by nature but by compulsion. They are driven to be communists in order to get national liberation. If we accept the Chinese Revolution we must accept the Indo-Chinese Revolution, and tell our friends not to waste millions of dollars on preserving a few square miles round Saigon."[27]

The dollars do not seem quite so important in 1966 as the lives which have been added to this grotesque bonfire: but Mr. Crossman has been too busy researching into the economic limitations which may not permit the rehousing of the British people to find time in which to continue to urge these very desirable economies upon the Americans. However, back in 1953 there were other voices from Mr Wilson's present administration which were not afraid to offer even stronger advice and criticism to the Americans. Mrs. Castle, for instance:

> "The foreign policy of the United States of America is to destroy communism ... That is a policy which does two things. First it says that the nationalist movements in Asia are all Moscow-inspired, Kremlin-financed, part of a great Russian plot. It fails completely to understand what is happening in Asia, the revolution which is taking place over large parts of the earth's surface – which, as hon members on this side of the House have shown quite dearly, springs from the natural needs and indigenous demands of the peoples themselves.
>
> Responsible organs of opinion in this country, discussing the problem of Indo-China, are complaining that the trouble is that we cannot get the people of

Indo-China to resist the Communist Movement, because the desire to resist is not there ... That is because the resistance movement reflects needs which are local and national."[28]

Possibly today, in the light of the intelligence which Mr Wilson has been able to offer about the origins and motivation of the English Seamans' strike, Mrs Castle has revised her opinion about the effect of natural needs and indigenous demands. In 1953, Labour MPs were not prone to such speculations as those of the later Mr Wilson on the effects of subversion. A certain scepticism infected them, arising possibly from a fairly healthy appreciation of the physical difficulties involved in subverting the restored conservative administration, against which all their bitter and justified reproaches seemed to bend like rubber knives or buckle like cardboard swords. For this reason, strong attacks were made upon the Government, which stubbornly refused to accept the logic of Messrs Attlee, Crossman and Castle. Among these was that of Jennie Lee, whose eloquence today seems stunningly appropriate:

"There are liberal Americans who are anxious to see Indo-China liberated from what they call old-fashioned colonialism.

We cannot talk to those Americans, when at the same time, we approach Washington with a begging-bowl held out, because money talks louder than words. I am grieved and shamed when I hear that the contribution which our country can make to international affairs is lost because of the clatter of the dollars falling into the begging bowl."[29]

Miss Lee is only partly right about this. Money does not necessarily talk louder than words: it depends who is listening. Her own past testifies to the truth of this cavil. For those in authority today, though, there can be little doubt that money talks very loudly indeed. It is not known for certain whether this still grieves Miss Lee. It does, without any doubt whatever, most surely still shame us all.

Where was Mr Wilson during all this time? He did not take part in this particular debate. But this does not mean that he did not share the opinions of his future ministerial colleagues: even a man of his agility cannot be everywhere at once. He did not break the line, though. In May, 1954, he did two Mayday meetings, one in Liverpool and the other in Manchester. First, the Liverpool one:

"not a man, not a gun, must be sent from this country to defend French colonisation in Indo-China ... we must not join or in any way encourage an anti-communist crusade in Asia under the leadership of the Americans or anyone else ..."[30]

In case this might be thought ambiguous, the next day, in Manchester, was added this:

> "It was right to issue a warning to the Government not to go any further in the subordination of British policies to the United States ... I believe at the moment the danger to a negotiated settlement in Asia is provided by a lunatic fringe in the American Senate ... Asia, like other parts of the world, is in revolution, and what we have to learn today in this country is to march on the side of the peoples in that revolution and not on the side of their oppressors."[31]

Mr Wilson had always a good eye for the winning side. By the beginning of 1954 it had become clear that the French were being routed by the forces of the Viet Minh. Even while he was speaking at Manchester and Liverpool, the final heroic 55-day battle of Dien Bien Phu was in progress. The French had had enough. For a race of empiricists, the British have been much slower than the schematising French to understand the facts of imperial collapse: and by May 1954 the French knew that their day in Indo-China was over. But four-fifths of their military bills were at that time already being met by the Americans: and the pragmatic empire-builders of Washington were ready at any time to make this five fifths of a very much larger total. President Eisenhower pondered on the feasibility of a 500-bomber strike against the Vietnamese forces at Dien Bien Phu. Indeed, the use of atomic weapons was carefully discussed. Less than a week before the Wilson declarations, the Americans were to have made their decisive intervention. We have it on the authority of Pierre Mendes France:

> "The United States intervention was to have taken place on the request of France, April 28th. The warships carrying atomic aviation material were loaded and on route. President Eisenhower was to have asked Congress April 26th for authorisation. Luckily the project of the US intervention was set aside by Britain and public opinion in the US."[32]

Britain, in this context, was the Britain of the Conservative restoration. Fortunately for the people of Vietnam and the peace of the world, the Conservative leadership were less deafened by the clatter of dollars into the begging bowl in 1954 than Mr Wilson's own team in 1964. To be fair, it must be admitted that the clatter of the dollars has taken on a neurotic significance for Mr Wilson, during the months since his October victory.

It remains true that before the American bombers were unleashed, the British Government of 1954 had intervened. Mr Wilson did not then instruct his supporters to "carry the banner then, but you do not need to carry it here: the right place to take that banner is to the Chinese Embassy."[33] In those days he marched "on the side of the peoples" in the Vietnamese Revolution, and "not on the side of their oppressors."

What accounts, then, for this singular change of front? The most obvious single answer is precisely, of course, the clatter of dollars, or, to be still more precise, the fear of the failure of that clatter. This was made perfectly plain at the famous speech in September 1964 to the Trades Union Congress.

> "You can get into pawn, but don't then talk of an independent foreign policy, or an independent defence policy ... if you borrow from some of the worlds' bankers, you will quickly find that you lose another kind of independence because of the deflationary policies and the cuts in social services that will be imposed on a Government that has got itself into that position."[34]

If not a handful, then at any rate for several planeloads of silver he left us. This explanation is, of course, rather strongly contested by the Prime Minister himself. At the 1965 Labour Party Conference, the South Nottingham delegate, Peter Price; put the matter in a nutshell:

> "I know the pound is important: I know the American loan is important; but so are the lives of Vietnamese people"[35]

This stung Mr Wilson. He exploded into a John Bull rebuttal:

> "I am surprised that this question can even have been put. At no time – and I say this categorically – has there been any attempt to link economic co-operation with any aspect of foreign policy. Patrick Gordon Walker, Michael Stewart and I can confirm that there have never been, whether in White House talks, in telegrams, in ambassadorial approaches, or even on the hot line, any attempts to link Vietnam with any aspect of economic or monetary co-operation, and to suggest that there have been is a libel first on the President of the United States; second, on Britain and the British Government. If I may quote Nye again, we are not gigolos."[36]

A number of questions arise out of this denial. First, are we in pawn or not? If we are not, then why all the hesitation about implementing Labour's domestic policy, why the transformation of the incomes policy into a machinery for wage restraint, why the retreat from taming property, why the assaults on trade unionism? If we are, was the warning to the TUC merely a rhetorical flourish? Which Wilson as we to believe; the solidarist with social revolution in Asia who excoriates pawnbrokers, or the statesman who never mixes business with foreign policy? Second, as cynics were already whispering before the premier had sat down, assuming that his claims about the virginal innocence of every syllable on the hot line were completely true, did that not make the whole matter worse? If we had moved from "the side of the peoples" to that of their oppressors for nothing was that in some sinister sense not worse than to have at any rate saved the pound at their expense? Of course, no one in his right mind could accuse her majesty's first minister of being a gigolo: he has hardly the appearance which is required for the job. Although he cuts a snazzy figure, it is fairly difficult to imagine even such a battered dowager as LBJ actually expending money for his embraces. To be utterly frank, none of those of us who had been listening to Mr Wilson during this speech had even the faintest reason to suspect his sexual conformity: it was his policies which we were concerned for about. The premier was aware of this, and it was presumably for this reason that he felt the need for a warm quotation from Nye[37] in which to wrap himself from the frigid blasts of disquiet which had been gusting up through the Labour Movement, as the killing accelerated and the Government's indifference solidified into open contempt.

If there ever were any doubt as to which Mr Wilson spoke the truth on this matter, it was finally settled when Mr Frank Cousins resigned from the cabinet on the issue of the legislation which was designed to buttress the entirely inequitable and retrogressive incomes policy. In his letter of resignation Mr Cousins, with a characteristic openness which makes a sharp and fitting contrast to the utterances of the prime minister, squarely states the plain fact:

> "We have slipped back to the usual position of Treasury control of our approach to questions of investment, spending and planning.
>
> That attitude cannot help us in a drive towards expansion of demand and has obviously driven us to the position where our international monetary transactions have been based on assurances of our intention to restrict internal demand. This is a wrong attitude and a contradiction of the philosophy upon which our party is based and so it must be opposed.
>
> Much of our domestic and external policy has been determined by the acceptance of that principle."[38]

We are in fact in pawn, in short: and for that reason, whether the American Government bombs, rapes, poisons or exterminates the people of Vietnam, the most that will ever come from the British Government by way of a gesture to humanity will be the type of 'dissociation' uttered up on the day after the bombing of Hanoi and Haiphong. That this sanctimonious gesture is upheld in the House of Commons by a speech (from the Foreign Secretary) about a 'long list of merciless cruelties by the Viet-cong'[39] is entirely to be expected. Mr Stewart has begun to gather a developed experience on how to dissociate himself while moving closer all the time to his dissociated mentor. At the Blackpool Labour Party Conference, he even went to the length of appealing for a cessation of the bombing raids by the US forces on the very eve of the rainy season, which made them operationally impossible.

The same pressures which bring about the need for such manoeuvres as these are of course felt here at home, as well as in the Mekong delta. The trade unions find themselves hoist with a severe system of wage control under the slogan of 'a planned growth of incomes'. Elementary trade union freedoms are placed in jeopardy. All the apparatus of the witch-hunt becomes involved in defence against the inevitable strikes which result from this.

Within this dreadful story there is one hopeful prospect. When people begin to feel the weight of these commitments dragging at their own freedoms, unease will turn to anger. But how long will this inevitable reaction take? While Labour's authentic spokesmen, in the unions and in the party, are groping for some answer to the disturbing problems of which they are becoming increasingly aware, how many peasants must be incinerated?

Labour's past contains many vital lessons which may help to ensure that it has a future. Not least of these is the lesson spelt out in detail by the actions of the old Labour left, now the establishment, in the days in which principle still counted for something in the Labour Movement. The idea of solidarity with the colonial revolution, spelt out by the young Wilson and his one-time mentor, far from signifying only a romantic attachment, is at the very heart of the solution to Britain's present problems. Only when the day of empire, including American empire, is past, can there be either peace or planned social development. If Labour in Britain will not embrace the future, it will be smothered in the past. And primitive, fierce, and infinitely brave as they are, the people of Vietnam, from their warrened dug-outs and earthen battle emplacements, embody in their desperate fight more of the undying liberal hope of mankind, more of the great and unexplored potential in humane culture, than has ever been forgotten by their most sophisticated tormentors.

Notes

1. cf Ellen Hammer: *The Struggle for Indo China*, Stanford UP, 1954

2. cf Michael Barratt Brown: *After Imperialism*, Heinemann, 1963. Mr. Barratt Brown, besides documenting the legacy of imperialism, sets out proposals for a strategy to replace it by a world-wide system of planned economic relations. A Labour Government might, once, have been expected to be interested in his proposals.

3. *In Place of Fear*, Heinemann, 1952, pp. 4-5.

4. Ibid, p4.

5. J.A. Rose in the *New York Times* Magazine Section, quoted in Russell D. Stetler Jr.: *War and Atrocity in Vietnam*, BRPF 1964.

6. *New York Times*, October 3rd 1965.

7. July 21 1965. For a terrifying dossier on American atrocities see Eric Norderi: 'American Atrocities in Vietnam,' in *Africa and the World*, July, 1966.

8. Currently the Americans are spending £4,500,000,000 a year on the destruction of Vietnam. On 14 April 1966 the *Sunday Times* carried these figures: 235,000 US personnel cost £517m in pay. Support forces (50,000) cost £110m; B52s costing £425 an hour fly daily ten-hour sorties to the North; the consumption of air-delivered munitions last Feb. was 2½ times the average monthly rate in the Korean war, itself proportionately the bloodiest war in previous history; US ground forces use £35m worth of ammunition a month; their air forces use £38 m. In 1965 the Americans lost 475 major planes costing £640,000 each, 165 lesser craft costing £70,000 each, and 320 helicopters at £90,000 each; which totals £345,000,000. The Americans give £350,000,000 in military aid to their Saigon puppets, and spend the same amount again in South-East Asian bases "associated with their operations in South Vietnam." As Pat Jordan commented in the May edition of *Vietnam Voice*: "Think what this would mean in aid to the Third World for its development plans."

9. The dead are not the only sufferers. Also the grotesque moral effect of the occupation upon the hapless town-dwellers of South Vietnam needs to be understood. See *Vietnam - The Dirty* War, Housmans, 1966.

10. In his speech to the Commons on July 8 1966, Mr. Stewart showed his arithmetical dullness as well as bis moral blindness. "As far back as 1960 the number of people, apart from the operation of the battle (sic) being murdered or abducted by the Vietcong was running at 6,000 per year; in 1965 it was 9,000 and in the first half of this year it was 5,000" he said. Even if one assumed an even escalation between 1960 and the present day, this would yield a figure around 45,000, killed and abducted. In other words, the Foreign Secretary accuses the NLF of killing and capturing a total of something over a quarter of the total killed alone by the puppet governments. But in his speech he continued, "These victims were not only civilians, but people who held any kind of governmental position or position of authority in the villages." By this he means that they were civilian functionaries: in fact, they were the usurers, landlords and oppressors of the villages. How many of them died, and how many were captured, and how many were reformed and integrated into the forces of the NLF, Mr. Stewart did not say. Nor did he say anything about the one million plus civilian casualties scored by the efforts of his allies. Nye Bevan once described Mr. Gaitskell as "a desiccated calculating machine." Desiccated, Mr. Stewart most certainly is. But in disrepair, into the bargain. Truly we have the worst of both worlds.

11. If anyone doubts this, they should read David Horowitz's graphic account of American Foreign Policy *The Free World Colossus*, MacGibbon and Kee, 1965.

12. *One Way Only:* a *Tribune* Pamphlet, 1951, p6.

13. Ibid, p7.

14. Ibid.

15. Report of the Labour Party Conference, Blackpool 1965, p155.

16. Report of the Labour Party Conference, Scarborough 1951, p121.

17. He was not mistaken about its tyranny: but it was a defensive tyranny, not an expansive one. The fact that Stalin advised both the Chinese and the Yugoslav Communists against revolutionary action (see Dedijer's biography: *Tito Speaks*) is only the best known instance of his general caution. All the cold war mythology of the aggressive Russian Empire has been effectively shattered by Fleming's work, and Horowitz, op cit.

18. *Hansard* CDXCVI (1952) col 989.

19. J. P. O'Connell 'Can Britain's Restless Rebel Take Over?', *Saturday Evening Post*, December 18 1954, p 82, cited in Krug: *Aneurin Bevan – cautious Rebel*, Yoseloff 1961, p 207.

20. Labour Party Annual Conference Report, Scarborough 1954, p70.

21. This is the Same Harold Davies, MP, who was starred for to appear at the 1965 Blackpool Conference as an apologist for Mr. Wilson's Vietnam policy. In the play *Waiting for Godot*, which Samuel Beckett must have written for the Labour Party, there is a stout character, determined and powerful, called Pozzo, who has a porterslave, mute and demoralised, who goes by the name of Lucky. Lucky is tethered, broken and frequently ill-used. He carries heavy bags for his master and remains quiet. But at the high point of the drama Lucky is licensed to burst into speech. All the lost hopes and devastated ideals of the poor creature come flooding out of him, but fragmented, in a shattering cascade of gibberish. Everything is jumbled up. The sight of this slave, humiliated even in his one moment that might have been glory, brings one to tears. The sight of Pozzo-Wilson at Blackpool last September, beaming from his eminence while Lucky Davies was payed out along his rope to the rostrum and then set up to babble through his tormented lines, was one of the most tragic, heart-breaking moments of recent Labour politics. It should not be forgiven. Thus men are broken, and it is not tolerable.

22. Labour Party Conference Report, Scarborough 1954, p77.

23. Ibid, p84.

24. Ibid, p75.

25. On the 28 March 1965 the *Observer* reported: "The angry young men of Muharraq have been on strike for nearly three weeks. Armed with stones and Pepsi Cola bottles, they have braved riot guns and instant-vomit gas to stage the first major disturbance in the Persian Gulf since Suez." The report went on to describe British helicopters "looking for … the flying shapes of schoolboy demonstrators."

26. House of Commons, Hansard, May 11th 1953.

27. Ibid col 1122.

28. Ibid col 1000.

29. Ibid col 1090-1091.

30. Reported in the *Daily Worker*, May 5th 1954, reprinted in *The Week* 5th May 1966.

31. Ibid

32. Speech in the National Assembly on June 10th 1954, quoted in Douglas Jenness: *War and Revolution in Vietnam*" Young Socialist Pamphlet, New York, 1965 p12.

33. Labour Party Annual Conference Report, Blackpool 1965, p199. Mr. Wilson has repeated this endearing smear at every possible opportunity. It would be pleasant if someone would inform him (a) that the Chinese are not employed in this war; (b) that far from being a Chinese puppet, there is every evidence that Ho Chi Minh is much more independent of his allies than Mr. Wilson has ever been; (c) That in any case the National Liberation Front, unlike Wilson's Britain, runs under its own steam.

34. TUC Report, 1964, p383.

35. Labour Party Annual Conference Report, Blackpool 1965, p195.

36. Ibid p197.

37. Perhaps the events of 1966 will have persuaded the premier that it is no longer judicious to continue calling upon the shade of Aneurin Bevan for this purpose. The discrepancies between utterance and performance are becoming more and more glaring. In case anyone still takes these genuflections of Doctor Jekyl to Mr. Hyde seriously, though, it may be proper to recall the memoirs of the late Hugh Dalton, *High Tide and After*. Dalton acidly describes Bevan's 1954 resignation from the Shadow Cabinet, following a public clash with Attlee on the question of SEATO:

"Bevan's action, taken on the spur of the moment and without consultation with his friends, disconcerted many of them. The vacancy on the Shadow Cabinet, due to his resignation, was filled under the rules by Harold Wilson, the runner-up in the ballot ... at the beginning of the session. Wilson was naturally anxious to accept this promotion. Otherwise he too would have been compelled to resign from the Shadow Cabinet, before he had even taken his seat in it. But he wished to be able to state publicly that he only accepted with Bevan's full approval. Crossman went to Bevan to seek his approval. But Bevan replied that he would regard it as an act of personal disloyalty to himself if Wilson accepted. 'So you regard Harold as expendable?' said Crossman. 'Yes, and you too,' Bevan replied." (Dalton, pp408-9)

38. *The Times*, July 4th 1966. A red-letter day for freedom!

39. *The Times*, July 8th 1966.

JOIN THE VIETNAM SOLIDARITY CAMPAIGN

The Vietnam Solidarity Campaign brings together representatives of those in Britain who have consistently and energetically combatted successive governments' support of American aggression.

Our President is *Bertrand Russell*; and our Chairman, *Ralph Schoenman*. The members of the National Council include Ken Coates, Chris Farley, Quintin Hoare, David Horowitz, Pat Jordan, Ted Knight, John La Rose, Ian Millar, John Palmer, Ralph Rosenbaum, Jim Scott, Ernie Tate, Tony Topham and Barbara Wilson.

If you wish to support the struggle of the Vietnamese people, your place is in the Vietnam Solidarity Campaign. If you are not already a member, fill in the form below and either hand it to the person distributing this leaflet or send it to our office. (Please use block capitals.)

Beyond
Wage
Slavery
by Ken Coates

Wage Slaves

Ken Coates

First published in The Incompatibles *(eds. Blackburn and Cockburn, 1967) and re-published in* Beyond Wage Slavery *(Spokesman, 1977)*

More than thirty years ago, a sensitive adult educationalist published a series of extracts from the writings of his students about their attitudes to their work. These students had all been active trade unionists, men of above average resourcefulness and intelligence. Their accounts of the feel of factory life were uniformly forbidding.

A minder in a cotton spinning mill described his work:

> 'The mule is fed by boys and the process-work of turning the partly prepared cotton sieves into yarn is controlled by the spinner who is termed the minder … The machine dominates my work. I have to follow every movement of the mule, and as the speed increases so must I. If I leave the machine the broken threads accumulate and the mule must stopped whilst the broken ends are pierced.'[1]

A colliery screen-hand wrote, in a distinctly familiar vein:

> 'Coal comes past me on an endless belt, and it is my duty to separate any dirt there may be from the coal. The belt sets the pace at which I must work. I have no feeling of power when working at the machine: on the contrary, I feel dwarfed, and I feel that the machine, instead of serving man, has become his master.'[2]

Another miner described his attempts to keep pace with underground machinery:

> 'One machine was vomiting more than I could clean up, the other had a larger mouth than I could fill. The outcome was a constant

worry: I was working always at the top speed without any sense of rhythm. I often wished that all machines and the men who made them were in hell burning.'[3]

These workers all went up to Ruskin College in the early 1930s. One who completed the course there some time earlier was the engineer, R. M. Fox, whose description of his work, published in 1928, is still vivid:

'The invariable comment when the leaving-off hooter sounds is, "there's the one I've been waiting for all day!" And in the morning when the starting signal is given, they mutter "Roll on the second one!" They look forward every day to the end of so many hours of life. Such an attitude towards work cannot embody the final wisdom of the ages.'[4]

This picture is one which I understand from the inside in a rather particular way: long before I ever meditated on it, I had become accustomed to the greeting which all Nottinghamshire miners exchange every morning: "How are you?" – "I'll be all right on Friday!" After nine years of such a customary greeting, I went to university. For several weeks I astonished students who asked me how I was by informing them that I would be all right on Friday. It was with a real sense of realisation that it dawned on me one day that Friday was no different from any other day in my new calendar, where freedom ran all through the week. This experience helps to persuade me that things are not so different today, and that the industrial regime of the 1960s is much less of an advance upon its forerunners than most public relations men are prepared to admit.

In 1965, another worker, from a tobacco factory, on his way up to Ruskin, wrote an article for *New Left Review* just before he moved:

'... The other day I overheard two old employees who had been in the factory to receive their pensions. They greeted each other as I passed. "How's it going, Bert?" said the first, "Lovely, Bill" the other, recently retired, replied. "Anything's better than that bloody hole." This may seem a paradoxical reference to a place where someone has spent forty years of his life …

It is probably wrong to expect factories to be other than they are. After all, they are built to house machines, not men. Inside a factory it soon becomes obvious that steel brought to life by electricity takes precedence over flesh and blood ... The onus is on the machines to such an extent that they appear to assume the human attributes of those who work them. Machines have become as much like people as people have become like machines. They pulsate with life, while man becomes the robot. There is a premonition of man losing control, an awareness of doom. The machines seem to squat restless in their oily beds awaiting the coming of some mechanical messiah ...

Sometimes I have an urge to open the nearest door and walk and walk and walk. I feel a need to get away from this atmosphere of here and now, where all that matters is the present, good or bad, and one must make the best of it. Nobody desires change. Everybody is looking into an endless flat future and thinking they could be worse off.'[5]

Of course, all this is impressionistic evidence. It is also tiresomely familiar. Satanic mills have been part of our landscape since the industrial revolution itself, and the romantic protest against them, however one-sided and utopian it has sometimes been, has provided a fearsome documentation. The alienation of this Nottingham tobacco worker was pinpointed by Herman Melville over a century ago, with his piercing if now depreciated metaphor of the cogs:

> 'Machinery, the vaunted slave of humanity, here stood menially served by human beings, who served mutely and cringingly, as the slave serves the sultan. The girls did not so much seem accessory wheels to the general machinery as mere cogs to the wheels.'[6]

The condition has also been thoroughly and blisteringly documented in the first volume of Marx's *Capital*. More recently it has been analysed and broken into a whole range of potentially accessible problems by Friedmann, while it has given rise to fierce complaint by the founder of cybernetics, who devoted a whole book to:

> 'a protest against the inhuman use of human beings'.[7]

It is hardly curious that clever and perceptive workers continue to write this sort of description of their lives, registering their humanity in their protest against the 'inhuman use' which is made of them. From time to time their complaints are heard by investigating sociologists; the problem of alienation, often somewhat hazily apprehended, is becoming increasingly frequently discussed by academics. What is strange is that there also exists a general and dominant mythology which hinges on the official belief that, with 'affluence' and modern man-management, this kind of difficulty is under control, and that factories have been transmuted into a new style of living. These complaints, for all their undeniable one-sidedness, indicate very plainly that in spite of half a century of declarations that Labour 'has ceased to be a commodity', the moral status of workers today is in no fundamental sense different from what it was a hundred years ago, while *Das Kapital* was still being read in galley-proof. Naturally, these harrowing commentaries by escapees from the mesh of factory life do not accurately represent the whole of it: it would be fair to say that even in the most estranged environment workers will discover some way of being involved in their work, some small sense of achievement, however attenuated, covert and harassed. What these repeated cries of pain indicate is that the *normal* condition in industry is one of semicaptivity: that inside the prison an occasional bird may sing is not denied.

In any case, individual descriptions of the feel of work are by no means the only evidence about the situation of labour in modern Britain. Lord Robens recently complained that voluntary absenteeism in the mining industry had reached 5.77 per cent of the industry's available manpower, equivalent to a permanent labour force of 27,000 men or an annual £46 million of output. And, in a controversial statement, the Chairman of the National Coal Board also queried the stringency of the criteria used by local practitioners for certifying sickness, on the grounds that involuntary absence has reached new heights. (If there is a heaven to which miners sometimes gain admission, undoubtedly it will include a little window on to purgatory, in which will be labouring, with exemplary fortitude and minute punctuality, all the unlamented legions of Coal Board bureaucrats, productivity-hounds and Labour politicians who ever incited other men to still further intensify a dreary toil which they would not, on Earth, even dream of taking, however lightly, and however temporarily, on themselves.)[8] But the collieries are not the only enterprises from which work-people temporarily absent themselves.

Over industry as a whole, sickness absenteeism has been steadily increasing during the past ten years. More than 300 million days a year are now being lost by employed men and women. Particularly important is the increase in psychoneuroses and psychoses. This, for male workers, rose from 13.2 million days of certified incapacity in the year 1953-4, to a provisional estimate of 17.66 million days in 1963-4. The rise in accident rates was even greater, from 12.66 million cases to 18.8 million during the same period. Other, physical, sicknesses have also tended to take a heavier toll in recent years. Dr. Beric Wright, commenting on these facts, points out that:

> 'all over the world, absentee rates are going up more or less parallel with the growth of social security benefits and hospital services. This overall increase cannot be entirely due to previously untreated disease. We ought as a nation to be fitter than we ever have been, but we are spending more and more time away from work.'[9]

Dr. Wright goes on to. advance a diagnosis which is entirely relevant to our argument:

> 'The problem ... is not one of disease, but of lack of job satisfaction and motivation ... This becomes clear from the study of the typical businessman. It might be assumed that he can afford to be ill and take long holidays. But the survey carried out by the Institute's (of Directors) Medical Centre showed that directors average between two and three weeks' holiday a year. Some take a month, but overall they do no better than their staff. And they certainly work longer hours. The Medical Centre now has three sets of figures about sickness absence ... these show that including *all* long and short-term sickness, the average director loses only between four and five days a year. Over 60 per cent of directors go for years without losing any time at all ... Their sickness rate is about a third that of the rest of the working population.'[10]

Something should be allowed for the fact that directors are their own masters, and can moderate the burdens they lay on themselves when they feel out of sorts, which their employees cannot do. We can allow a little more for the fact that there may be grounds for including under the heading 'work' for directors such burdens as business lunches, sundry rounds of golf, and various other chores which other people might regard as play. On top of this there is the far more telling fact that directors usually vet and submit their own reports on their own activities, a boon not granted to lesser men, whose activities are reported on by others, often without their being given access to the results, and sometimes without their even knowing that reports are being made. Even so, Dr. Wright's argument is not so far-fetched as many workers might think it. 'The more responsible a job, the more strongly motivated its holder, and the more persistent his work', runs its thread. The story is plausible. True, Dr. Wright goes on to attempt to square the circle, by insisting that 'Governments must govern, managements must manage, and everyone needs to work'. The obvious cure for endemic malingering, if the doctor is right about the example of the directors, would be to distribute their mana of responsibility far and wide throughout the population, in the hope that strong motivation and the virtues of persistence would be distributed with it. Instead, Dr. Wright thinks it necessary to concentrate power, and presumably with it civic and industrial virtue. Yet in spite of this foible, the rest of the diagnosis makes sense. What is remarkable is not that things are as he says they are, but that anyone should expect them to be otherwise. Rational employees might be expected, on working out the balance of advantage, to become disciples of the Good Toiler Schweik, inveterate and skilful malingerers to the last man. The wonder is not that some do, but that most don't. If responsibility carries with it commitment, helotry produces withdrawal: and when Dr. Wright appeals for the sharpening of managerial authority, the stiffening of the division of function, he is in fact appealing for an intensification of the very problem he is trying to solve.

Sickness is by no means the only avenue through which the frustrations of factory-life may be partially eased. There are innocent escapes, like day-dreaming and the football pools. There are also more violent solutions. One of these is little-documented, but I suspect, significant. It consists of individual sabotage. A worker who is hard-pressed by the speed of his machine may find a way to cause it to stop. The first time I observed this happening I was a boy in a colliery in the Midlands. I was sent to a conveyor-head on the coal-face which was rather difficult to operate, since the seam through which the face was running was very and rather badly faulted. I arrived to find a lad sitting by the gear-head, wielding a seven-pound hammer. He had stopped the belt from running and was carefully whacking at the metal stitches which joined two long sections of belt together. Raw, I asked him what he was doing. 'Won't that break the belt?' I said. 'What the hell do you think I'm trying to do?' he replied. When the conveyor in this seam broke, it did not assure lads like this belt-driver of an easy time. Far from it. They had to race about up and down the face, snaking on their bellies all the way, and working much harder than usual. The boy was registering his protest against boredom, he was getting some of his own back on the machine which dominated him, and he was demonstrating his indispensability to the colliers down the face who normally took his efforts for granted.

In all these integrated protests the psychologists who study small group behaviour might labour for months to find a co-ordinated pattern of response. But there is one central question which needs to be asked: why did he not contemplate the feelings of the manager who was striving to raise output, or of the Coal Board who were currently trying to beat a fuel crisis of major proportions, or of a government which was trying against odds to restore a shattered economy which still rested on coal? To ask it is to dismiss it. It is safe to say that these important matters never even entered his head. Why should they? Who could truthfully say that they were problems in which he had even a fractional interest? By sabotaging all these worthy drives, this one boy was making his own life more difficult, but more interesting. Doubtless a delinquent solution. But how many millions of such delinquent incidents are there every day in British industry? Sabotage of this kind, it should be emphasised, is purely individual reaction. There have been times when sabotage has been used as a collective, trade union, weapon: notably the Luddite episode. It was an integral weapon in the syndicalist arsenal, both in the shape of temporary or permanent disablement of machines, in the broadcasting of discreditable commercial secrets, and in the practice of ca'canny and obstructionism. But in his book, *Strikes,* G. C. K. Knowles argues, rather convincingly, that it 'generally characterises a weak trade union movement, where ... it is difficult to prevent the use of blacklegs or to maintain a long strike'.[11]

Paradoxically, a principal obstacle to personal withdrawal of these kinds is precisely the development of solidarity among the workers. This also takes place as a reflex response to their treatment in this alienated environment. Not only do the loyalties which workers form to one another greatly reduce absenteeism and increase the degree of attention paid to mutual tasks and safety, but often men have found ways to relate themselves to what they have rightly regarded as a hostile society, precisely through the institutions which they have formed to protect themselves from it. If one examines the progress of such fierce rebels as Ben Tillett, John Burns, Ernest Bevin and Ray Gunter, from subversive fire-raisers and rabble-rousers to establishmentarian reconcilers, dousers of conflict, disseminators of official pieties, one can quickly see that it has only taken place through the medium of solidary opposition, which has been contained within the hostile social structure. Unions have formed not only a front-line defence against the regime of alienation and exploitation, but also a bridge from the condition of withdrawal to 'involvement' in a controlled way in the policing, for Authority, of what is for it a fundamentally lawless territory. They are thus inherently ambivalent.

During the early years of the postwar boom, which effectively disoriented a whole generation of leading socialist propagandists, it was popular to assume that the attainment of full employment had solved all the basic problems which have been traditionally posed in socialist discussion. As C. A. R. Crosland has put it:

> 'The status of the worker, in any sense, has been rather substantially enhanced as a result of full employment, rising real wages, social security legislation and a general change in the social climate ...'[12]

Within this view of things, not only had poverty been dissolved, but 'democracy and social justice' were on their way. For Crosland, the principal significance of the problems we have been discussing would be the evidence that they offer of lack of 'job satisfaction'. He would tackle them on two levels: on the low range by 'improving the standard of personnel management,' and as a longer-range goal by 'unravelling the natural group relationships' at work in order to 'align these with the technological necessities of the work process'. This bizarre devaluation of the problem is a classic example of what Marx would have denounced as 'commodity-fetishism'. Rather than align technique with human needs, Crosland's crude and philistine approach is inevitably the reverse; it does not envisage for one moment a *human* society in which things serve people. But even Crosland is prepared to admit the historical concern of socialism with this goal:

> 'Historically, the aspiration towards a "juster" organisation of industry has been enshrined in the demand for industrial democracy and workers' control. This has a long history in the Labour Movement ... reaching a climax the stormy decade before the First World War when even revolutionary syndicalism briefly caught the imagination of the British unions; while Guild Socialism, a more prudent and pacific version, took a strong hold on the minds of younger socialist writers ...'[13]

However, Crosland by no means infers from this that 'justice' might require that attention be paid to these pioneers: on the contrary:

> 'If we wish to revive this issue, we shall not derive much help from the old literature ... (it) was ideologically rooted in a theory of "wage slavery" *which has no relevance to present-day conditions.*'[14] (my italics)

It is in the light of this comfortable conviction that much of the debate which has troubled academic sociology, concerning affluence and the changing class structure, has been conducted and as a result has been incapable of revealing much more than surface platitudes. 'A washing machine is a washing machine is a washing machine,' David Lockwood has written. His words might with profit be branded upon the rumps of most psephologists and a good many political commentators.

The relationships between employer and worker which the first Guild socialists described as 'the bondage of wagery' has not in the least been ameliorated by motor cars and refrigerators. On the contrary. While no one would deny that there has been an absolute improvement in the standards of living of workers in all the advanced capitalist countries, which has continued throughout most of the past two decades (and which has only been arrested during the epoch of advanced, modernising technical innovation inaugurated by Crossland and his colleagues when they assumed political office), the important thing is that this absolute improvement has not been accompanied by any significant *relative* improvement in the rewards of Labour as opposed to those of Capital. What really matters in evaluating this situation is not simply the yardstick of comparative consumption, which is often misleading. The key to an understanding of the psychology of industry is the yardstick of comparative *accumulation*, or agglomeration of power.

The original Marxist conception of exploitation never concerned simple money robbery; it always involved itself with the alienation of the product of labour from the control of the labourer, in which workers produce, over and above their own livelihoods *at whatever level of 'affluence'*, a volume of capital which, under alien direction, concentrates ever greater economic force against them in ever fewer hands. Conceived in these terms, 'exploitation' has been continuously intensified and aggravated throughout the whole history of capitalism.[15] The growth of scale of modern industry is clearly conjoined with the distillation of corporate political and social power, which has not been diminished in any way by 'high', or near-full employment, wage-levels. Decision-takers, deriving steadily augmented authority from direct and indirect titles to capital, cluster in a tightening throng at one pole of society; at the other pole are massed the vassals, who, in spite of the fog of a vast ballyhoo of cynical devices for 'participation' or 'involvement', feel the continuous pressure of attempts to cut back, erode and remove any traces of real rights which they may have been able to grasp at their own immediate level, over the shaping of their own tasks and direction. Of course trade unions have been able to seize some serious powers at the workshop level, over working arrangements and the disposition of the labour force, during the intensive competition for labour which has persisted for most of the post-war period.[16] But these powers, of which shop stewards are rightly jealous, are under constant fire from authority, both in management and the State at large. And while it would be quite wrong to minimise the strength and self-confidence of the trade unions in this persistent struggle, it would be absurd to overlook the fragmentation which has been induced in their ranks by the same economic and political processes. If they were consciously bent upon the destruction of the power of capital, the trade unions could find means to accomplish it: this no one doubts. But within the higgling of contending interests inside the present power-structure it seems absurd to speak of 'trade union power' in the same breath as the power of capital. In the past few years the monolithic National Union of Mineworkers, with near thirty members of parliament, including a number of ministers, under a Labour government upon which it has a thousand claims and ties, has found it impossible to secure the fulfilment of the wholly specific promises it had been given before victory in the elections. A sympathetic Minister of Power recently burst into tears at a confrontation between trade union and government spokesmen, but grim and implacable behind him sat Mr. Douglas Jay, the voice of the Treasury and the bankers.[17] When all the miners in the land weigh less than a handful of bankers, it is premature to assume the rout of management prerogatives.

Both C. A. R. Crosland and H. A. Clegg, who have in numerous books and articles celebrated the virtues of permanent trade union oppositional power, have during the Wilson administration been lending every possible practical assistance to the crusade to roll these powers back.[18] The inconsistency in their behaviour reflects a deeper inconsistency in their ideas. These ideas found a popular expression in Michael Shanks's account, *The Stagnant Society*, which was, in the terms of this kind of literature, a bestseller. In retrospect it may be thought that Shanks not only puts a key part of the Crosland-Clegg view into a nutshell, but also provides a convenient epitome of the basic industrial relations assumptions of the Labour Government:

> 'There is no greater morale booster for a worker than the feeling that he too is consulted on policy questions and plays his part in influencing managerial decisions. Of course, in any form of democracy there is an element of humbug. Our rulers never, in fact, allow us as much power as they pretend to. The sovereign people can only be permitted to exercise its power on certain limited occasions and within certain defined limits – otherwise the operations of government would be paralysed. Nevertheless, the illusion of power is good for us, besides imposing important restrictions on our rulers.
>
> This applies to industrial democracy, where the element of make-believe must of necessity be greater than in political democracies. Because of the highly technical nature of the decisions which have to be taken, the management must retain ultimate control of the policy. Moreover, the analogy which is often drawn between industrial and political democracy breaks down on two vital points. The first is over the diversity of aims. Ultimately, we all have a common interest in the survival of our political community. But in a factory this may not be so. Only the employer has an interest in preserving the factory at all costs – and even he may be anxious to sell out. But the workers' interests might well be best served by increasing wages and decreasing hours of work to the point where the concern might be driven bankrupt – provided there were other jobs in the district for them to go to.
>
> This brings us to the second reason why industrial democracy cannot be equivalent to political democracy. The political rights of the individual in society derive largely from the fact that he is compelled to live in it. But the

worker in industry can always 'vote with his feet' by moving to another factory. The unit of society, in other words, is not all embracing. This means that the worker cannot with justice claim the same rights *vis-a-vis* his employer as he can as a citizen *vis-a-vis* his government.

Industrial democracy, in other words, is a matter of tactics rather than of high principle. It is in no sense immoral to run one's business as a rigid autocracy – but it is probably foolish. It is equally foolish, however, to surrender one's ultimate power of decision to a group of workers, or even to all the workers. Industrial democracy cannot be like a two-party political democracy, in which today's opposition may be tomorrow's government. In industrial democracy a permanent administration confronts a permanent opposition – and as everybody knows, in parliamentary terms this is a most healthy situation. To look at this matter sensibly, we would do well to forget all about the mother of parliaments and the far-flung analogies of the pundits, and consider the issue on its merits.

If one is to talk sensibly of industrial democracy then the first thing is to deflate it and empty it of ideology. It is the fact and not the form of consultation that matters.'[18]

Of course, in this passage, Shanks ducks all the main problems. He outflanks his opponents by a simple device: he narrows the base of his model of industrial democracy to the point where it becomes possible to derive a whole series of completely discrepant analogies. The real unit which socialists aspire to democratise is not, as he is claiming, the factory. It is the economy. If it is true to say that members of a factory can 'vote with their feet', and most of us would claim that that was only true within very straitened limits, then the proper answer to this is that within his own analogy people who don't like Wapping can go to Broadstairs. (With similar difficulties, be it added.) The moment one begins to argue about 'society' the parallel area of dispute becomes the economy. It is absurd to pretend that members of 'the economy' can leave *it* any more easily than they can leave 'society'. If the State marks out the frontiers of 'society', then, to be sure, it is easier by far to leave society than the economy, for the very good and simple reason that not the State but the market marks out the shape of economic frontiers. In this case the reverse of Shanks's argument is true: it is far more easy for English feet to vote for Australia or Japan than to vote their way out of the economy. To argue democratic control of the economy is not to argue against factory democracy: factories could and should be democratically administered. But to establish norms of workshop democracy in an uncontrolled and undemocratic economy, is to conduct a permanent Canute-like dialogue with the ocean of the market.

Sometimes the tide will conform to our desires. The important times are those when it does not. Every day, mild fluctuations in demand wreak havoc in existing traditions of factory organisation. It is only if the economy at large is *both* planned and democratised, that the extension of democratic forms to the workshops has any permanency. As far as the Shanks argument is concerned, factory democracy can be vulgarly related to democratic central planning much in the same way that, within his own inadequate analogy, local government might be related to national government.

More woefully ill-founded though is Shanks's conviction that, in the sense that the opposition can never be allowed to win, there can be no two-party democracy within an industrial democracy. If the controllers of an economic plan are democratically controlled, they must be subject to organised criticism, backed by a free press and the liberal standards of open comment. If they are so subject, the possibility cannot be excluded that they might be displaced. In any of the existing centrally planned economies one cares to think of, it is fairly plausible to assume that some, at least, of the planners *would* be displaced if effective popular controls of this kind were established. Whether a democratic plan would necessarily require two or more institutionally established parties it is difficult to say in advance: no such plan exists as a convenient model. Probably its norms would require more of an unleashing of shifting but articulate caucuses and lobbies, forming and reforming according to the emergence of new social needs and pressures. These themselves would engender successive controversies and then settle them as they arose. But none of this is what Shanks is talking about. When he appeals for this whole problem to 'be deflated and emptied of ideology', those reading him might be tempted to offer a quiet 'Amen'. The fact that 'a permanent administration confronts a permanent opposition' in this best of all possible worlds, is completely ideological, in the precise traditional meaning of the word. *Why* can our industrial controllers never be displaced by popular vote when their policies cause disquiet? Because they are appointed to and fixed in their positions by the institution of property. Property alone within the structure can displace them, yet it is so much of a taboo that in this vital discussion it cannot even be mentioned. Every single form of rebuttal of democratic arguments which is now being deployed against trade unionists demanding real extensions of industrial democracy could equally have been and indeed probably was, invoked by the squirearchy in its staunch resistance to the most elementary democratic demands within the political field.

This complex of arguments forms a pattern. The orthodox 'revisionist' critics of socialism (who have captured at any rate the industrial relations policies of the Labour Government) have been from the beginning prepared to recognise widespread alienation, which they have seen purely as a psychological condition, a form of individual withdrawal.

They have indeed been prepared to appropriate as their own the call to 'radically improve the status' of the working population, and to 'transform the quality of industrial life'. But they have diagnosed the condition simply as a response to modern technologies, without seriously considering how such technologies came to be enforced, and what conditioned their employment. It has always been assumed by them that it is 'natural' for people to adapt to the requirements of the market in this field. In the words of Brecht, their failure has been a refusal to

Inquire if a thing be necessary:
Especially if it is common.

Had they been able to do this, they might have even gone on to learn

When a thing continually occurs
Not on that account to find it 'natural'.

Implicitly accepting an impermissible framework for their judgements, they can only seek limited solutions to global problems. They are, for instance, prepared to explore all kinds of experiments in factory group dynamics, in order to adjust workers' errant minds to the mechanical imperatives against which they rebel.[20] Just as social psychologists during the war were able to employ group discussion techniques in order to brainwash housewives into feeding their husbands with offal, so this school of thinkers posits a labour force realigned, in small chunks, to a severe appreciation of the need for more production and its own self-abnegation. This is what Crosland means by 'alignment with the technological necessities of the work process'. To help sell this placebo, labels like 'industrial democracy' can be applied to it. As Shanks revealingly confesses, this involves multiplying 'humbug' by 'make-believe'. But there is a limit to the potency of group manipulation, and the problem, truly posed, has never been one of how people may adapt to machines in the abstract. It has been one of adapting to someone's machines.

To explore what this means, consider two greenhouses. One, in a back garden, contains a happy fanatic who saved money to build it and now spends every spare minute nourishing tomatoes which he could possibly buy cheaper in the market. While he is in this greenhouse, this man would probably describe himself as 'free'. Yet he is certainly 'working'. The other greenhouse is one of a long row in a nursery. Two labourers pass on the way into adjoining doors. 'Roll on Friday' we hear them saying. Our particular man enters his work-place where we observe that, after carefully scanning around him, he settles comfortably down and falls to the reading of the *Daily Mirror*. He is not working, but he is 'at work', and would certainly prefer to be reading the *Daily Mirror* elsewhere. He is behaving in an alienated manner. But can we say that greenhouses are alienating? Of course not: our first man cannot spend long enough in them. He is his own master. The other two are working for someone else. Ignore this simple fact at peril: for the whole essence of the alienation we have been describing is that property, the private control of public resources, is at the heart of it. Of course, greenhouses can be personal belongings. In this they differ from, say, a four-million pound production-line in a vehicle factory which can never, for any of its individual operatives, become really 'my' machine. But such a costly complex *could* become 'our' machine, and if it did, this would merely bring the juridical norm into line with what has long been a social need. Until this happens, every factory is a flagrant assault on the categorical imperative: 'I ought never to act except in such a way that I can also will that my maxim should become a universal law.' If those words were to be enforced in any working enterprise for half an hour, it would cease to function altogether. Socialist revolutions in full flood apart, capitalist industry is the most sustained and awe-inspiring collective effort which men have ever made; yet its ethos is such that members of the collective only traditionally use the words 'we' and 'us' when they are making hostile demands upon its directors.

None of this is to say that all forms of work will become pleasant once we nationalise the means of production, distribution and exchange. The contrary: their very unpleasantness, in a really open democracy, will hasten the social effort to abolish them. The effort to do this has always been seen by socialists as involving a double onslaught: efforts must be made to plan a technological explosion, capable of blasting out continuous all-round cuts in working hours; at the same time there must also be a systematic transfer of increasing ranges of consumer goods to welfare forms of distribution, gradually but remorselessly replacing money as the normal means of personal transactions, and increasingly relegating it to the role of an accounting device between various public corporations. The effect of these onslaughts would be a vast increase in *free time*, which, in such conditions as Marx frequently pointed out, 'is the most productive time of all'. This, in turn, would lethally undermine the division of labour itself, which has hitherto given rise not only to the impositions of class and rank, but also to the conditions which Ruskin so tellingly described:

> 'We have much studied and perfected, of late, the great civilised invention of the division of labour; only we give it a false name. It is not, truly speaking, the labour that is divided; but the men: divided into mere segments of men – broken into small fragments and crumbs of life; so that all the little piece of intelligence that is left in a man is not enough to make a pin, or a nail, but exhausts itself in making the point of a pin, or the head of a nail. Now it is a good and desirable thing, truly, to make many pins in a day; but if we could only see with what crystal sand their points were polished – sand of human soul, much to be magnified before it can be discerned for what it is – we should think there might be some loss in it also. And the great cry that rises from all our manufacturing cities, louder than the furnace blast, is all in very deed for this – that we manufacture everything there except men; we blanch cotton, and strengthen steel, and refine sugar, and shape pottery; but to brighten, to strengthen, to refine or to form a single living spirit, never enters into our estimate of advantages.'[21]

Ruskin may have approached this terrible reality in a one-sided manner, but at least he faced it. Our present generation of 'socialist' leaders do not even know what it is about. They may have thought about it, briefly, once; and in mitigation we can accept that to deal with it no doubt requires a long-range strategy. They are all busy people. However, not thinking about these long-range problems makes the range still longer and the haul uphill still harder.

By foreshortening its range and lowering its aim, Labour in Britain has set a cruel trap for itself. Immediate, 'practical' problems have for so long dominated the minds of the Labour establishment that they have no independent criteria by which to respond to them. No one in the present government has time to think about the overcoming of the division of Labour. But if no one thinks about such matters then the goals of the movement become devalued. For all the loud noises we have had from Labour leaders about 'equality' over the past fifteen years, every evidence appears to show that this notion is strictly limited to piety of a most abstract kind. The complete failure of any prominent spokesman of the Labour Party to discuss this kind of problem in fundamental terms, during the whole of the past two decades, reveals a definitive retreat from the most crucial front in the battle for Labour's aims.

This refusal to think about these ultimate problems blocks Labour leaders from opening up the vision of the members of the movement. At the same time it forces them to accommodate to a position in which their short-range moves are completely blind. They come to rely entirely on the given priorities of the established system. And so, they come to reduce all political choices to administrative alternatives. In this way, the 1964 Labour Government found itself with the strategic aim of 'restoring the economy'; after which (in some way which has neither been specified nor, one suspects, agreed) 'we will pay ourselves a dividend'.[22] Instead of becoming the reason for beginning to create a new one, the difficulties of the old economic order became a pretext for placing in jeopardy even the limited programme of amelioration which had previously been envisaged. Not only has the incidence of poverty been increasing, but there are signs that this is happening at an accelerated rate. Professor Townsend, who calculated recently that some 7.5 million people were living at or below the standard available on National Assistance, is now publicly speculating abouts the increase of this figure by another million. In this serious condition, the policies of retrenchment which have been imposed upon the administration add their own quota of misery. The deliberate creation of artificial unemployment, referred to under the repulsive name 'shake-out', marks out the ultimate capitulation to the logic of the market, to the primacy of property over all humane interests.

A man's hopes are his moral boundaries. He will rarely press beyond them. If someone merely aspires to put a new roof on his kitchen, not only is it easier to fulfil this dream than to bring about a world in which *every* cook may learn to govern the state, but, when the roof is on, you will not find prime ministers in the kitchen by accident. In the event, in 1964, even the kitchen roof could not be seen to. Worse. Having accepted the administrative priorities, the restoration of the old order to good health required the new ministers to make incisions in the economic body. Cuts could not be inflicted upon capital's prerogatives without stepping outside the administrative routine which had by now become more demanding with each submission made to it. And so arose the need for first piece-meal, and then wholesale attacks on the living standards and liberties of the very people the Government had been elected to protect.

The word for this is 'betrayal'. It is an emotive word, but, unfortunately, it is accurate. Yet the first and fundamental betrayal took place a while ago, almost unnoticed: it was a betrayal of socialist theory, since which the events 1964 and onwards have only made manifest something which was gestating, latent in a small flow of books and articles, for a decade and half before.

Having inherited the leadership of a vast mass organisation of working people, the present dominant caucus had not the remotest idea of an aim for the whole complex. Because their horizons were so limited, they reacted like any sealed-in provincial village community, and embellished their own immediate social arrangements with polite and decorous descriptions to soften the realities. In the village everyone will tell you that much can be improved, that no one is complacent, that many reforms are needed, and so on. Similarly Mr. Crosland was in favour of uplifting the status of the workers, just as Mr. Shanks would spread more widely the humbug of democracy, just as all the world and especially Mr. Harold Wilson would love to blow warm blasts of modernising wind through every enterprise. But workers are not merely deprived of status by some genteel scale. They are, as every line of this essay is meant to argue, wage slaves. There can, if this is true, be no easy continual uplift of the people without a fundamental structural change in society as a whole. A wage slave does not cease to be a wage slave when he can buy a refrigerator. Roman slaves might be thin or fat, sad or cheerful, employed to entertain their masters' lions as dinner or their masters' wives as lovers; wage slaves too come in all sizes and conditions. Some even drive to work in motor cars. As they trod the grape harvest, the Roman slaves on the *latifundiae* probably ate some too. You cannot tell a wage slave by his looks. You can tell him by the fact that on Monday he says 'Roll on Friday'. He is defined by the fact that he lives in little islands of freedom called 'leisure'.

That these, to an outsider, may be more and more coming to resemble the surrounding sea of 'work' is not so surprising. It is hard to be a five-day slave, free at weekends. Recently in the same week, I visited a pharmaceutical factory employing some thousands of girls, and a fun-arcade at Skegness. In both places, rows and rows of girls stood poring over rows and rows of little machines. The first enterprise was for bottling, sealing, and labelling pills; engaged in it the girls were 'producing'. At the second, which was for taking away the six-pences earned in the first, the operatives were 'consuming'. Work and leisure, production and consumption: fully *human* beings would have to reason with subtlety to discover the difference. Wage slaves know it intimately; it is the first fact of their existence. If wage slaves who earn above average pay feel the freer for that on Friday night, they will most probably feel all the more enslaved on Monday morning. A Derbyshire colliery under-official won £20,000 on the football pools two years ago, and having assembled a fair-sized crowd in the pityard, he ceremonially burnt his pit-clothes in front of them. They knew what he meant.

* * *

In sum, if slavery is a social relationship and not an absolute level of distress; and if slavery may be discovered wherever the will of one man is involuntarily and arbitrarily subordinated to that of another; then we remain bound to the same basic problems which the Labour movement faced, one hundred years ago, when Marx offered it this excellent advice:

> 'At the same time (that they defend themselves with vigour in all partial battles for improved conditions) … the working class ought not to exaggerate to themselves the ultimate working of these everyday struggles. They ought not to forget that they are fighting with effects, but not with the causes of those effects; that they are retarding the downward movement, but not changing its direction; that they are applying palliatives, not curing the malady. They ought, therefore, not to be exclusively absorbed in these unavoidable guerrilla fights incessantly springing up from the never-ceasing encroachments of capital or changes in the market. They ought to understand that, with all the miseries it imposes on them, the present system simultaneously engenders the material conditions and social forms necessary for an economic reconstruction of society. Instead of the *conservative* motto: "A fair day's wages for a fair day's work!" they ought to inscribe upon their banners the *revolutionary* watchword "For the abolition of the wages system!"'[23]

Notes

1. A. Barratt Brown, *The Machine and the Worker* (London, 1934), p.85.

2. ibid.

3. ibid, p.86.

4. R. M. Fox, *The Triumphant Machine* (London, 1928), p.35.

5. D. J. (Dennis Johnson), 'Factory Time' in *New Left Review*, 31 (1965), pp.51-7.

6. Herman Melville, *The Tartarus of Maids* in Collected Short Stories (London, 1950).

7. Norbert Wiener, *The Human Use of Human Beings* (Boston, 1950).

8. An honoured place among these toilers will be reserved for Harold Wilson, who will need a fair slab of eternity to demonstrate how easily he could dispense with 'conservatism' on the shop floor in order to boost the dynamism of British Industry. It is perhaps unfair to predict that Purgatorial Industry may also slacken its pace when it comes under his inspired tutelage.

9. 'The Sick Society', Dr. Berle Wright, in the *Director* (October 1966), pp.90-L

10. ibid, p.92. For an account of the Report of the Institute's Medical Centre see the *Director* (May 1966), p.270ff.

11. G. C. K. Knowles, *Strikes* (Oxford, 1952), p.13. The best known advocate of sabotage as a trade union weapon in this country was William Mellor, cf. the appropriate chapter in *Direct Action* (1920). Recently the idea has been discussed in the militant journal *Solidarity* in somewhat similar

terms. Since this essay was written a major study of *Sabotage* has been written by Geoff Brown (Spokesman Books, 1977).

12. C. A. R. Crosland, 'What Does the Worker Want?' in *Encounter* (February 1959), p.10.

13. Crosland, *The Future of Socialism* (London, 1956), p.343.

14. ibid, pp.343-4.

15. Those who doubt this interpretation of Marx should carefully re-read *Wage Labour and Capital.* An extract may serve to point his attitude both in the field of consumption and accumulation:

> 'A house may be large or small; as long as the surrounding houses are equally small it satisfies all social demands for a dwelling. But if a palace arises beside the little house, the little house shrinks into a hut. The little house shows now that its owner has only very slight or no demands to make: and however high it may shoot up in the course of civilisation, if the neighbouring palace grows to an equal or even greater extent, the dweller in the relatively small house will feel more and more uncomfortable, dissatisfied and cramped within its four walls.
>
> A noticeable increase in wages presupposes a rapid growth of productive capital. The rapid growth of productive capital brings about an equally rapid growth of wealth, luxury, social needs, social enjoyments. Thus, although the enjoyments of the worker have risen, the social satisfaction they give has fallen in comparison with the increased enjoyments of the capitalists, which are inaccessible to the worker, in comparison with the state of the development of society in general. Our needs and enjoyments spring from society; we measure them, therefore, by society and not by the objects of their satisfaction. Because they are of a social nature, they are of a relative nature ...
>
> Real wages may remain the same, may even rise, and yet relative wages fall ... If, therefore, the income of the worker increases with the rapid growth of capital, the social gulf that separates the worker from the capitalist increases at the same time, the power of capital over labour, the dependence of labour on capital, increases at the same time.'

From *Selected Works* (London, 1945), vol. 1, pp.268-73.

16. For a balanced treatment of this, see Tony Topham, 'Shop Stewards and Workers' Control' in *New Left Review*, 25 (May-June 1964), pp.3-16.

17. cf. *The Scottish Miner* (February 1966).

18. Compare Clegg's discussion of these matters in *A New Approach to Industrial Democracy* (Oxford, 1960) with his part in framing the Devlin and Pearson Reports on the decasualisation of dock workers (Cmd 2734, August 1965) and on the Seamen's Wage Claim (Cmd 3025, June 1966).

19. Michael Shanks, *The Stagnant Society* (London, 1961), p.160-1.

20. Crosland, 'What Does the Worker Want?' loc. cit., pp.16-17.

21. Ruskin, *The Stones of Venice*, Section II, chapter vi.

22. As James Callaghan pointed out to the Fabians at a gathering during the 1963 TUC: 'A Labour government must not rush its fences ... its first job must be to get industry moving again(!). Then we can start paying ourselves a dividend' (*Guardian*, 4 September 1963).

23. Karl Marx, 'Value, Price and Profit' in *Selected Works*, vol. 1 (London, 1945), p.337.

Michael Barratt Brown
and Ken Coates

The 'Big Flame' and What is the IWC?

Institute for Workers' Control

Pamphlet Series No. 14

What is the IWC?

Ken Coates

First published in The 'Big Flame' and What is the IWC?, *Institute for Workers' Control Pamphlet, No. 14, 1968. The IWC was launched following a long period of discussion, consultation and preparation, at a point where the idea of workers' control developed a significant following in the labour and trade union movement in Britain.*

All over the world, unrest is mounting. More and more people are finding the political and social arrangements which they have inherited to be totally inadequate. As men have gained greater knowledge and increased their technical skills, the world-wide division between rich and poor has become wider and more stark. In the colonial and former colonial countries, forced economic underdevelopment, which means poverty for whole populations, gives rise to rebellion after rebellion. The revolutions in China and Cuba, and the twenty-five year-old war in Vietnam, are simply the most extraordinary instances of what is becoming a world-wide struggle against hunger and colonial exploitation. But in the rich countries, the former centres of world-wide empires, other forms of acute discontent are expressing themselves. Foremost among these is the sharp dissatisfaction with the dominance of a totally undemocratic power-structure, ultimately based solely on the ownership of wealth, over an economy which is becoming more and more complex and socially interlocked. Factory workers and industrial technicians alike find that, as their work requires them to act in increasingly co-operative ways in their particular tasks, at the same time the government of their collective becomes increasingly dictatorial and arbitrary. The more skilled a man becomes, the more he is likely to resent the rule of a moneyed industrial autocracy which knows little and cares less about the tasks in hand, but concerns itself only with the concentration of wealth and power. And that is not all. War to the knife, which is the law of the competition that impels this system to produce, results in the accumulation of victims. Mergers and takeovers have not only concentrated industrial power on a scale which defies any form of socially accountable control, but they have produced wave upon wave of "re-organisations", dismissals, redundancies: they have dislocated whole communities. Men find themselves facing premature early retirement, or they find themselves abruptly without employment. Even when such shocks are cushioned by welfare payments or pensions, the loss of human dignity and self-respect involved in them is beyond calculation. And frequently the victims of these convulsions find not only that they have neither civil nor even beggars' rights in relation to the enterprises in which they have invested their working lives: but also that they face deprivation, and sometimes, poverty, into the bargain.

It is in this context that the words Workers' Control have come to take on a new and vivid meaning. Industrial democracy has become a watchword which has a profound relevance to the world of economic autocracy in which we are now living. Indeed, in every major capitalist country, the concentration of financial power has become so great, and the difficulties of administering so irrational a system have become so marked, that the State has increasingly been called upon to intervene directly, as the open political arm of business interests, to curb the independent functions of trade unions, to hold down wages by public fiat, and to implement whole successions of 'plans' to assist in the conglomeration of major enterprises and the augmentation of business power.

The trade union answer to these pressures has been, in every major capitalist country, divided. Old-fashioned unions, often top-heavy with officialdom and sluggishly, if at all, responsive to the needs of members, have tended to react defensively to the combined pressures of businessmen and governments, and to succumb after what have in fact amounted to ritualistic complaints. But the more dynamic organisations have been searching for ways of replying in an aggressive way, of evolving a counter-strategy to extend trade union powers where authority seeks to whittle them down, and to assert workers' rights where management seeks to establish its own "prerogatives".

Wherever one looks there are signs of this kind of response. In West Germany, trade unions like those of the metal or chemical workers demand a significant expansion of the workers' rights in the system of 'co-determination'. In Italy, more and more struggles break out in the factories about the workpeoples' rights to control speeds of work, allocation of tasks, and similar questions. In every country, redundancy raises the question of the trade unions' right to control hiring and firing. In practically every country, as was graphically borne out in the British

Seamens' strike, the imposition of incomes policies and "productivity bargains" provokes the counter-demand "open the books", so that the workers can, for the first time, judge the effect of such arrangements on their employers' ability to meet demands. And in France, as all the world knows, the culmination of these processes brought a spontaneous general strike, in which factory after factory was occupied by its workers, and, while managers were locked in their offices, workpeople began an extensive and pressing nationwide discussion on workers' control.

At the same time as the rich capitalist countries reverberate with this argument, so also the richer socialist countries begin to echo it. The concentration of power into the hands of unrepresentative elites in those countries has been, quite obviously, economically counter-productive, to say nothing of its catastrophic political consequences. And so, in Czechoslovakia openly, and covertly all over Eastern Europe, there arises the demand for Workers' Councils with effective control of the enterprises, and the equally pressing insistence on the need for democracy in planning. In Yugoslavia, where this debate began, the argument continues fiercely and publicly: while in the Soviet Union itself there are all the signs that the stiffening of Governmental control and doctrinal rigidity reflect a serious growth of democratic pressures in the factories. Every move which is made in Eastern Europe to develop this argument has its immediate repercussions in the West, and vice-versa. And since the economic and political difficulties of bureaucratic planning seem to be acute, there can be little doubt that this process will escalate.

In Britain, the workers' control movement has emerged from these conditioning factors. Starting in 1964, with a conference of some 80 socialists in Nottingham, a public debate has grown to embrace most major trade unions, the Labour and Liberal Parties, and even a corner of the mass-media of communications, which are, of course, a crucial preserve of autocratic control. Beginning in response to stimuli from Yugoslavia and Algeria, where self-management experiments excited British socialist thinkers, the movement has been confronted by a whole series of developments which have reproduced the traditional arguments for industrial democracy on a quite new plane, and given them a force which is becoming increasingly obvious and relevant. The post-war industrial revolution has produced a new technologically educated labour force, to which "managerial prerogatives" are an affront without mitigation. But the uneven development of this revolution has made the process of "modernisation" all the more convulsive in the backward sectors of industry, thus forcing workers to look towards control demands if they are to succeed even in the most elementary measures of self-defence. The fact that the neo-capitalist strategies of incomes policy and corporate "planning" have begun to show savage teeth, has forced workers to begin to revalue their assessments of the political utility of the organisations they have built, and to look for complimentary forms of industrial and political action with which to meet the next offensives which have been unleased upon them. During this time, the discussion on workers' control has grown from conferences of eighty socialist journalists and academics, leavened by occasional trade union leaders, to cover gatherings of over one thousand trade union delegates. The seven conferences which have so far been held have brought together workers in more than twenty different industries, and produced a whole mass of documentation on conditions in those industries, and a stream of pamphlets and articles by workers engaged within them.

Arising out of this ferment, and as a result of a decision of the Sixth Conference for Workers' Control, the Institute for Workers' Control was formed in 1968. Its function is to act as a research and educational body, to co-ordinate discussion and communication between workers' control groups and trade unions, to provide lists of speakers and to publish important materials on the subject of industrial democracy and workers' control. Membership of the Institute is open to all individuals who are interested in workers' control and who pay an annual subscription of three pounds, for which they receive all the publications of the Institute. It is also open to trade union and other working-class organisations who wish to affiliate, upon payment of a fee based on a sliding scale for local, district and national organisations. The Institute is governed by a Council which is elected at its general business meeting, open to all individual and affiliated members. Of course, the Institute does not commit itself to the majority or minority views of the groups or unions which support it, and where there is a plurality of views upon a question it will, subject to the state of its resources, publish them all. Voting, therefore, either at Council or General meetings, will normally concern administrative questions, unless there is a very general consensus upon the issue under discussion. The Institute does not seek to replace or usurp the policy-making functions of trade unions or the political organisations of the Labour Movement, but rather to provide them with a convenient and open forum upon a crucial issue. For organisations or individuals who wish to support the Institute, but who do not wish to concern themselves with its administration, associate membership is open at thirty shillings a year, which carries with it a subscription to the Bulletin of the Institute. In industries or localities where there is a developed interest in workers' control and industrial democracy, workers' control groups have been formed. These will normally affiliate to the Institute on the same basis as other local or district committees of trade unions or political bodies, and will therefore carry the same rights as those bodies in relation to the administration of the Institute.

Besides publishing a whole series of pamphlets and books, and issuing a monthly digest and a quarterly Bulletin of articles and information, the Institute convenes seminars for specific industries wherever it is requested to do so. Important seminars of dockworkers, busmen, farm workers and steelworkers have been held, and many other seminars are projected. At the same time, the Institute has taken the responsibility for convoking, jointly with the journal *Voice of the Unions*, the annual Conferences on Workers' Control in which the different industry seminars meet and exchange views. The seventh such Conference, held at Sheffield, had one thousand and thirty-two trade union delegates, and marked a serious step forward in the study of the relevance of ideas of industrial democracy to the problems of many groups of workers. The workers' control conferences are open to all who wish to participate in the movement for workers' control, and their seminars produce reports which are, wherever possible, published by the Institute, if necessary with both majority and minority views. Naturally, the nature of such a Conference precludes it from arriving at decisions which bind the participants: but nonetheless, the value of so wide a forum is becoming increasingly apparent.

Of course, the crisis in which the British Labour Movement is caught requires the development of serious analyses, programmes and forms of organisation over a range which cannot possibly be covered by the Institute. But it seems clear that in the process leading up to this development, the ferment of ideas will be greatly assisted by the kind of work which it is undertaking.

Further materials on the Institute for Workers' Control
can be found at ***www.socialistrenewal.net***
and ***www.spokesmanbooks.org***

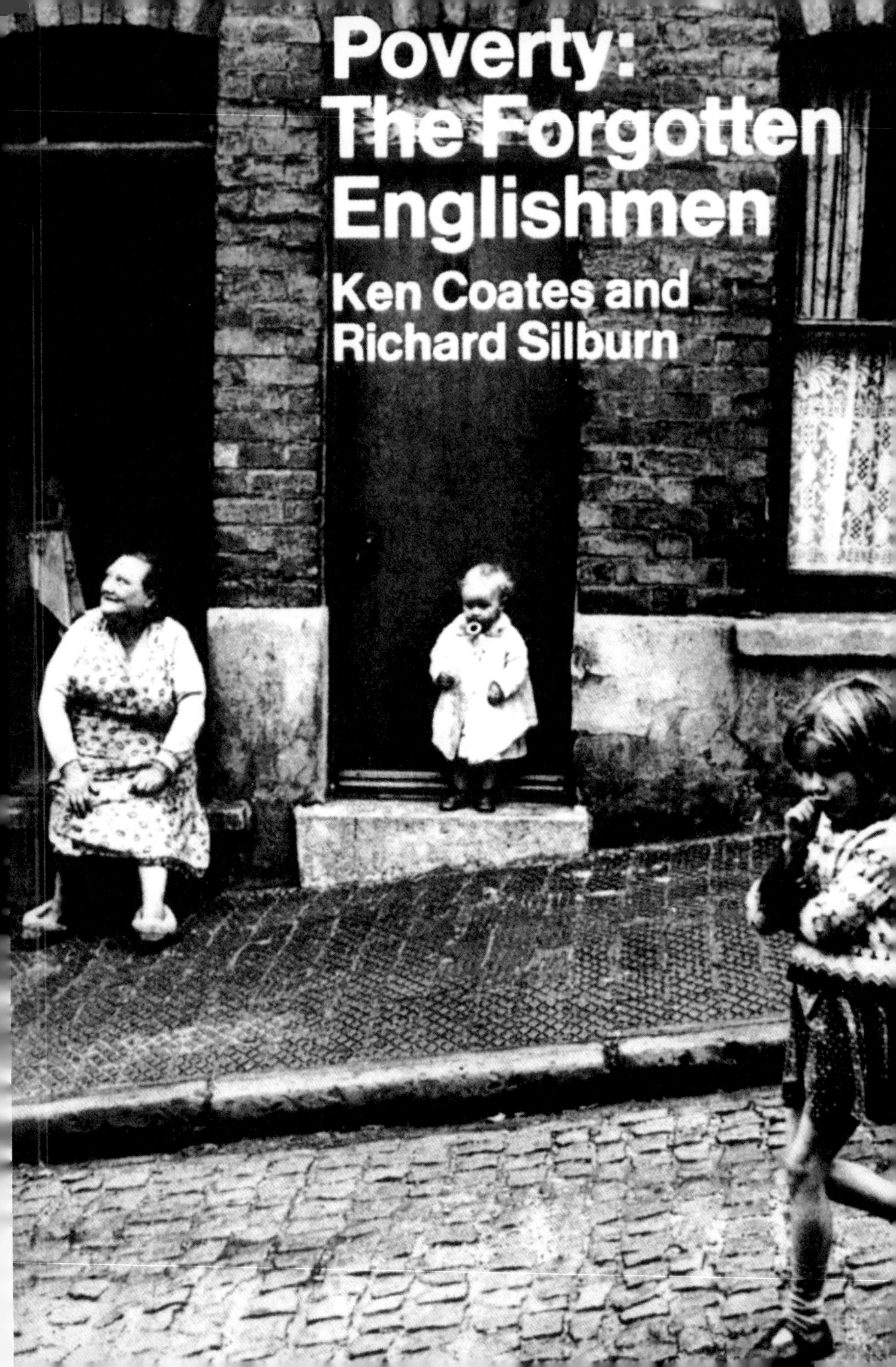
Poverty:
The Forgotten
Englishmen
Ken Coates and
Richard Silburn

The Way We Still Live Now

Ken Coates

Published in Socialist Leader, *August 29 1970. Ken Coates worked extensively on poverty in Britain, most notably in two works written with Richard Silburn:* St Ann's: Poverty, deprivation and morale in a Nottingham community *and* Poverty: The Forgotten Englishmen.

Mr. Wilson has come and gone. The winds of innovation have passed through Whitehall and ruffled up the major industrial combines, merging some here and rationalising others there. Today men who were powerful six years ago are wont to be still more powerful. Men at the burgeoning middle level have more opulent roadhouses to choose from, when they entertain their friends on the expense account.

The other day I was helping put together a film in St. Ann's. We were looking for young mothers, who could describe life at the other extreme, in the struggle to keep slum children clean and healthy. We found them, and in time they will say their piece on telly. We also found some old ladies, whose plight we weren't discussing, so they won't appear. But before the Labour Party Conference undertakes its post-mortem on What Went Wrong, its delegates ought, both for their own good and the good of the cause, to meet some of them, because they might help us to answer that question.

Mrs. James, we will call her, is an old, old lady indeed. She is 87, and she lives in a row of houses which we will call, no more fancifully than it is in fact called, Bluebell Terrace. Bluebell Terrace is one of several short rows which are stretched parallel across a short terrace cut out of a hillside, butting into a brick cliff which walls up a higher range, on which other terraces can be seen dangling above.

The terrace is wide enough to carry six or seven two-up, two-down cottages in each row. These cottages have back doors facing little files of broken outside lavatories, and front doors facing the backs of lavatories of the next row. Each yard is approached by steeply cramped black brick stairways, rising off a street whose other side gives on to another terrace. Mrs. James lives with her son, who "earns good money", some £20 a week, and she can't wait for the demolition men to come, because she has arthritis which is greatly worsened by the damp conditions which affect all the houses in the row.

The houses are not damp because it is raining in, which it is, but because the damp runs down the terrace from the hillside and rises up through all the floors. When you tread on the black bricks in the yards, you can make them squelch. Inside the houses, umpteen thicknesses of paper under the lino or the carpet all go mouldy, even though everyone has a blazing fire in mid-July. Mrs. James took us up to see her son's bedroom, where she has to keep a bowl by his bed in case it rains. The rent is 26s. a week. The landlord won't mend the roof because the house is scheduled for clearance. Clearance might not take place for two years. Mrs. James is 87.

But Mrs. James is a woman of great resources, and she keeps cheerful. The lady we will call Mrs. Target, next door, is in worse case. She is only 57. We met her dragging herself up the steps from the street, pulling a little shopping basket on wheels. She, too, has arthritis, and is, indeed, one can truthfully say, crippled by it.

She took us into her little house, which is kept beautifully, and showed us the parlour, with its fire up the chimney, and the rising damp crawling up the wallpaper all around. She showed us the mouldy cupboard, right by the fireplace, which she had lined with cooking foil in order to try, vainly, to make it usable. She told us her story. She had worked in a department store until recently.

She had the voice of a John Lewis partner, and was clearly habituated to respecting herself. She had to stop work because of the arthritis. She lived on £6 a week relief. When she got behind with her electricity bills, and asked the Supplementary Benefits people to help, they told her she must learn to budget and refused. "It was a chit of a thing, an eighteen-year-old, who told me," she said. As she described the house, she began crying uncontrollably. A lonely woman, there is no one to whom she can turn to ask for help in dealing with the landlord, the corporation, or the relieving authorities.

She opened the stair door to show us the two top rooms. She began to crawl upstairs like a wounded dog. "Why haven't you a stair-rail?" we asked. It came away from the wall six months ago, and the landlord won't re-fix it because it is her responsibility. For six months Mrs. Target has been fighting her way up and downstairs on her hands and knees. She could be forgiven if, during this time, she didn't notice the election. The outcome could scarcely affect her for the worse.

Next door to Mrs. Target, in the house by the cliff wall, is yet another old lady, who didn't speak to us, but looked at us a bit resentfully when we spoke to her. "She's a recluse," said Mrs. Target. "Her house is the worst of the lot; the water just runs down the walls in streams. It's quite terrible."

In the first house in the row, hanging straight over the street, by the little steps, is Mrs. Thompson. (This is not her real name either.) She is a widow. Her husband died last year. He was 58. He had bronchial pneumonia. "We sent him away earlier on, and he got ever so much better," she said, "but when he came back the doctor said we should all leave here." Mrs. Thompson's rent is 15s. a week.

In the new houses which the corporation is stacking 27 to the acre across St. Ann's, rents will vary from just over £3 a week upwards. Two-fifths of the people of St. Ann's live at or below the standards set by public relief.

Mr. Greenwood's callously stupid remarks about the solution of the housing problem aside, it is clear that no one can solve the slum problem without at the same time attacking the present total distribution of income and wealth in this country. And it should be plain that this distribution will not change unless we attack also at the same time, the power-structure upon which rests the whole existing system of wretchedness and greed. If the old ladies of St. Ann's could speak at the Blackpool Conference, perhaps we would see this truth.

If the Labour Party is content to discuss how Mr. Wilson can win the next election, and stop at that, it deserves to be totally ostracised by every decent man and woman in the country. The only discussion that makes sense is one which attacks the problem of socialising power and wealth, and in that light, evolves a strategy against poverty which can kill it for all time. In a word, Labour must rediscover a path to socialism.

Is this suggestion a sick joke?

Socialism and the Environment

Socialism and the Environment

Ken Coates

Published in Socialism and the Environment, *Spokesman, 1972. This volume grew out of the international conference on "The Quality of Life" organised by the German Metal-workers' Union, I.G. Metall and was translated into several languages including German and Japanese.*

Somewhat belatedly, the socialist movement has begun to face up to some of the issues which are involved in the increasingly urgent debate on the environment. In Britain, the argument has broken out across the whole spectrum of the left, involving Wayland Young in the Fabian Society, C.A.R. Crosland from the front bench of the Parliamentary Labour Party, John Lewis and the readers of the Communist Party's newspaper *The Morning Star*, and some few voices of the New Left, including those which speak in this collection of papers. Crosland has sprung to the defence of working-class standards of life, to urge that trade unionists have a right to take their holidays in Majorca even if (as he implies in a characteristically snobbish aside) this implies the proliferation of fish and chip shops in that once blessed haven.[1] Trade unionists might well have been grateful for this advocacy during the days in which Crosland's own administration was busily restricting their purchasing power in the interests of the defence of sterling: but they will need stronger defences than Crosland's newfound "populism" if they are to resist the next onslaught that will fall on them, which will undoubtedly seek legitimacy in the appeal to environmental conservation.

Of course, there is an ecological crisis. Its precise boundaries and significance remain to some extent open to argument, since there may well be some case for caution in the extrapolation of existing trends over a prolonged time-scale. As Professor Kapp has pointed out, a computer set to work in 1872 would have predicted that the density of horse-drawn traffic would by now be so great as to render all our cities impassable:

choked as they would be with an impenetrable deposit of horse-dung.[2] The new technologies have been developing with remarkable speed, and much of the discussion of their likely effect is bound to be to some degree conjectural, not only until their side effects and other implications have had some time to manifest themselves, but also until their longevity can be assessed, and their degree of liability to supercession by still further new technologies estimated. Yet it is impossible to dismiss as simply misplaced certain of the central arguments of what has become the ecology lobby: while this movement contains its own bizarre and reactionary voices, and while it frequently betrays a lack of sociological sophistication, it has nonetheless produced a volume of hard evidence … which already demands not only scrutiny, but also action.

More than a century ago, Marx repeatedly warned against the fact that:

> "all progress in capitalistic agriculture is a progress in the art, not only of robbing the labourer, but of robbing the soil; all progress in increasing the fertility of the soil for a given time, is a progress towards ruining the lasting sources of that fertility. The more a country starts its development on the foundation of modern industry, like the United States, for example, the more rapid is this process of destruction. Capitalist production, therefore, develops technology, and the combining together of various processes into a social whole, only by sapping the original sources of all wealth – the soil and the labourer."[3]

The works of the Ehrlichs, Commoners, Meadows and others, whatever other effects they may have, assuredly serve to provide at any rate a partial documentation of the results of the evolution, over a hundred years of blind rapacity, of capitalism's extraordinary "success".

Traditional socialism has in its theoretical arsenal two responses to this state of affairs. The first of these concerns the critique of the market economy, which, for a by no means negligible part of the ecological lobby, seems, however inconsistently, to remain a basic presumption, a sacred cow. Labour movements will soon discover this truth, because the administrators of the market economy, once alerted to the environmental problems their institutions have created, will spare no efforts to present the bill for them to the very workpeople who are the main sufferers from the ill-effects both of the problems themselves and the institutions which have given rise to them. It is not impossible that we shall live to see Mr. Roy Jenkins restored to office by virtue of the vices of his antagonists, attempting to freeze the busmen's wages in order to prosper the cause of national conservation. To avoid this state of affairs, socialists must take the offensive, not merely to ensure that capitalism is presented with its own bills, but also to determine that it be forced into liquidation as soon as possible.

There is a second traditional socialist insight which is crucial to the consideration of this issue, if the whole argument is not to be allowed to become a pretext for a new conservative authoritarianism. This is linked with the first, but is by no means reducable to it: it concerns the basic assumption of Marx, which was that capitalism saps not only the productivity of the soil, but also that of the labourer. Of all the resources available to mankind, the only virtually infinite one is that of human potential. Before one can give a definitive answer to the question of how many human beings can survive in a given space with given materials, one has to know what kind of human beings are under consideration. Presumably there was an optimum population as well as a maximum population which was capable of survival in the environment confronting paleolithic men. Whatever specific figures might be put on these populations, they were vastly smaller than those which could apply to primitive agriculturists, and these in turn were very much less than those relevant to civilisation, in the dawn of metal technology.

Man and his environment have always existed in reciprocal interaction, and the same constellation of natural elements have been proved capable of bearing radically different meaning for men at different levels of intellectual development and technical prowess. There is every reason to believe that each technology has its frontiers of potential; but we shall never be able to delineate those frontiers fully until we have answered first the question of how far technologies themselves are contained and distorted within the restrictive presumptions of divided and exploitative societies. Other societies than modern capitalism have collapsed. None could be said to have fallen for want of technology in the abstract: indeed history is full of accounts of ruined civilisations which were structurally incapable of utilising and developing the techniques they had already begun to discover.

The Greeks made elaborate toys incorporating some of the basic principles of steam engines at Alexandria: but they had no need for mechanical motive force when there was adequate slave-power on call, so that their discoveries had a purely academic significance. The development of Ancient science has been shown to have repeatedly run into cul-de-sacs, not because of any want of abstract intellectual capacity, but because the social structures of Greece and Rome created life-styles and expectations among the leisured classes which militated against experimentalism and applied practical intellectual activity in many fields.[4] In war, or in Government, the inhibitions may have been less formidable than they were in husbandry, medicine, and the practical arts of economic production: even in war, however, the class structure exercised its pernicious enfeebling influence over time. To remain in this comparatively narrow field of enquiry, we would be bound to recognise that neither the Greek nor the Roman civilisations floundered because of their technological rigidity, but that they fell because of the contradictory pressures generated within their oppressive social structures, which exercised their own baleful influence on technological development.

Again and again throughout history we find instances of this same phenomenon. In the writings of Ibn Khaldun, the Arab scholar who founded historical sociology in the 14th Century, we find an account of the cycle of governmental styles in hydraulic society, as dynasty succeeds dynasty and replicates its trajectory, through the generations, from popular upsurge to oppressive tyranny, from restorer and custodian of the irrigation works to parasite, war lord and vainglorious builder of state monuments among the recurrent droughts and floods produced by the neglect of water conservation. The Ch'in dynasty in China had sufficient technology to consolidate the unification of the country by unifying its canals: it did not have adequate politics or social science to prevent the recurrent neglect and abuse of that technology, and the recurrent cycle of "good" and "bad" government which was later to be noted by Ibn Khaldun in the somewhat different circumstances of the near East.

Even when advanced techniques have been imported neat from other cultures, class structures have frequently proved insufficiently plastic to utilise them. This is true even in the military domain, where opportunism is normally well-developed. A classic case is that of the introduction of firearms into the Mamluk kingdom: the development of the arquebus, general throughout Europe for more than a century before the final confrontation between the Mamluks and the Ottomans, was meaningless to a military caste which identified status with cavalry and could not delegate critical responsibility to mere foot-soldiers. Throughout crucial struggles the decisive weapons could only be wielded by slaves. The Mamluks were routed.[5]

Modern capitalism has liberated an explosion in technical capacities, and has created the preconditions for a global society. But it has no more solved the problem of class antagonism, of internecine social war, than did the Ancients with their slaves, or the oriental despots in the great river-based civilisations. Both inside the great capitalist metropoles, and outside them in the subordinated territories over which they hold sway, class struggles are a fundamental fact of life. That the ascendent class is today an entrepreneurial one only adds the burden of market domination to that of political subordination. In such a context, technology is *always* distorted.

Social priorities emerge by a process of aggravated indetermination, to determine that millions shall starve while inconceivable wealth is pledged to the task of lunar exploration. More ingenuity is lavished on research into the production of harmful detergents than on the investigation of cancer, while the goal of enabling a few men to traverse the Atlantic in three and a half hours assumes greater importance, and demands much greater investment, than that of enabling the majority of citizens in a small country like Britain to cross their own capital city in the same time.

In modern capitalist industry, which produces an increasing number of technical miracles which virtually no-one wants, the vast majority of human beings develop only a tiny fraction of their capacities. Large numbers of production processes exist which can pre-empt the waking hours of an enormous labour force, often for some transparently silly purpose, without stimulating in their victims anything other than the most basic mechanical skills and a developed capacity for alienated day-dreams. This artificial diminution of human beings is one of the major triumphs of capitalist industrial organisation, and must be considered as having some weight in any explanation for the astonishing longevity of the system. The process is never complete, and there are welcome signs that it is less and less able to function adequately, as technologies demand higher levels of skill in at least part of the labour-force, and as competition stimulates appetites which it cannot slake. Even so, the manifold deprivations inflicted upon the human victims of capitalism begin with, and culminate in, the restriction of their potential for self-development. Any ecology which ignores this fact ignores the fundamental problem, and can only be expected to develop into a form of elitist anti-humanism. The present significance of the movement for workers' control and socialist self-management is not that it already provides the answers to this problem, but only that it faces the question. Unless this question is faced, the only conceivable strategy for preserving the environment from the ruin which is predicted for it is a narrowly restrictive one, based on curbing the elementary appetites of the many, while quite possibly stimulating all the silliest and greediest fads against which ecologists rightly complain, in order to develop the "proven" capacities of the few.

Does this mean that the Malthusian echoes which are to be heard on all sides lack all foundation in science? Hardly. Malthus remains as wrong as he ever was, but there is a population problem for capitalist-imperialist society, and it may well be "solved" by the inhuman processes predicted by so many ecologists. If we say that developed people can make more of an unpromising environment than undeveloped people, this does not mean they can levitate themselves above all material problems. But the major material problem of the modern world remains that of its social structure, which generates a whole series of obstacles to the solution of all other material problems. First, it thwarts personal human growth and therefore the progress of art and science. Mute inglorious Miltons abound within it, because it mutes them. But secondly, thwarted people are more easily constrained to develop thwarted needs, to seek surrogate satisfactions, and commonly, to compensate for the frustration of their spiritual, intellectual needs by the generation of quite peculiar material appetites. This opens up the whole question of what is involved in the concept of "need", and to this we shall have to return.

Further, the same atavistic social arrangements commonly prevent the utilisation of any technology but the most "advanced", whose relative advancement may be, in human terms, that is to say, in terms of its practical usefulness to a given people within a particular terrain, highly questionable, but whose ascendancy is determined by its market superiority. The weight of this deformation of rational technique is felt above all in the undeveloped countries, where it is joined by the weight of controlled non-development of vital resources. To the extent that the World Health Organisation makes marginal improvements in life-expectation, in the birth-rate, and in overcoming child mortality, in these countries, while UNCTAD fails to do anything at all to reverse the trade imbalance which is constantly aggravating their adverse economic position, medical technology merely intensifies the contradictions which have prevented the social order from liberating any appropriate scientific response to the paramount needs of those territories. There is only one answer which is realistic for such countries: it is revolution. Revolution alone will tackle the economic development crisis: and in the process it will not fail to tackle the population problem, not for Malthusian reasons, but in response to the demands of revolutionary women for their own rights to develop as creative people.

In such revolution can be seen some key elements of the solution to the wider environmental crisis. The law of uneven development which produced the industry of Pittsburgh alongside the plantations of Cambodia, and the living standards of Detroit car-workers alongside those of Vietnamese rice-growers, is paralleled by a strange form of combined development.

As American Armies took the field in Korea and Vietnam, resting on the hyper-developed technology of their extraordinarily powerful economic base, so they produced a reaction among their antagonists. The Vietnamese, whose economic development at the beginning of the conflict was as scant as is imaginable, found themselves confronting a colossus. In fighting it, they were compelled to develop a politico-military machine of equal complexity: a human collective which could match the most sophisticated computer hardware which was ranged against it. This extended and intricately co-ordinated division of political and military labour could never have evolved from the paddy-fields alone. It arose to meet a specific and all-too-apparent challenge: but having evolved, it manifestly will not simply dissolve with the overcoming of that challenge. Such an extended and sophisticated machine has many uses other than military ones, and its effect on economic development when peace is won is likely to be explosive. Will it traverse the same paths in spoliation of the human and natural environment as its opponent? There is surely ground to doubt this. To begin with, it will commence reconstruction in a context in which the gross environmental ill-effects of American military technology will be major problems, and this will have the result of stimulating an unparalleled conservationist effort. To switch this on and off at random will prove quite impossible: and since the will to rehabilitate the habitat will become a national priority, it will obviously affect the development plans which follow. If Korean experience proves anything, it reveals the astonishing productive potential we may anticipate in Vietnam: the evolution of both countries will require close monitoring by socialists and environmentalists alike during the coming decade.

In the light of such studies, there may well be strong grounds for doubt about some of the more overtly Malthusian assumptions of ecological theorists. As a general commentary on these ideas, we could do worse than recollect Engels' account of the controversy of his own time, set down in his famous letter to Kautsky:

> "There is, of course, the abstract possibility that the number of people will become so great that limits will have to be set to their increase. But if at some stage communist society finds itself obliged to regulate the production of human beings, just as it has already come to regulate the production of things, it will be precisely this society, and this society alone, which can carry this out without difficulty. It does not seem to me that it would be at all difficult in such a society to achieve by planning a result which has already been produced spontaneously, without planning, in France and Lower Austria. At any rate, it is for the people in the communist society themselves to decide whether, when, and how this is to be done, and what means they wish to employ for the purpose. I do not feel called upon to make proposals or give them advice about it. These people, in any case, will surely not be any less intelligent than we are.
>
> Incidentally, as early as 1844 I wrote (*Deutsch-Franzosische Jahrb.*, p.109):

> 'Even if Malthus were altogether right, it would still be necessary to carry out this (socialist) reorganisation immediately, since only this reorganisation, only the enlightenment of the masses which it can bring with it, can make possible that moral restraint upon the instinct for reproduction which Malthus himself puts forward as the easiest and most effective countermeasure against over-population.'"[6]

Engels' last paragraph has a particular relevance to our own discussions: for sure, capitalism has survived (for twenty years? … fifty years? … seventy years?) longer than he anticipated, and its ecological crisis *would* demand structural changes before remedies could be forthcoming, even if it were to prove far less severe than Professor Ehrlich thinks. Exactly *what* population can be maintained in post-capitalist India, or Indonesia, is clearly a matter for some study, and we should certainly not dismiss the idea that this is a far more pressing problem in 1972 than it was in 1881. At the same time, we should equally certainly not dismiss the idea that the liberated ingenuity and creativity of millions of Indians or Indonesians can still exercise a powerful and positive effect on the final terms of the equation, when they come to be elaborated.

While my own bias would be towards considerable scepticism about the meaning of population projections, for the reasons I have given, which imply that China may well support more millions still if need be, while Africa and Latin America will scrimp and starve far lesser population increases, simply because restrictive social conditions prevent people from finding ways to help themselves: nonetheless it seems to me that there is one key area in which the ecological debate compels socialists to take careful stock of their basic theoretical equipment. This concerns the problem: what constitutes a *need*? If everybody needs to fly in Concorde, then they can't: that seems superabundantly plain. We shall drink up all our oil in short order if only a proportion of the world's VIP's come to the conclusion that this is amongst their urgent necessities. The notion that everyone in the world needs a car presents a similar problem. With somewhat less clarity, we can see a whole series of like difficulties looming up when we look at the likely availability of useable resources in a number of other fields. This appreciation must require at least some intellectual effort by socialists about their fundamental goals.

* * * *

The classic statement of the socialist aim is that of Karl Marx:

> " ... after the enslaving subordination of the individual to the division of labour, and therewith also the antithesis between mental and physical labour, has vanished; after labour has become not only a means of life but life's prime want; after the productive forces have also increased with the all-round development of the individual, and all the springs of co-operative wealth flow more abundantly – only then can the narrow horizon of bourgeois right be crossed in its entirety and society inscribe on its banners: From each according to his ability, to each according to his needs!"[7]

This celebrated watchword has a very plain meaning: bourgeois right will be superceded when society has developed to the point that it can sustain the free personal development of its members to the point that each makes voluntarily his own contribution, which represents the best of which he is capable, in the light of his *personal* estimate of his ability: while each receives according to his needs which, in the context, can only be those which are felt, subjectively, to exist. In this sense alone can we make sense of Marx's own view that, for him, communism represented a step beyond the realm of necessity. Of course, Engels tells us that freedom is the recognition of necessity, an aphorism which has caused no little confusion.[8] In this insight, "recognition" has a peculiarly Hegelian meaning, and can only be adequately understood in the light of Hegel's own dictum "to undestand is to pass beyond". Lenin certainly saw all this when he annotated Hegel's Logic during the early months of the First World War, and wrote in its margins "Freedom = Subjectivity".[9]

Marx had written about "a first phase" and a "higher phase" of communist society, and had given his view that the reign of subjectivity would begin in the higher phase, with the final abrogation of "bourgeois right". His schema was substantially modified in the Soviet Union after 1934, with the announcement of the inauguration of "socialism" at the conclusion of the farm collectivisation programme. The full socialisation of property was identified as the consolidation of Marx's "first phase"; and a new principle was announced as relevant to this: "from each according to his ability, to each according to his work". This formula is a subtle modification of that of Marx. "Work" is not a quality which is evaluated purely subjectively: on the contrary, for a vast majority of workers in the Soviet Union it can be very precisely assessed, and quantified, according to what are claimed to be "objective" criteria. True, there is the age-old problem of arriving at a calculus which can permit estimates of the relative worth of physical and intellectual work: and the Russians have reached no deeper into the heart of this difficulty than have the industrial psychologists of Western capitalism. Indeed, Elliot Jacques' nostrum of a "time-span of responsibility" which would pay people according to their capacity to operate without supervision, for all its manifest logical shortcomings, seems a severely practical measure compared to those applied in the USSR, when things are no better advanced than they were in the division of labour between Sidney and Beatrice Webb at the turn of the century. "Sidney" said Beatrice, "is responsible for the matters of fact in all our researches, while I am in charge of matters of principle." "Who, then," asked a curious disciple "determines which is which: what is fact and what is principle?" "Oh" came the reply, "that is a matter of principle, and so it is bound to be my concern."

Somewhat similarly, the calculation of the relative value of mental and manual work in Russia appears to be quite squarely and definitively the responsibility of mental workers. Hardly surprisingly, Mme Furtseva's salary has thus been estimated to reflect far greater social effort than that of a coal-miner. But if "work" is in truth difficult to evaluate objectively, it is certainly evaluated externally as far as the operative is concerned. At the same time, the word "ability" bears a very different meaning when it is juxtaposed with "work" than it held when it was linked with "need". Marx thought of ability in the same way that he thought of need, as a quality subjectively assessed. But just as whole batteries of work-study men can with greater or less degrees of apparent justice pin cash amounts on units of work performed, so, in such a context, "ability" becomes an externally adjudged, and therefore, to a degree, externally limited; matter. This gross devaluation of the socialist goal reached beyond the initial verbal modifications of 1934, to culminate in the revision of the Russian Communist Programme at the 22nd Congress of the CPSU. In the discussion of this Programme, which marked a considerable departure from Marxist orthodoxy, N. S. Khruschev made it plain that under communism the phase "to each according to his needs" certainly did not mean "that each individual could claim just what he liked." Since the new society was due by 1980, this was a provident reservation, even if it might have drawn a blistering criticism from the author of the *Critique of the Gotha Programme*.

Yet, if communism in its classic literature is about the rule of "subjectivity", at no point did Marx reject the view that in all human society individual personality is developed in social interaction. "Needs" for him, were largely learnt behaviour. Describing the formation of needs under capitalism, he was extremely specific on this matter:

> "Our needs and enjoyments spring from society: we measure them, therefore, by society and not by the objects of their satisfaction. Because they are of a social nature, they are of a relative nature..."[10]

Under capitalism, this relativity takes competitive forms:

> "A house may be large or small; as long as the surrounding houses are equally small it satisfies all social demands for a dwelling. But if a palace arises beside the little house, the little house shrinks into a hut. The little house shows now that its owner has only very slight or no demands to make; and however high it may shoot up in the course of civilisation, if the neighbouring palace grows to an equal or even greater extent, the dweller in the relatively small house, will feel more and more uncomfortable, dissatisfied and cramped within its four walls."

Does this mean simply that Marx thought everyone must keep up with the Joneses? Hardly: he was concerned to illustrate the extent to which appetites are evolved, beyond simple natural needs (whatever they are) to increasingly *social* conventions. Two post-Marxian insights need to be taken into account in updating this intuition: first, the extent to which the creation of needs has itself been institutionalised, in the development of a specific industry concerned with advertising and marketing. This is one-sidedly considered, from different sides, by Fromm in his book *The Fear of Freedom* and by Marcuse in *One-Dimensional Man*. Secondly, there are artificial social limits to this learning-process, which have come to be explained in conventional sociology by the concept of reference groups. Some such concept is needed to account for the fact that in all our cities slums and palaces have been jostling side-by-side, in narrowly adjacent districts, for a century or more, and yet incendiaries from the poor districts are extremely uncommon in the rich ones, while expropriations of the mansion-holders and penthouse dwellers are almost unheard of, except as hippy escapades. However we may wish to develop these later ideas, there will be few people who wish to resist the basic notion that men learn their needs in social interaction.

The debate on the environment raises the possibilities of a studied attempt by authority to intervene in this process for "social" purposes. In this connection there is already a developed arsenal of techniques not only in the advertising business, but, from another side of the problem, in the institutions of the welfare state. The danger of elite pressures for the control of "anti-social" appetites and the "social" manipulation of needs is all too painfully apparent. We could well reach a situation in which a managed or "concerted" capitalism developed an ideology of need-control which was not a thousand miles in its assumptions from the surrogate-communism of Mr. Khruschev. It is for this reason that socialists who are alive to the problem of environmental development need at the same time to pay close attention to the refinement of their own concepts, not in order to dilute them, but in order the better to insist on the democratisation of all those areas of decision-taking, extant and about-to-come-into-being, in which these considerations are going to figure. If it becomes plain on investigation that this or that resource will largely disappear in ten or twenty years, the labour of adapting to such a problem must be a truly social, truly collective one, and not a response by a narrow interest group. No such decisions can be taken collectively without open and public argument, since no such decisions are without differential ill-effects on different social groups. The more true it is that there are serious resource problems, the more necessary it becomes that strict social accountability be imposed on every authority involved in access to those resources. The graver the threat of pollution, the greater the concerted social effort required to meet it, and the more profound the need for democratic means to arouse the conviction that the effort is necessary. And the larger the problems of adaptation to new natural imperatives, the more need for creative involvement by wider and wider sections of the affected population.

Industrial, political and social democracy are not, in this sense, dispensible attitudes, transitory systems of administration. They must be at the very core of any strategy for the defence of man's environment, if we are not to see a situation in which the very squalor of capitalism becomes a pretext for riveting its basic institutions and impulses even more firmly and inflexibly on an increasingly reluctant society. In reaction to the spoliations of capitalist industrialism, nineteenth century socialism developed a set of ideals in which the generous impulses of men could once again recognise themselves. If these impulses are to be curbed by a new authoritarianism, if capitalism is to seek ways to enter a Spartan age where the vicious dogmas of Malthus have the force of law, then not only will we see a painful restriction of human appetites, but we shall almost certainly lose the battle for the environment as well. To state the prospect is to show how unthinkable it is.

Notes

1. Cf. Michael Barratt Brown: *Must We Build More Cars and Dishwashers Before We Can Have More Roads, Schools and Houses?* Spokesman, No. 12, May 1971.

2. Professor Kapp was introducing his paper at the Fourth I.G. Metall International Conference: "The Quality of Life", held at Oberhausen, Germany, during April 1972.

3. *Capital*, Volume I, (Torr Edition) pp. 513-4. Cf. also Volume III (Kerr, Chicago), where Marx claims that "the whole spirit of capitalist production, which is directed toward the immediate gain of money, contradicts agriculture, which has to minister to the entire range of permanent necessities of life required by a network of human generations." (page 724) and the same volume, pp. 944-5. Marx also made a number of other references to the problem in his *Theories of Surplus Value*, the third and final volume of which has recently appeared, and which contains a rudimentary index.

4. Cf. *Greek Science* by Benjamin Farrington (2 volumes, Penguin, 1949) and the same author's *Head and Hand in Ancient Greece*, Watts, 1947.

5. Cf. David Ayalon *Gunpowder and Firearms in the Manluk Kingdom*, Valentine, Mitchell, 1956.

6. Engels' letter to Kautsky, 1 February, 1881. Reproduced in *Marx and Engels on Malthus*, edited by R.L. Meek, Lawrence and Wishart, 1953, pp. 108-9.

7. *The Critique of the Gotha Programme*, Foreign Languages Publishing House, Moscow, n.d., p.22.

8. In fact, the motto originated with Spinoza, but was taken up by Engels in *Anti-Duhring*.

9. Cf. *Lenin's Philosophical Notebooks*, contained in Volume 38 of the *Collected Works*, F.L.P.H., Moscow, 19.

10. *Wage-Labour and Capital*, in Karl Marx, *Selected Works*, Vol.1, Lawrence and Wishart, 1946, pp.268-9. Richard Silburn and I have discussed this insight in the context of modern research in our Penguin Special: *Poverty: The Forgotten Englishmen*.

11. Op.Cit. p.268.

Brussels, December 1993: participants in the first ever European Disabled People's Parliament, initiated by Ken Coates MEP and others.

KEN COATES
AND TONY TOPHAM
THE NE
UNIONISM
THE CASE FO
WORKERS' CONTR

Towards Self-Management

Ken Coates &
Tony Topham

Published in The New Unionism: The Case for Workers' Control, *1972.*
Theory and practice of 'self-management' had been put to the test in Yugoslavia, Algeria and in the spirit of the Prague Spring where it met challenges, abandonment and crushing defeat under the tracks of invading tanks. It interested and motivated many of those involved with the Workers' Control movement in Britain. Despite challenges, initiatives for 'self-management' or 'direct democracy' reappear. Coates and Topham probe why this is the case.

'No man is good enough to be another man's master,' wrote William Morris. It is a profound thought, if a simple one. In a world in which masters dominate, the social arrangements over which they preside are so arranged as to obscure its truth. Myths are created, with the prime object of justifying the right of rulers to rule, owners to own, managers to manage. These myths cannot succeed in their prime object, however, if they do not, at the same time, achieve a secondary effect: the undermining of the self-confidence, critical judgement and independent initiative of all those over whom rule is exercised.

This is a common story. In the United States black people have been dominated, ever since the overthrow of direct slavery, as much by their own carefully implanted sense of inadequacy as by the force at the disposal of authority. When Malcolm X and his friends began to preach 'Black is beautiful', and the movement for Black Power started rolling, the first and key element in the upsurge of the black population was a new self-recognition. Black people had to recognize themselves, but they also had to learn to like what they recognized. In the same way, the movement for Women's Liberation has to begin with an attack on all the complex of attitudes held by women which contribute to their subordination. And with working people, things are not fundamentally different. It is a mental police force, first and foremost, which holds the trade unions in a subject role. Whilst workers take for granted their right to political suffrage, they are prevented, by attitudes which pervade their whole upbringing, from conceiving industrial suffrage as natural or just.

What are these mental policemen? In the old days they were savagely distorted religious ideas, which not only placed God over Heaven just as the King ruled the State, but went further, to uphold the notion that the King derived his own authority directly from God, to whom alone he was accountable. If there are modern workers who believe in God, there are few among them who would be prepared to accept that He appointed the Chairman of the Board of Directors, and fewer still who see the lineaments of divinity in the inconsiderate and impolite fellow who, all too often, is entrusted with the immediate supervision of their work. More subtle myths, rationally founded, are required to justify the present industrial order.

We must necessarily examine two of these. The first is the myth of 'intelligence'. Some men, we can all see, are cleverer than others. You have to be clever to run a factory. If you are clever, provided you are not *too* clever, you'll get on. All these commonsense perceptions have now been systematized into an extensive theory of intelligence, which, however often it is questioned or discredited, still persuades many people that they are too stupid to know how to conduct their own collective affairs. The theory, in its crudest form, states a number of propositions. One is that intelligence is a quality which is secreted in individual heads. Another is that the capacity to secrete it is determined genetically, so that it can be inherited. A third used to be that this capacity was fixed, and unchanging, so that it could be objectively measured by an intelligence quotient. An extension of it, commonly made, is the fourth proposition that people in subordinate roles occupy them because they are inadequate in intelligence, and could not do other than what they are doing. All four propositions are questionable. We prefer to regard intelligence as a social product, resulting from the social interaction of people. Whilst all kinds of characteristics can be inherited, most people are capable of learning up to the highest standards, provided that the learning starts early enough, that the teaching is effective and that the process is not subject to counter-influences from the labour market, which discourage the learner and distort the role of the teacher. Because it is a social development, the capacity of people to show individual intelligence, is very variable indeed, and can be drastically affected by changes in the social environment. And people in subordinate roles occupy them because people who aren't in them like to keep things that way.

And yet it remains true that workers need to learn much before they can manage their own factories. If teaching facilities were made available to them by the factories, they could acquire the right knowledge relatively simply. But the factories are organized in ways which prevent them from being taught, so that the whole process of management appears to be out of reach.

The second myth is that property is the whole basis for a free society. This myth used to be a great deal truer than it is today. In the Middle Ages, when 'town air was free air' and the guilds were at their height, a workman would own his tools, his shop and his product. Apprentices would learn their skills and subsequently become masters. Property in scissors, needles and cloth was indeed the very foundation of the freedom of the tailor, or the glover, in such a society.

But property in the vast concert of machines which are currently working towards the manufacture of the RB-211 aero-engine is a very different story. Those who own this equipment can only do so at the expense of the freedom of all those who have to work it. Unless this ownership becomes truly social, that is to say communal, it is bound to restrict the general freedom, not advance it.

None of these arguments prevents many workers from seeing things differently. If you ask ten engineers at random whether they believe in, say, the nationalization of the engineering industry, at least three or four of them will say 'No': and when pressed for a reason, answer: 'How would you like it if you worked all your life to build up a sweetshop, and the Govemment came along and took it?' Of course, sweetshops aren't aircraft industries and might well be left for ages to the control of individual shopkeepers, who might, indeed, feel the freer for the fact. But when workers make this equation, which is wrong, they do so because it corresponds to the 'normal' assumptions of the culture they inhabit. It is 'normal' for factories to be privately owned and autocratically managed. It is 'natural' for workers to be allocated to jobs which do little or nothing to develop their capacities, and subjected to disciplines which are calculated to restrict their initiative to minimal levels. If these things are usual, then they all too easily become accepted as unavoidable and, even when resented, may well be seen as, in some sense, 'fair'.

Yet the idea that no man is good enough to be another's master constantly recurs. It can be traced throughout the history of industrial capitalism, from its very dawn. The goal of social self-management has never really been purged from the body of the trade unions, or the political parties of Labour. With every crisis of the established order, it is wont to reappear. It is repeatedly announced to be dead, outdated or primitive. Men who have renounced it repeatedly secure preferment after the fact. Its partisans are frequently reviled and sometimes persecuted. None the less, it keeps coming back, and has done so ever since the beginning of socialism.

The lineaments of self-management are to be found clearly exposed as far back in British Labour history as the struggles of the Grand National Consolidated Trades Union.[1] In August 1833 the Manchester building operatives were locked out, in the famous dispute about the 'document' (in which employers tried to forbid trade-union membership, and required that all employees sign a statement that they did not, and would not, hold allegiance to a union). In his address to these workers, Robert Owen said:

> The turn-out of the building operatives, and the existing differences with their masters, will, I doubt not, tend greatly to effect a permanent good for both parties. It affords a fair opportunity for you, the producing classes (and masters and men are both producers), quietly, calmly but most effectively, to make a stand, at once, and put yourselves in your right position, and thereby gradually accomplish the great change required: that is, that individual competition, the bane of the producing class, shall cease among you, that your children shall be well trained and instructed in all that is useful from their birth, that they may become men and women possessing superior dispositions, habits, manners and conduct, and that whatever is injurious or inferior may speedily be removed out of society …

By December, the union men of Derby were 'turned out', and they went well beyond Owen to declare:

> Fellow countrymen, we are going to set the Derby people to work – we decline to contest the matter with the masters – we remove ourselves totally away from them. Every penny shall be applied to a reproductive end. The silk trade and the bobbin-net branch shall have warehouses and machinery of their own, and every thousand pounds of yours shall not only be maintained without diminution but shall be increased by the industry of Derby –
>
> With this view we call upon the machinists and working engineers of Glasgow and elsewhere to bethink themselves of the propriety of supplying a steam engine or engines to work the power looms. We call upon the men of Nottingham, Leicester, Macclesfield, Manchester, Congleton and Leek, to look out for, and supply, such machines as may be of instant use to the silk-throwsters, the spinners, the weavers and bobbin-net work-people; if each will contribute in this way, the groundwork will be established of a weekly increase ... Of the unemployed builders in Derby suffering from this persecution, we intend to select as many as the fund will admit of … to erect workshops and factories, and, it may be, dwelling houses, for the use of this Grand Union Association.[2]

But even the most successful attempts of the Owenites, to equip their own

Builders' Guild-Hall in Birmingham, came to grief.[3] Repeated experiments in communes, and lower-level attempts to establish producer co-operatives, all tended to failure on the same general ground: even if the famine of capital among workpeople could be partly relieved by wealthy donors, the division of labour outside the experimental units was more ruthless and more productive because it was arranged around more concentrated capital investment. So one tended to work harder in communist co-operation for less material reward.[4] The lessons of the failure of the communist colonies, and the weakness of the producer co-operatives were carefully discussed in the International Working Men's Association. In 1868, at its Brussels Congress, the International resolved:

> If we are such partisans ... of trade unions ... it is not only from regard to the necessities of the present, but also the future social order. To explain, we do not simply consider these as necessary palliatives (note that we do not say remedies), no, our views are much higher. From the bottom of the chaos and misery in which we struggle, we lift our eyes to a more harmonious and happy society. Then we see in these trades unions the embryos of the great workers' companies which will one day replace the capitalist companies with their thousands of wage-earners, at least in all industries where collective force is used and there is no middle way between wage-slavery and association. (As has been shown by recent strikes, Union funds may be used for setting up co-operative productive societies.)
>
> Yet it must be noted (and this is an important point) that the productive associations to arise from the trades unions will not be the trifling societies that the present-day associations are. These latter, excellent, we admit, as example and precept, do not seem to us to have in fact any great social future, any part to play in the renovation of society, for, consisting only of a few individuals, they can only end … by creating beside the bourgeoisie or *third estate*, a *fourth estate*, having beneath it a *fifth estate* yet more wretched. On the other hand the productive societies arising from the trades unions will embrace whole industries … thus forming the new corporation … founded on mutuality and justice and open to all.
>
> … This transformation of trade unions will take place not in one country alone, but in all, or all at least that are at the head of civilization…[5]

Within three years, one of the foremost nations 'at the head of civilisation' had given remarkable support to this prophecy. The Commune of Paris, during the short period of its rule, before its bloody suppression, went far towards implementing the principles advanced by the IWMA. On 16th April 1871, it decreed that those factories abandoned by their directors should be investigated and enumerated by the workers' *trade councils* 'to present a report on the practical means of exploiting again at once these deserted shops, not by the renegades who have left them but by a co-operative association of the workers once employed therein'.[6]

The Commune itself, elected by universal suffrage throughout Paris, set other rival patterns, recorded by Karl Marx in these words:

> The majority of its members were naturally working men, or acknowledged representatives of the working class. The Commune was to be a working, not a Parliamentary body, executive and legislative at the same time. Instead of continuing to be the agent of the central Government, the police was at once stripped of its political attributes, and turned into the responsible and at all times revocable agent of the Commune. So were the officials of all other branches of the Administration. From the members of the Commune downwards, the public service had to be done at workmen's wages.[7]

From this time on, the struggle for self-management was linked in workmen's minds with the struggle for the transformation of political institutions, up to and including the State itself. And necessary though this overall political transformation has remained, it has to be recorded that it has frequently been posed over and against the goal of self-management, in a manner which has had grave consequences not only for the development of cooperative democracy in industrial organization, but also for the maintenance of democratic controls of any kind over political processes themselves. The upsurge of the soviets in Russia, first in 1905 and then in 1917, was always linked in the minds of socialists with the example of the Paris Commune. But although the soviets were authentic and spontaneous workers' organs, once their rule had been established in the October Revolution, the dominance of the norms established in Paris in 1871, and cogently reaffirmed in Lenin's tract *The State and Revolution*, was short-lived.[8] However one evaluates the process by which the power of the soviets passed to the Communist Party, and the power of the Communist Party became concentrated in the hands first of its leadership, and ultimately of its leader, two linked facts must be squarely faced. First, the hostile encirclement of the new Soviet Union, and successive armed interventions, created a siege society and a quasi-military style of government: and second, at an early stage in this development, effective democracy in the factories gave place to increasingly centralized management, under diminishingly effective trade-union surveillance. The most baneful effects of these processes, it should be said, were not during the worst days of the Civil War, during which time social disruption was unbelievably acute but the socialist culture of the Revolution remained vividly alive and present. It was during the long years of rebuilding and the launching of the industrialization programme that the autocracy of the party leadership crystallized (while the principle of autocratic management in industry became firmly established) and ultimately transformed itself into personal dictatorship over the whole State, in which the only effective means of communication between the Government and the people was through the eyes and ears of the secret police.

Libraries of books have been written about this evolution. For our purposes, it is enough to say here that it powerfully assisted in the demobilization of the Labour movements of the majority of advanced countries during the inter-war years, and in the immediate post-war period after 1945. Sidney and Beatrice Webb were able to write of a 'New Civilization' in which all nonsense about workers' control, let alone self-management, had been finally refuted. Herbert Morrison was able to take himself to a Labour Party Conference in order to justify the London Passenger Transport Board as the best conceivable model for public enterprise, by genuflecting to the 'Russian experience'.[9]

It was not until 1948 that a major sector of the communist movement began to rediscover the central importance of self-management in the development of a new society. Lucien Goldmann has described this event with characteristic force: 'It will be the glory of the Yugoslav socialists to have been the first to introduce self-management into the real economic policy of a socialist state. Without doubt self-management seeks to correspond with the idea of freedom and human development which has always regulated the thoughts and hopes of socialists.'[10] When the Yugoslav communists were expelled from the Cominform by Stalin in 1948 they were faced with the immediate prospect of diplomatic, political and economic isolation. Since the country was neither economically self-supporting nor technologically developed, it could not remain in that condition without risking serious social and economic crisis. At the same time, there was a clear short-term need to mobilize to the full the internal human resources of the country, since no immediate external aid would materialize to fill the gap left by the withdrawal of the country from the Eastern bloc and from access to Russian economic assistance. The system of self-management of enterprises and social institutions was the Yugoslav answer to this problem of mobilization: through this method, the Government and the Communist Party aimed to raise the level of managerial skills in a society still backward and limited in its experience of industrial growth and organization. At the same time, self-management developed enthusiasm and commitment to the country's success and to the political leadership, and was a living demonstration that the Yugoslavs had rejected Stalinism not only at a diplomatic level, but also as a model for socialist theory and practice. Finally, the decentralization of command from the Stalinist ministries in Belgrade to the republic; the local communes and the individual enterprises, although controlled and limited during the 1950s, met a further need of the system; namely, to find a means of tolerating and harmonizing the nationalist and particularist tendencies of the different republics and nationalities within the country, without resorting to a repression and recentralization which the Party had rejected alike on ideological and economic grounds.

Thus, self-management of the factories, combined with a measure of internal decentralization of planning and resource allocation, represent a brilliant solution to many of the regime's most pressing problems. That this solution – in the absence of a political system which would have allowed democratic planning to evolve in place of bureaucratic planning – also led to the growth of market relationships between the self-managing enterprises and institutions, seemed in those early days only to confirm the advantages of the chosen road. For market relations encouraged the emergence of financial incentives: methods of payment, and differentials, which stimulated both individual and collective effort to raise productivity – the overriding need of the stricken and isolated economy. Moreover, a market system enabled the regime to adjust its relations with the still dominant peasant farming sector, collision with which could have produced a permanent social tension at the heart of the society, if it had been subject to the drastic methods of a siege economy. There is no evidence now to suggest that at that time (we are speaking roughly of the decade between 1951 and 1961) the Yugoslavs consciously recognized that the encouragement of market relations also prepared the economy for easier 'harmonization' with and penetration by, the economies of the capitalist Western world. During that period indeed, the regime – and particularly President Tito personally – strove vigorously to create a neutral bloc of countries which could establish its economic and diplomatic independence of both the Western and Eastern spheres of influence. The combined effects of CIA subversion and the objectively determined dominance of Western capital in the Third World, however, undermined the edifice which Tito aimed to build with Nehru, Nasser, Sukarno and the rest. Meanwhile, the Titoist heresy of 'separate roads to socialism' remained a recurrent threat to the internal security and cohesion of the Eastern European countries, thus ensuring that Yugoslavia could not adjust to an international division of labour by reharmonizing its economy with those of the Comecon members. This combination of circumstances determined the country's eventual orientation towards the Western world economy, and in particular towards the countries of the Common Market. Lacking the self-sufficiency of a Russia or a China, and not being able – because of internal differences of nationality and culture – to impose the stern controls which had been developed in, say, Cuba, the Yugoslavs were drawn inextricably towards the West. Their 'separate road to socialism' became diverted by external as much as by internal forces.

This experience should lead socialists in the West to a number of conclusions. First, that the self-management system of the Yugoslav workers' councils was always incomplete and vulnerable whilst set in a market economy. Secondly, that the obligation of socialists and trade unionists in a Western capitalist society, towards the Yugoslav working class, is a dual one. Trade unionists should not only appraise and defend its great positive contribution towards the global, historical experience of socialist theory and practice, but should also recognize that they, too, are involved in the negative evolution of that experience; whilst capitalism thrives and dominates the world economy, neither the Yugoslavs nor any other small nation can embark with impunity upon an unambiguous attempt to emancipate human beings from alienated, market, relationships. Thus, the deterioration of self-management in Yugoslavia is not only the concern, but also in a sense the responsibility, of workpeople in the West. Finally, we should acknowledge that despite the serious inroads made into the system, which have now reached the stage of invasion of the basic socialization of the means of production (Yugoslav enterprises now issue interest-bearing bonds for sale to individuals and institutions), the Yugoslav working class is the heir to an ideology which is anti-bureaucratic, and which stresses the principle of self-management, and is therefore uniquely equipped, amongst the countries which have undergone a social revolution, to stage an aggressive defence of the values it has been taught.

There is no necessity for us here to enter into a detailed description of the formal structures of Yugoslav workers' self-management. They have been amply documented elsewhere.[11]

Suffice it to remind readers that all economic and social organizations are managed by elected workers' councils, with which the ultimate legal authority for the whole range of decisions normally associated with boards of directors and boards of governors in a capitalist society is vested. Elaborate internal devolution of decision-making within each enterprise has been developed; there are workers' councils for separate departments, and collective decision-making on a number of matters has been handed down to the work group itself. As business methods have developed, so has the process of mergers between enterprises, so that multi-plant, cross-industry combines are increasingly common; for them yet another level of self-managing councils is necessary. It is not, we believe, the increasing scale and complexity of self-management institutions which threaten the reality of their power, but their subjection to market forces. To 'manage' the market, a new breed of businessman, the salaried executive, has come into being, who often has considerable scope to increase his income through commission, expenses, personal savings and 'speculation'. He may be formally accountable to the workers' council; but is able to place before it the necessities of the market, which become commercial restraints on the exercise of socially based decisions. Indeed, the social nature of economic decisions becomes itself obscure: the market assumes the same blind but imperative power as it has in a capitalist economy, and consequently the workers' council (where it does not abdicate its authority to a board of 'experts', a step which the law now tolerates) becomes alienated from its constituency; status and class differentiation reappears, and the working class withdraws from its commitment to the aims of the system.

Reinforcing these tendencies, which have gathered full momentum over the past eight years or so, the banks have emerged as dominant influences over the decisions taken by productive enterprises. The availability of loans and credit is crucial for expansion and prosperity of the enterprises; the criteria of the banks are increasingly commercial rather than social. In line with the consistent purpose of the regime in these later years (to insert the Yugoslav economy fully into the international divisions of labour), the State's management of external economic relations has been more and more 'liberalized', which has meant that the infant industries of the country feel the weight of competition from advanced economies, and that the currency has been subject to frequent devaluations. Pursuing the logic of this evolution further, the Yugoslav Government has ammended the laws on self-management on several occasions to allow more and more foreign, mainly West German and Italian capital, to invest in Yugoslav enterprises.[12] Where this occurs, the law on the supremacy of the workers' council may be suspended, whilst the foreign investor is permitted greater and greater leniency over the repatriation of his profits.[13]

A critical phenomenon which has now assumed serious proportions is the level of urban unemployment and rural underemployment.[14] Indeed this would be twice as serious were it not for another equally negative feature; the mass exodus of Yugoslav workers, involving both skilled workers and professional grades, to work in the factories and institutions of Western Europe, notably in West Germany. Yet further tensions are created for the hard-pressed leadership and for President Tito himself by the reappearance in strength of nationalism, which has thrived on the divisive influence of market-oriented and uneven development in the different regions of the country. This may take the form of revanchist neo-fascism, in the case of the Croat organization of the Ustasa, which is now active in the emigre Croat working-class communities in Western Europe. It had an appalling record of genocidal attacks on Serbian and other minorities in Croatia during the Second World War. In another form, nationalism threatens the cohesion and purpose of the Yugoslav League of Communists itself, as Tito has made clear in recent speeches attacking these tendencies. This is a critical factor as the long years of Tito's dominance over the Party and the State near their end. Clearly a collective leadership must succeed to power on his death or retirement, and clearly collective leadership requires a minimum of common commitment amongst the leaders to the interests of the Federal economy.

In all this gathering crisis, the victim at present is the working class and its instruments of self-management. Yet a strange phenomenon is occurring. The Yugoslav trade unions, which in the past have been the transmission-belt for State and Communist League priorities, have begun to assume an independent role. They have, in recent years, frequently expressed support for unofficial strikes, which have often been directed against the formal authority of the workers' council and the elite managerial class; and they have instituted post-strike inquiries in which 'heads have rolled' – figuratively speaking, of course. Last year the miners' union took a further step by actually declaring official a stoppage in that industry.[15] In 1971, the central body of the Federal Trade Union hierarchy itself was in direct controversy with the Government over the injustices of an incomes policy imposed to curb inflation. The divisions between new business-bureaucracy and old political-bureaucracy, between nationalists and federalists, between North and South, town and country, middle class and working class, are reflected in the political leadership and in the trade unions.

The outcome is impossible to assess, but we may be sure that it will not take the form of a simple reversion to capitalist relations, with the trade unions becoming the only and purely defensive expression of workers' interests. A new synthesis between socialist politics, trade-union practice, and self-management aspirations could emerge to challenge and halt the drift towards the re-Balkanization of Yugoslavia. Hopefully, the Yugoslav experience of self-management has still much to contribute to our understanding of the transition to socialism. Certainly we learn from the struggles of that country and its working class, that self-management does not easily detach itself from the concrete historical, political and economic circumstances in which it appears. The Western working classes do not inhabit economically handicapped Balkan countries in which most of the economic and technological cards would be stacked against them.

The salvation of the Yugoslav experiment could have been achieved by its extension to neighbouring countries, and the creation of an expanded economic base powerful enough to inspire the Labour movements of the Western capitalist-countries, as well as the workers of the Soviet Union itself.

An abortive but brave attempt to follow the Yugoslav example, also inspired by the Paris Commune, was made in Algeria after the victory of the National Liberation Front over the French forces. In 1963 the abandoned properties of French settlers were seized by the new government of Ben Bella and placed under self-management administration.[16] A 'bureau for the animation of the socialist sector' was established and manned by dedicated and intelligent socialists, and a serious effort was made to extend the principles established in Yugoslavia to the Algerian economy. But with the fall of Ben Bella, his proteges were exiled from the country or imprisoned, and the young self-managed firms and enterprises entered into a swift decline.[17] If the Yugoslavs suffered from this blow, it was nothing compared to what came after, in 1968.

The centralized and heavily bureaucratic political and economic machines that had been established in the early post-war years in Eastern Europe on the Russian model, had been accelerating towards open crisis throughout the 1960s. Czechoslovakia, the most industrially advanced country in the socialist bloc, suffered particularly under a remarkably sclerotic political hierarchy, headed by Antonin Novotny, which maintained a ludicrously rigid and top-heavy planning system and a command economy. The early post-war successes of this economy having exhausted themselves, it lapsed into an irremediable stagnation. Developing theories already tentatively advanced in the Soviet Union by 'liberal' economists, the Czech theoretician Ota Šik began to argue the case for a renewed role for the market in the Czechoslovak economy.[18] Having developed his ideas on this theme, he began to canvass them not only in the Communist Party; but also in the factories, where they became linked with the demand for autonomy by managers, and self-management by workers. The political movement of the Prague Spring gathered rapid momentum, and every aspect of social life experienced a radical democratization. For the first time in many years a socialist country found itself engaged in profound debate, openly conducted, about its goals and direction. Not a voice was raised for the return of capitalist forms. But keen concern was revealed, everywhere, for the achievement of the long-withheld democratic promise of socialism, in both industry and society. Workers' councils were formed in the factories and laws were drafted giving them substantial administrative powers. These were never implemented. In August 1968, the armies of five Warsaw Pact nations, headed by the Soviet Union, occupied Czechoslovakia, arrested the leaders of the Czech Government, and began a prolonged process of 'normalization', or, to be more precise, of restoration of the same abnormalities which have become the established institutions of the Soviet Union and its Eastern European allies.

But in Eastern Europe, and in the Soviet Union itself, socialism with a human face remains a potential challenge to those who inhabit the morally empty corridors of present power. We do not doubt that the challenge will find new expression in practice, throughout those territories in the future.

Meanwhile, in France in May 1968,[19] and in the subsequent Italian hot summer,[20] Western Europe began to see the pattern of a new kind of political awareness; directly challenging the old order. Workers' control, self-management, are ceasing to be the dreams of a mere coterie of idealists and are possessing the imagination of whole sectors of the European work-force. Even in England, things are moving.

The extraordinary struggle of the workers of the Upper Clyde shipyards, who, in their struggle to safeguard their employment, have raised the whole question of workers' control to a new level, has already triggered off a series of quite unparalleled actions, in which, from Plessey's at Dumbarton down to the River Don Steel Plant in Sheffield, and in enterprises from Bristol to Essex and from South Wales to London, workers' rights to control their jobs and to affect or set aside the investment decisions which determine them have been dramatically asserted. The main obstacle that prevents the incorporation of such episodes into an overall challenge to the whole social order is the domination under which the political councils of the Labour Movement suffer: domination by generations of men intellectually impoverished by the Cold War and its debilitating ideologies.

During the 1950s British Labour leaders converged on the discovery that socialism was all about equality. True, they tended to measure this in cash, and, true again, they were prone grossly to exaggerate their successes in realizing it, since they were misled by the official statistics of the day, provided in the main by the Inland Revenue.[21] England, they thought, was going through an egalitarian revolution, because the taxman showed that the range between the top and bottom levels of taxable income had been somewhat diminished. Indeed, incomes subject to tax were to some extent equalized: because a highly trained school of accountants were dedicating a developed (and expensive) expertise to the purpose of 'reducing' the size of units of income, precisely in order to shed as much as possible of the burden of taxation. But all this was very largely irrelevant to the facts of the distribution of wealth in Britain: and totally unrelated to the distribution of effective social power. Since, however, they believed themselves to be architects of the best of all possible social worlds, members of the Labour Establishment studiously abstained from discussing questions that might disrupt this comfortable assumption, and, instead, prescribed a simple solution to all such problems as they deigned to acknowledge. Poverty recurs? Frustration rules work? Even when they were forced to recognize such questions, the same mixture as before, only less of it, was all these pundits could ever bring themselves to recommend. In this way Labour leaders not only discredited themselves but also, to a certain extent, some valid ideals. Equality is a good goal, but not for reasons of dogma. The reason to move towards an equal society of free men and women is that the potential of individual people cannot be realized outside one. Inequalities invariably engender, just as they rise out of, the exploitation and manipulation of one man by another. When one person can subordinate another to his will, he diminishes both the other and himself in the act. When, together, men form common aspirations and find ways to move towards them, their development is mutually extended. For these reasons, the trite cry of 'equality of opportunity' is usually not only ill-thought-out, but self-defeating. Normally, it is a call for an equal start in the rat-race.

The real question is how to take people out of the rat-race and put them into the human race. Equality of opportunity can mean something valuable and real if it is interpreted as requiring that all men and women should have the optimal chance to develop their capacities to their fullest potential. There is no good reason not to assume that potential to be infinite: although how far it can be realized will depend on the human evolution of society as a whole. What is clear today is that the finest achievements of humanity remain, to the vast masses of human beings, a virtually closed book: and, even to the fortunate elites for whom they have some reality, they are refracted through a haze of misery and deprivation. Men in advanced civilizations commonly do not develop even a fractional part of their present capacities. Indeed, they are actively prevented from developing, because they could never accommodate to the routines of present industrial life if their abilities were ever even partially awoken. Production in our society has nothing to do with the development of human personalities and talents: it has everything to do with the subordination of those personalities and talents to the mechanical needs of the manufacturing processes.

The enemy, in this case, is the division of labour itself: that very social arrangement which stimulated an unprecedented growth in human powers, has become, increasingly, a fetter on those powers. At the beginning of modern political economy, Adam Smith pointed out that the difference between a porter and a philosopher depended primarily upon the use which society had made of their talents, rather than upon the 'original' state of those talents themselves. Nothing in modern psychology in any way effectively undermines this cry of faith. But industry creates the actual psychology of today's men, and, as Adam Smith again saw, the scope actually afforded to men to become either porters or philosophers is determined in the market available for those respective talents.

What stops human beings from making war on the division of labour? Modern communications media could make us all linguists, mathematicians, musicians at will. Electronics could reduce the hours of compulsory social labour to hitherto unimaginable minima. Every factory could become a school, and a true school at that, not an educational prison for preparing wage-slaves to accept their lot. Why don't we move in this direction? The main reason for social inertia, for failure to attack the crucial problem of human underdevelopment, is that the division of labour has solidified into a class structure, which, crystallized around institutions of property and manipulative indoctrination, has become self-perpetuating. Industry would be better run, even in the improvement of its levels of productivity, if it were based on the growing awareness and increasing initiative of all those at work within it. But such awareness and initiative are incompatible with the irrationalities of the power structure which industry serves, and so they cannot safely be allowed to grow.

Socialists, confronting this situation, face two linked but separable problems: they must move to overcome the division of labour, so that 'every cook may learn to govern the State' (and every labourer can control his enterprise's investment); but simultaneously they must seek to overcome the power of the market, by extending the principle of free distribution of goods to ever-wider limits. True equality can never be quantified, because all men are truly different from each other. Appetites, needs and interests differ, and will differ the more as opportunities for social, which is to say spiritual, fulfilment, widen. Equal rations are merely equally applied constraints of unequal demands, so we may be sure that the market will not finally succumb to a higher order by the imposition of policies artificially restricting appetites. Openly or covertly, legally or illegally, the market will continue, albeit with restricted scope, until society can cope equally with all the multiform needs which it is increasingly engendering. But if we can see that men have unequal needs for wooden legs yet still have equal need of access to medical treatment, cost what it may, we should also see the need to apply welfare norms of distribution to housing, public transport, fuel, food and to any new services an advanced civilization can create. Welfare or free distribution requires social planning, which can only be effective in the long run when it involves not merely the consent, but also the active involvement, of every citizen.

Self-management as a model will necessarily require the solution of the difficulties involved in this progress. Today, all this is still the music of the future. But it will be heard: it must be heard, if humanity is not to relapse into a new and unthinkable barbarism. We know enough to comprehend that we must live better. We do not yet know how to begin doing so. But unless we strive forward, there is no doubt that the technologies we have already unleashed can destroy us all, and probably will. The quest for self-management is the quest for humane, socially conscious control over technological development. Only in a self-managed society may we begin to see rational approaches to the solution of some of the world's most pressing problems – pollution, environmental development, unemployment, poverty, alienation in work, and so on. The more prolonged the reign of the market system and its concomitant divisions of labour and authority, the more threatening will those problems become.

Notes

1. Cf. Rarmond Postgate, *Revolution from 1789 to 1906* (Harper Torchbooks, 1962), pp. 90 *et seq.*; also Cole and Filson, *British Working Class Movements: Select Documents* (Macmillan, 1951), pp. 241-91.

2. Postage, op. cit., p.93.

3. G. D. H. Cole, *Robert Owen* (Ernest Benn, 1925), pp. 203-7.

4. Cf. *Workers' Control*, ed. Coates and Topham, pp. xxviii-xxxvii, for a documentation of these experiments.

5. International Working Men's Association, Resolution carried 15th September, 1868. Cf. Postgste, op. cit., pp. 383-4.

6. Postgate, op. cit., p. 297.

7. Karl Marx, *The Civil War in France* in *Selected Works*, Vol. 2 (Lawrence & Wishart, 1945), p. 459.

8. For key documents, see Ernest Mandel, *Controle Ouvrier, Conseils Ouvriers, Autogestion* (Paris: François Maspero, 1970), pp. 85-154; also V. I. Lenin, *On Workers' Control and the Nationalisation of Industry* (anthology) (Moscow: Foreign Language Publishing House, 1970). For a convenient short analysis, see Isaac Deutscher, *Soviet Trade Unions* (Royal Institute of International Affairs, Oxford University Press, 1950).

9. Cf. *Workers' Control*, pp. 285 *et seq.*

10. Speech to the Stockholm Conference of the Russell Foundation on Czechoslovakia, February 1969: published by the Bertrand Russell Peace Foundation.

11. For example in Fred Singleton and Tony Topham, *Workers' Control in Yugoslavia*, Fabian Research Series 233 (1963); Roy Moore, *Self-Management in Yugoslavia*, Fabian Research Series 281 (1970); *Workers' Management in Yugoslavia* (ILO, Geneva, 1962); Jiri Kolaja, *Workers' Councils: The Yugoslav Experience* (Tavistock, 1965); Paul Blumberg, *Industrial Democracy: The Sociology of Participation* (Constable, 1968), Chaps 8 and 9; and *Yugoslav Workers' Self-Management*, ed. M. J. Broeckmeyer (Dordrecht, Holland: Reidel, 1970).

12. See Tony Topham, 'Yugoslavia's Peaceful Road to Capitalism?', Institute for Workers' Control *Bulletin*, Vol. 2, No. 5.

13. See Fred Singleton, 'Workers' Self-Management and the Role of the Trade Unions in Yugoslavia', *Trade Union Register* 1970.

14. 311,000 were unemployed, out of 3.5 million normally employed in the social sector, in 1968. Figures in Singleton, op. cit., p. 236.

15. See Fred Singleton, 'Socialist Yugoslavia's First Official Strike', *The Spokesman*, No. 8 (December 1970).

16. Cf. Michael Raptis, 'Le Dossier de L'Autogestion en Algerie', *Autogestion*, No. 3; also *International Studies in Industrial Democracy: The Algerian Experience* (Institute for Workers' Control, 1971).

17. Cf. Arslan Humbarici, *Algeria – A Revolution That Failed* (Pall Mall Press, 1966), pp. 114-27. Also Clegg, *Workers' Self-Management in Algeria* (Allen Lane, The Penguin Press, 1971).

18. Cf. *Czechoslovakia and Socialism*, ed. Ken Coates (Bertrand Russell Peace Foundation, 1969), especially the essays by Mandel, Guerin and Bodington, and the lectures by Šik; also Ludek Rychetnik, *Two Models of an Enterprise in Market Socialism* (Institute for Workers; Control, 1971).

19. Cf. Andrée Hoyles, article in *Trade Union Register* 1969 (see Chap. 4 n. 17 above).

20. Cf. Stephen Bodington, 'Struggles of the Workers' Movement in Italy', *The Spokesman*, No. 11 (April 1971).

21. For a summary of the evidence on this matter, see Coates and Silburn, *Poverty: The Forgotten Englishmen*.

Ken Coates on graduation from the University of Nottingham. Ken's route to university involved access to day release classes from the pit, followed by the award of a state scholarship. His dissertation, 'An Essay on Marx's Concept of Alienation', drew heavily on Marxist theory alongside his experiences as a miner.

Education as a life-long experience

Ken Coates

First published in Peter Buckman (editor), Education Without Schools*, 1973. Re-published in Ken Coates,* Beyond Wage Slavery *(Spokesman, 1977).*

What is the relationship between education and industry? This is a crucial question, but it is quite commonly avoided by educationalists, and particularly by educational reformers. Whenever we do meet it, it is usually to find that those asking it have subtly transformed it in order to assume an answer which is not too discomfiting either to the teaching profession or to industrialists. Of course, the question 'what does industry need from education?' poses quite a different set of problems to those we need to discuss. 'How can education better serve industry?' is the sort of conundrum that arises with every new phase of technological development: more schools, more colleges and universities must be opened to provide more scientists, more administrators and more technically qualified workpeople, we are told at intervals of about a generation. The priorities in such questions are upside down and back to front. To see things the right way up, and to begin the pursuit of *education,* we must ask 'what sort of factories do our schools need?'

In the abstract, taking formal schooling at its best, there are few teachers who will not, when pushed, lay claim to the fundamental liberal commitment that their role is to stimulate the fullest possible development of their charges. The school, they feel, is properly an incubator of the free personality. That is to say, teachers commonly assume, or to be more accurate, think they assume, that they should treat their students each as an end in himself, and never as a mere means to serve some greater goal: whether that goal be the imagined good of the State, or the anticipated productivity of the Economy, or even, in these agnostic days, the alleged purpose of the Almighty. The old Jesuit boast that given care of a child until he reached the age of seven, he would be kept forever in the faith, is seen by the dominant educational consensus of today as almost the very epitome of evil. True, there are some who would explicitly repudiate liberal pretentious, but there are numerous good liberal swearwords to describe the results of such apostasy. 'Indoctrination', 'manipulation', 'brain-washing', 'propagandising' all spring to mind.

To remain on an equally abstract plane, there is not a factory, an office, a mine or a depot in the land in which these basic liberal assumptions can hold sway for a fraction of a moment, not even on Christmas Day when everyone is on holiday. No employer can treat his employees as ends in themselves, whose free personal development is the prime object of his enterprise. Indeed, no employer, however powerful, can easily imagine being so treated himself, even though it is his will or the will of the elite grouping of which he forms a part, which has determined, often in precise detail, the major life options which are open to, or closed from, his subordinates. Few employers today actually *tell* their workmen that they are paid to work, not to think: but none are able to predicate their activities on any assumption other than that the goals and strategies of the enterprise, insofar as they are determined by anyone at all, must be rigidly monopolised by its directorate. Throughout the majority of modern industry, it is fair to be far more precise than this: individual initiative by an employee is commonly seen as at best an embarrassment, at worst a disruption, while the personal development of employees is considered a matter for their own pursuit, as best they can arrange it, in those parts of their lives which are called 'leisure'. Industry still seeks square pegs for square holes, and round pegs for round holes. Even in the comparatively rare cases where jobs are 'enlarged', or rotated, the modern division of labour remains, for the overwhelming majority of people, an absolute barrier to the development of their productive, or creative, capacities in any field other than the narrow strip to which they have been allotted. Proficiencies which can be learnt in days or weeks frequently become life expectations. Such horizons can only tend to reduce people, unless they find ways to rebel against them.

The brutalising of work tends to turn leisure into passivity, or into an aggressively private activity: the alienated antithesis of compulsory labour. Modern industry, modern capitalism, far from constituting a celebration of the freedom of the individual, in fact represents a most systematic and extended denial of the basic conditions of that freedom.

But these are abstract statements, statements moreover of tendency, and they represent only part of the truth. The complex reality is that conditions of unfreedom repeatedly stimulate moods of rejection. Good schools reinforce this rejection, which will only hold out new hopes of fulfilment when subjection no longer remains the rule.

It remains true that the liberal educational goals are at root, in flagrant contradiction to the basic assumptions which regulate our economic life. The result is that today, far from education – individual development in co-operative activity – reaching out through working life to become a life-long experience, it is still true that industry constantly exerts itself to reach its clammy hands down into the schools, in order to make wage-slavery as life-long, and as inescapable, as it possibly can. Of course, there are gross difficulties in the process. Although it is true that there are still all too many infant schools in which five-year-olds are aligned in ranks in wet playgrounds and whistled into assembly, a ritual which is only meaningful as house-training for the factory and the clocking-in queue, yet it remains quite undeniable that modern pedagogy (which is the more necessary to industry as it desperately roots round to find expanded off-square pegs to fit the new precision-made eccentric holes of modern technology) is persistently rolling back the age at which authoritarian discipline can be introduced. Opening the 1972 Conference of the British National Union of Teachers, the President of the organisation claimed that in recent years there had been 'a new spirit in the schools. The primary school today' he said, 'is a place of adventure, experiment, liveliness, joy, and a felicitous co-operation between child, parent and teacher.'

Such progress notwithstanding, and there is still room for a great deal more of it, the school still serves its masters. The more co-operative and participatory that teaching techniques become, the more grossly they will be out of phase with the roles for which their victims are being prepared. The raising of the school leaving age may see a rise in the age of secondary school mutiny: but mutiny remains as likely as ever to nullify even the best pedagogic intentions as the transition from classroom to workshop becomes imminent. In the best imaginable case, if the schools were to succeed in wholly dedicating themselves to the stimulation and liberation of imagination throughout the whole school-life of their pupils, then those pupils would be powerfully tempted to drop out of the society into which they were subsequently evicted. There are reformers, like Paul Goodman, who welcome this prospect. To me it seems an unlikely blessing. Denied access to any satisfactory outlet for productive effort, and denied facilities for creative communication unless they show exceptional talents, such rebels are likely to develop into shallow hedonists, whose lives will be prone to sterile introversion and dependency. If hedonism is a life-style, it is scarcely a *human* life-style: evolution could well have been arrested with the emergence of the common cat, or for all we know, the garden slug, leaving ample possibilities for self-satisfaction at this sad level of expectation. If it were possible for schools to ignore industry during the whole period of compulsory education, and it is not, it would still be ethically impermissible for them to tolerate a factory system which would give their pupils the choice of forgetting the most important things they had learnt, or lapsing into social parasitism. In fact, up to now, this discussion implies, if anything, far too rosy a picture of the state of school autonomy from the industrial power-complex. The whole system of public examinations has no imaginable educational function, but is indispensible to the Labour Exchange. Tests of certain kinds can help both teachers and students: but they help best when the student understands that perhaps their most crucial function is to help the teacher overcome his own inadequacies. There never was a mark awarded that said anything incontrovertible about the ability of a student, because 'ability' is a term which includes a vast area of potential which can never be measured until after it has been realised, and which can (and should) remain open throughout a lifetime: but every mark ever given does say something quite final about the level of actual communication that has taken place between a teacher and his charge. 'Bring out number, weight and measure' said Blake 'in a year of dearth'. The mania for evaluation of students' performance would be a healthy event, if it were a self-critical pedagogic device. As it is, it tends to present a recurrent libel on the capacities of those 'evaluated', which has the effect, all too often, of self-fulfilling prophecy, convincing its victims that *they* suffer from incapacities which are not in truth their own, but their institutions'. Of course, if an employer wants a French-speaking secretary, he has to know that she can in fact speak French before he can employ her. Exams will be with us for a while yet: but we should know for what they were spawned, and refuse them the dignity of an *educational* rationale. Yet, in a negative way, they show us what vast developments are possible, by revealing some fraction of the *needs* which our current school system can never begin to meet. It is precisely when we are confronted by the results of measurements of 'performance' that we become aware of the pervasive influence of social status on the school structure. Poor kids do badly, rich kids do well. As J. W. B. Douglas reports in *The Home and the School:*

> 'When housing conditions are unsatisfactory, children make relatively low scores in the tests. This is so in each social class, but whereas middle-class children, as they get older, reduce this handicap, the manual working-class children from unsatisfactory homes fall even further behind; for them, overcrowding and other deficiencies at home have a progressive and depressive influence on their test performance.'

Bad housing is important as an indicator of this phenomenon, but its real root is occupational. Unskilled workers are badly paid, which is why they live on poor estates or in slums. Slum housing is certainly a handicap, but it is not an insuperable handicap on its own. Half-blind Sean O'Casey saw more colour in the world from a Dublin tenement than most duchesses can find in a room full of Titians. Abraham Lincoln was reportedly conceived in a log cabin, but his step-mother taught him to read the Bible, *Pilgrim's Progress,* and *Robinson Crusoe.* You have to apply other clamps to the imagination than poor housing if you are to achieve any success in the effort to paralyse it. In British slums, the majority of fathers and mothers have never been introduced to Bunyan or Defoe, or for that matter to any other major writer in our language, so it is hardly surprising if their children read late, and with difficulty. For years it was fashionable to consider this fact as the outcome of genetic determination. The unskilled were not culturally deprived because they were poor and unskilled, but because they were born that way. This was not the view of the classic theorists of industrialism. Adam Smith, who began his greatest work with the celebration of the productive merits of the division of labour, was well aware of its baneful influence on the labourer. His insights on this matter were enlarged in different ways by Owen, Ruskin, and Marx, to say nothing of the whole pleiad of romantic novelists, poets, and publicists. What is perfectly clear is that as factories stabilised themselves as the predominant form of productive unit through society, so the divergence of talents was widened, and transmitted across generations. The industrial division of labour became the solid foundation of an industrial class system. For all its one-sidedness, there are few descriptions of this process which are more compelling and more far-sighted than that of de Tocqueville, in *Democracy in America:*

> 'When a workman is unceasingly and exclusively engaged in the fabrication of one thing, he ultimately does his work with singular dexterity; but at the same time he loses the general faculty of applying his mind to the direction of the work. He every day becomes more adroit and less industrious; so that it may be said of him that in proportion as the workman is improved the man is degraded … When a workman has spent a considerable portion of his existence in this manner, his thoughts are for ever set upon the object of his daily toil; his body has contracted certain fixed habits, which it can never shake off: in a word he no longer belongs to himself, but to the calling which he has chosen. It is in vain that laws and manners have been at pains to level all barriers around such a man, and to open to him on every side a thousand different paths to fortune: a theory of manufactures more powerful than manners and laws binds him to a craft, and frequently to a spot, which he cannot leave: it assigns him a certain place in

> society beyond which he cannot go: in the midst of universal movement it has rendered him stationary.
>
> In proportion as the principle of the division of labour is more extensively applied, the workman becomes more weak, more narrow-minded, and more dependent. The art advances, the artisan recedes ...'

This savage prophecy has not been by any means fulfilled in full, for two good reasons. First, for the reason that people *will* resist de-humanisation, however high the cost of resistance, and however long the odds against their success. The whole story of trade unionism, and the entire vicarious history of the socialist movement, bear witness to this fact. As a result of it, the basic liberal humanist ideals survive the process which de Tocqueville traced, which is of course, at one level, itself the result of the operation of the liberal doctrine in economic life. Secondly, the prophecy fails because the story of the development of industrial capitalism is an account of the unleashing of a succession of technological upheavals, during which the division of labour is recurrently recast. On one side this results from time to time in the demand for new skills and higher educational levels: but at the same time, on the other side it repeatedly gives rise to the displacement of old skills and the social rejection of all those people whose inflexibility (whether because they are old, or because they have been inadequately taught in their youth) keeps them below the threshold of profitable employment. So-called technological unemployment is not a new phenomenon, although in its recent forms it has the capacity to create wider unease in the body politic than heretofore. Its true source is not abstract technology, which, being inanimate, is socially neutral, but specific technologies in the service of capital, whose dominance depends upon the control of equipment and processes, and upon the subordination of the interests of people to the imperatives of its balance-sheets.

Adam Smith had adumbrated three component benefits of the division of labour: it augmented productivity by specialization, increasing the proficiency of workmen by intensifying their dexterity; it saved time by cutting out transfers between operations; and it facilitated the introduction and development of machines. To these three principles, Charles Babbage, in *The Economy of Manufactures,* added a fourth:

> 'That the master manufacturer, by dividing the work to be executed into different processes, each requiring different degrees of skill and force, can purchase exactly that precise quantity of both of which is necessary for each process.'

With this perception rose the possibility of the whole school of scientific management as subsequently developed by F. W. Taylor in the United States. The more intensively processes could be controlled, the more dependent roles were created for employees, and the less the industrial currency of the liberal ideal of an integrated human personality. Babbage recorded the process in 1832 without noticing the implication of his words:

> ' ... if the whole work were to be executed by one workman, that person must possess sufficient skill to perform the most difficult, and sufficient strength to execute the most laborious of the operations into which the art is divided.'

Just about fifty years were to elapse before Taylor was to refine this insight to the point where he could insist, without shame, that:

> 'One of the very first requirements for a man who is fit to handle pig iron as a regular occupation is that he shall be so stupid and so phlegmatic that he more nearly resembles an ox than any other type.'

The logical result of such specialisation was clearly expressed in the dire anti-utopia of H. G. Wells' *The Time Machine*, in which exploration of the future revealed that effete aristocrats and feelingless plebians had evolved into two distinct and incompatible species. If the logical result is not to be anticipated in the actual outcome, we owe the fact both to human resilience and to the contradictory implications of advancing techniques. While Taylorism in its classic prescriptions gained a considerable following, in spite of protests, in the mass production industries of the Ford school, subsequent work methods have evolved alongside electronic techniques to produce quite different notions of job control. Nevertheless, Taylorism was an innovatory discipline which cast a long shadow before it, and even today, in the discussion of job-enlargement, rotation of tasks, 'participatory' reform, and kindred expedients, the ghost of scientific management can still be heard speaking in a variety of accents it is true, but with no diminution of its anti-human intent. It is the same ghost which speaks in the debate on educational methods and reform of the schools. 'More means worse', it says. Selection and specialisation are its necessary watchwords. Its cardinal principle it transfers from Babbage's factories to the secondary modern schools and the lower streams of the alleged comprehensives which spring up on all sides. 'Spend no more than is necessary on human formation' it whispers. Surplus of training is dysfunctional: over-educated operatives are indisciplined and refractory. In a square hole, square people are optimal, and tendencies to deviate into roundness must be rigidly clamped out.

Yet all the time, industry needs education. A modest explosion has recently taken place in certain forms of continuation courses, in adult classes of a particular kind, in shop steward training, and in technical education, since the passage in Britain of the Industrial Training Act, which levies a toll on firms in order to ensure that if they do not train their own workers, they will be forced to pay to train other people's. A much bigger convulsion is called for but is unlikely to take place. But all this effort, and most of the proposed effort which will not be undertaken, is conceived within the essential framework of the constricting assumptions we have been discussing. We *could* have a real transformation in education *at* work, but the price would not be simply the universalisation of day-release courses, desirable though that may be. A genuine transformation would involve education *in* work, self-education, community education, in the generation of real moves towards collective self-management of industry. Only such a revolution would abolish the stultifying role-patterns which are imposed on work-people, and only such a revolution would open up the possibility, and the need, for every man to seek the continuous enlargement of his powers and his basic knowledge of the world in which he was working.

Universalist education is incompatible with the rigid division of labour which forms men into porters and philosophers, and aligns them into opposing social classes. Both in work, and in whatever preparation which enlightened people come to agree it may be necessary to make for work, the division of labour as we understand it is more than a net disincentive to free personal development. Within it, 'equality of opportunity' comes to mean the will o' the wisp of an equal start in a fundamentally unequal race: and all the nobility of the watch-word is transformed into sleazy apologetics. Free development of each personality to its outer limits means the systematic encouragement and fostering of talents, and this will never begin until factories begin to be schools, and self-governing schools at that. Only then will schools cease to be factories for the engineering of human beings into employees. Perhaps a hundred years ago this was a utopian message. Today, it is direly practical: the only resource which we possess in virtual abundance is that of human potential, and yet it is that resource which we squander with even greater profligacy than we eat up the earth's finite material resources. Mankind will soon need all the wits and creativity which it is stifling every day in modern industry, and its appendage, modern education, if it is to find the way to live out another century.

Bertrand Russell
Peace Foundation

European Nuclear Disarmament

Bulletin of Work in Progress

No. 1 1980.

30p

Making Peace in Europe

Ken Coates

Published in Tribune, *12 March, 1982*

"We are entering the, most dangerous decade in human history. A third world war is not merely possible but increasingly likely." It was with this sombre warning that the appeal for European Nuclear Disarmament [END] was launched at the end of April 1980. At the time, some people thought these words exaggerated. They have, however, been amply confirmed in the months which have followed. The arms race has surged ahead without control, and a series of crucial decisions have worsened the prospects for avoiding nuclear war. The perilous doctrine of "flexible response" continues to dominate the arms procurement policies of the super-powers and, although both intermittently deny adherence to the doctrine of limited nuclear war, material preparations for such a war continue remorselessly.

The invasion of Afghanistan, the shelving of the decisions of the Strategic Arms Limitation Treaty II, the decision to "modernise" the so-called theatre nuclear weapons deployed in Europe, the steady emplacement of new SS20 missiles in the European part of the Soviet Union, the traumatic developments in Poland, where the second largest Warsaw Pact army has imposed martial law in order to prevent an evolution which was viewed as hopeful by the large majority of thinking people in Western Europe – all these events have contributed to raising the fearful spiral of conflict, and all are rightly greeted with dismay by those who are working for the preservation of peace.

In response to this threatening situation, the END appeal called for the removal of all nuclear weapons from the entire political territory of Europe, East and West alike. This proposal does not imply that a comprehensive nuclear-free-zone can be established all at once. Indeed, it positively encourages all reasonable proposals for agreements to create lesser nuclear-free zones, whether in the Balkans, the Baltic, Nordland, Central Europe, the Mediterranean, Iberia, or in any other relevant areas. The ultimate objective of a nuclear-weapon-free continent it shares with the Socialist International, which enshrined this call in its Madrid resolution of November 1980; with a variety of churches and peace movements; and with the protocol of the United Nations Special Session on Disarmament of 1978, which specifically insisted on the usefulness of nuclear-free zones as steps towards general and complete disarmament. But, at the same time, the END appeal supports all relevant disarmament initiatives, and every other rational step towards the improvement of East-West relations.

In soliciting support from European signatories, the Russell Foundation, which took the responsibility for circulating the appeal, proposed a European Convention of all those political, religious and social forces which shared these broad objectives. Hundreds of distinguished men and women from every country in the continent endorsed this proposal.

In the 18 months during which the appeal for European Nuclear Disarmament has been published and discussed, numerous other proposals, many of them very similar, have attracted very significant support in one country or another. Huge mass movements against the deployment of the new "theatre" missiles have simultaneously grown up in Britain, Holland, Germany, Italy, Belgium and Scandinavia.

Significant opposition to the extension of the alliance systems has been registered in Spain and in Greece (which has seen the phenomenal PASOK victory in the October 1981 election, bringing to power a Greek Government totally committed to the policies which inform the END appeal, one of whose earliest signatories is the new Prime Minister, Andreas Papandreou).

Endorsing the call for a Balkan nuclear-free zone, President Ceausescu of Romania has specifically underlined the need for the withdrawal of intermediate-range missiles from both West and East. The October 1981 mobilisation of peace demonstrations produced extraordinary responses: 250,000 people in London, 500,000 in Rome, 200,000 in Brussels, 300,000 in Bonn. Why, since so many millions of people are already joining forces, do we need to press ahead with the call for a representative European Convention?

Such a meeting is, in fact, more urgent than it was in the earliest days of the appeal. Of course, it is necessary to arrive at a point where peace movements can begin to co-ordinate their several separate national efforts at an international level. But the pre-requisite for effective coordination is ample discussion. We need to explore each other's minds.

Taking even those who agree on the general basis of the END appeal, it is already clear that there are rather many different possible approaches to the task of removing nuclear weapons from our countries. There are also considerably different assessments of the political balance in the continent, which affect our possible responses.

Some Western peace movements already seek unilaterally to leave the NATO alliance. Others judge this to be an unhelpful step. There are many nuances of view about the proper relationship to seek with East European citizens and Governments. In short, all the Western peace movements are already profoundly pluralistic, bringing together people of many churches and political practices, different national experiences and different cultural traditions. We need to establish lateral links, across national boundaries, between churches, between trade unions, between women's organisations, and other relevant constituencies. Already doctors and scientists have established powerful international networks, which can have a salutary influence on the development of the argument, country by country. We have to reach out to countries where the argument is less strongly developed, and we need to pool the experiences, not only of the movements in those countries which belong to the alliances, but of the peoples of the morally powerful group of neutral and non-aligned states.

But there are other reasons that we need to talk with one another, which revolve around how we all find our orientation in a divided continent. What is involved in our positive goal of a nuclear-free Europe, and how can we advance it? Alva Myrdal has explored many of the key issues in her paper on *The Dynamics of European Nuclear Disarmament*. What other pertinent considerations apply? What arms control initiatives make practical sense, and how can popular movements help to advance them?

It cannot be too strongly stressed that these positive policy questions need to be focused in joint discussion quickly. The opposition to particular items of modern weaponry is powerful, and rightly so. But command decisions on such issues are changeable, and may under the weight of massive pressure, be quickly changed. It is quite possible for NATO to avoid land-based emplacements for the new generation of missiles, because they could all be adapted to sea-based deployment. Such a move would rightly be seen as a vast concession to the European opposition, but it would not thereby render Europe any safer. The sea-borne missiles would still be trained against the Soviet Union, which would still therefore maintain its countering arsenal, trained upon the cities of our continent. Some European areas would become more, not less vulnerable. It is the arms race and the confrontation between European nuclear blocs which must be ended, and not simply one or another horrific component of the opposing technologies.

The opening talks in Geneva and President Reagan's proposals for the "zero option" reinforced our need to explain this issue. Discussing Reagan's proposals, *The Times* accurately styled them "the zero gambit". The danger is that the Geneva talks will be a continuation of super-power gaming across the conference table, rather than a genuine effort to reverse the arms race.

All these issues urgently need discussion. A convention would not be expected to resolve such questions by formal resolutions. Before that can be done adequately, the different national peace movements must be allowed time to focus on their own ideas in a thorough process of debate and discussion. But if we do not talk these matters through at the international level, we shall reduce our contact to a process of marching and demonstrating, which is not enough to maintain the physical momentum of the movement, still less to develop its thinking.

For this reason, we propose that the European Convention should consist essentially of two kinds of workshops. The first of these will be the issue-centred seminars, addressing policy problems, discovering the range of positions which exist, exploring their differences and similarities, and enabling their proponents to come to know each other's views better.

It would be pointless to try to bind people to views that they do not hold, or to mandate movements to support policies with which they do not agree. The Convention should make no pretension to determine policy, but it should become a forum for sharing opinions.

The second type of workshop will concern affinity groups: churches, women's organisations, trade unions, municipalities, and similar interest groups. The job of these meetings would be to enrich the lateral contacts, across national frontiers, between disarmament supporters in particular professions or social organisations. In this way, the discussion can be enlarged in a kind of telephone exchange which enables each to communicate freely with all, rather than simply in a centralised framework of interconnected nationally structured peace organisations.

The Rome consultation which discussed all these ideas agreed that the European Convention should be called in 1982. A liaison committee was appointed, and remains open to participation by any organisations or individuals in Europe who approve the original appeal.

This committee held its first meeting in Milan in December 1981 and, as a result, it has been agreed that the Convention will meet in Brussels from July 2-4 1982.

We appeal to all those who approve of the END appeal to ensure that they are represented at the convention, and to join in the work of preparing it by participating in the liaison committee if possible. The agenda of the convention will be agreed in the liaison committee, and all participating groups will have the right to convene seminars of either type in the proposed structure.

SOCIALISM IN THE PRESENT-DAY WORLD SOCIALISM IN THE PRESENT-DAY WORLD SOCIALISM IN THE PRESENT

SOCIALISM IN THE WORLD

samir amin

expansion ou crise du capitalisme?

živojin rakočević

reflections on capitalism: development and borders

göran therborn

the prospects of labour and the transformation of advanced capitalism

ken coates

the common ruin, barbarism, or exterminism?

mounir chafiq

les politiques arabes et la cause palestinienne

james petras

toward a marxist theory of industrial development in the third world

UDC YU ISSN 0350-8234

44 '84

Common Ruin, Barbarism or Exterminism?

Ken Coates

First published in Socialism in the World, *Number 44, 1984. This journal grew out of a series of international conferences, convened in Cavtat – a town on the Adriatic coast – initiated by the Yugoslav journals* Socializam, Socialist Thought and Practice *and* Marksizam u svetu. *Its first number (1977) features Ken Coates's article, 'Prospects for Socialism in Britain'. Coates was a regular attendee at the Cavtat conferences and encouraged others from Britain to do so.*

"The history of all hitherto existing society is the history of class struggles. Freeman and slave, patrician and plebian, lord and serf, guildmaster and journeyman, in a word, oppressor and oppressed, stood in constant opposition to one another, carried on an uninterrupted, now hidden, now open fight, a fight that each time ended, either in a revolutionary reconstitution a large, or in the common ruin of the contending classes."[1]

One hundred years after the death of Karl Marx, these opening words of *The Communist Manifesto* sound to many people more like the premonition of doom than the hopeful exhortation they were intended to be. "The common ruin of the contending classes" no longer presents itself as a distinct prospect, but must appear as a distinct possibility as we peer at one another between the nuclear emplacements which sprout all over Europe in the middle of the 1980s.

In the early months of the first World War, writing in the prison to which she was confined for defending Marx's internationalism, Rosa Luxemburg composed her pamphlet *The Crisis in German Social Democracy,* which subsequently became better known as *The Junius Pamphlet*.[2] In this tract, she harked back to Engels' statement "Capitalist society faces a dilemma, either an advance to socialism or a reversion to barbarism". For Luxemburg, "This world war means a reversion to barbarism … either the triumph of imperialism and the destruction of all culture, ... de-population, desolation, degeneration, a vast cemetery; or of the victory of socialism". Those who drew the human balance sheet of the first World War could not fail to confirm Luxemburg's appreciation of it. While her pamphlet was being clandestinely printed, the battle of Verdun was raging over a 20 mile front. A 5 mile movement along this front cost 281,000 German lives and 315,000 French lives. On the 10th July, Luxemburg was re-arrested, so that she was again in prison during the battle of the Somme, which was continued until the 14th November, costing 419,604 British and 194,451 French casualties. German losses were estimated at half a million.[3] Over four dreadful years, the unimaginable carnage cost an estimated 272,290 million dollars.

"Barbarism" is in common parlance a mild description for such universal mayhem: although it is grossly unfair to real barbarians, for whom slaughter was a heavy physical labour, unameliorated by the mechanical arts. Today, the process of slaughter is more efficient than ever. Vastly increased military expenditures bring within reach casualty lists besides which the first World War seems almost a benevolent event. Luxemburg did not believe that the barbarism she denounced would amount to "the common ruin of the contending classes": "we are not lost", she said "and we will be victorious if we have not forgotten how to learn". In 1918 there were still generations left with time to learn.[4] But in the present age of nuclear weapons, pessimism seems to many people to be a more rational stance. Herbert Marcuse, for instance:

> "Intensified progress seems to be bound up with intensified unfreedom. Throughout the world of industrial civilization, the domination of man by man is growing in scope and efficiency. In our days, this trend appears as incidental, transitory regression on the road to progress. Concentration camps, mass exterminations, world wars, and atom bombs, are no 'relapse into barbarism', but the unrepressed implementation of the achievements of modern science, technology and domination. And the most effective subjugation and destruction of man by man takes place at the height of civilization, when the material and intellectual attainments of man seem to allow the creation of a truly free world."[5]

It was this kind of understanding which provoked Edward Thompson to ask "If 'the hand-mill gives you society with the feudal law; saw mill, society with the industrial capitalist' what are we given by those satanic-mills which are now at work, grinding out the means of human extermination? I have reached this point of thought more than once before, but have turned my head away in despair. Now, when I look at it directly I know that the category which we need is that of 'exterminism'."[6]

Thompson is right that the military organization of the modern world is a live and growing *social* phenomenon. Speaking with irony, he parodies the left by saying: "As for the bomb, that is a Thing and a Thing cannot be a historical agent."[7] But an important part of the left has known for a very long time that things may become social agencies. The mechanical production lines associated with Fordism, for instance, were accurately identified by Gramsci, and again by such writers as Mallet and Goldmann, as developing an associated consciousness which had direct results on the agencies of social change. Bertrand Russell who was well known to be agnostic about many of the principles of Marxism, insisted almost fifty years ago that:

> "Changes in the technique of war have had more influence upon the course of history than is supposed by those whose attention is mainly centred upon economic causation. There has been, since the beginning of organized fighting, an oscillation between the superiority of the defensive and superiority of the offensive. Broadly speaking when the defensive is strong civilization makes progress, and when the offensive is strong men revert towards barbarism. Another oscillation has been between the importance of mere numbers and the importance of skill and elaborate equipment. In the Middle Ages, the knight in armour was an expensive unit, and the world was aristocratic; gunpowder abolished chivalry, and led by slow stages to citizen armies and democracy."[8]

Of course, military expenditure has reached such phenomenal levels that all social organization is grossly distorted through the iron mesh which extrudes the society of militarism. World military expenditures run at more than 19,000 dollars per soldier, compared to less than 400 dollars educational expenditure per school age child; there are more than 550 soldiers in every hundred thousand people, but the same population enjoys the ministrations of only 85 physicians.[9] World military expenditures have risen from 503 billion dollars in 1975 to 532 dollars three years later, and 561 billion dollars at the beginning of this decade. They are scheduled to continue to rise and they have indeed already passed 618 billion dollars per annum.[10] These statistics are the monetary reflections of vast human organizations, each one of which imposed its own pattern of debility on the community structures of the society which supports it.

In 1982, the United States had something over ten thousand strategic nuclear warheads and the USSR about 7,400. (In 1962, at the time of the Cuba crisis, the balance of strategic warheads had been 70 in the USSR and 2,000 in the USA). The present balance of tactical nuclear weaponry is even more awe-inspiring: especially when one considers that the weapons styled "tactical" are commonly considerably more powerful than the bombs which devastated Hiroshima and Nagasaki in 1945. The United States apparently deploys some 20,000 such tactical weapons against 10,000 Soviet weapons.

If we are looking for evidence of barbarism, it is already to hand: even before the outbreak of nuclear war, this vast procurement of nuclear weapons is correlated with economic decline, rising unemployment, and growing starvation in the poorest countries of the world. At the beginning of the decade the OECD estimated that world-wide economic aid was running at 36 billion dollars, or 8% of the world military budget of 1980. Meantime, perhaps a billion people live on the verge of starvation.

For all these reasons, Edward Thompson is right to deny that the bomb is simply a "thing". The bomb determines; and those who make, develop and deploy it fit into; a social division of labour. At this point, however, Thompson moves his argument forward: "No doubt we will have one day a comprehensive analysis of the origins of the cold war, in which the motives of the agents appear as rational. But that cold war passed, long ago, into a self-generating condition of cold-warism (exterminism) in which the originating drives, reactions and intentions are still at play, but within a general inertial condition…" Such a process, Thompson reasons, has left the plane of rationality, not because individual leaders are insane (although sometimes they are) but because there exists this "inertial thrust" towards war, drawing its force from the deep structured militarization of the contending societies. "The USA and the USSR do not *have* military industrial complexes: they *are* such complexes."[11]

As we have said, the nuclear armament of these powers have, since 1962, moved very much closer to parity. The conventional wisdom in the West, when Mr. Krushchev turned aside from the naval confrontation with which Kennedy responded to the initial deployment of missiles in Cuba, was that the theory of deterrence had been justified. At one level, this theory embodies a truism, so that Krushchev's decision to turn back was hardly surprising. But as competent practitioners of the same theory of deterrence, Krushchev's colleagues drew all of the requisite lessons in order to avoid repetition of such humiliation.[12] The hundredfold development of their strategic nuclear arsenals in the following 20 years is, to be sure, evidence of an insane competition, but it is unfortunately not "irrational", but entirely "normal" within the rules of that game. Of course, all of us would desire that things were different, and that the arms race were being run in the opposite direction, towards the dismantling of all nuclear weapons. To outlaw the game would be sensible: to incarcerate the players is beyond anyone's powers, so we have no option but to develop rational pressures towards a world order which does not engender such follies.

It is in the light of this need that we must evaluate Thompson's assessment that "the USA and the USSR do not *have* military industrial complexes: they *are* such complexes." These formations, he concedes, have a "leading sector" of weapons systems and supports, which protected by official secrecy, enjoy "low visibility". Speaking in such terms may indeed have been justified while such low visibility was the rule, because the metaphor served to warn of the existence of a great menace. But in sobriety, now that we are able to hear the voices of millions of peace marchers, we are bound to see some exaggeration in this warning formula. At one level this exaggeration has been adequately chronicled by Zhores and Roy Medvedev in their response to the *Exterminism* article.[13]

The Soviet complex, they say, is not a "state within a state", but a subordinate state unit. On the other side, competition between services, as well as transnational corporations, ensures that the military-industrial complex in the USA retains a sinister, inverted pluralism, which generates "overproduction" of arms systems. Perhaps as seriously, competition between exporters of civilian nuclear installations increases the trend to military nuclear proliferation: a trend which has been solidly resisted by the Soviet administration, but abetted, not only by private contractors, but also by actual states in the West.

None of this is to deny the scale of the Soviet input to war preparation: starting as it does from a lower civilian basis, it pre-empts a far larger proportion of Gross National Product than is required to maintain the vast American output of weaponry. The Soviet system finds these resources, presumably with difficulty, by central command out of a planned economy. The process has been clearly described by an American journalist, Robert Kaiser, who spent years in the USSR on behalf of the *Washington Post*.

The military economy is not apart from the rest; it is the cream on top of the rest. Its accomplishments are the ultimate tribute to the music-school approach to the allocation of resources. The military economy gets the most resources and makes the best products.

To a great extent, the military equipment is made by the same factories that produce goods for the civilian economy, and yet the military equipment is usually much better. The difference is quality control. When a factory is filling a military order, an officer is on the premises. If it's a big order, there may be a number of officers. They are empowered to reject any item if they think it is substandard, and the factory must either make it right or produce another one. I learned about this from an engineer with extensive experience in military industry. He had once been in a transistor factory, he told me, which was trying to fill a military order. The Army's inspector would accept only two or three of every 100 transistors the factory was making. The man who worked in the factory that makes electrical equipment for ships, described earlier, told me what happened when his enterprise had a contract from the Soviet Navy:

> "The Navy people don't mess around. An ordinary customer is different. You can tell him, 'Take it easy, we'll have it ready for you tomorrow,' things like that. But the Navy man won't listen to that kind of talk. When he comes, everybody bows down to him and listens to him as though he were a god. What he says goes."[14]

How different is the American process! Competition drives it forward, and as two prominent specialists tell us, this may "be so fierce that without expansion many companies would not be able to survive."[15] Cyclical crises accompanied by price movements, uneven development and utilisation of capacity, and inflation provoke mergers, rationalization, transnational links and takeovers, and conglomerate product diversification. The multinational corporations which rocketed into life in the USA and Western Europe after the second world war, drew life from, and ultimately caused the extinction of, the postwar Keynesian world order, by recruiting nation states in their support whilst undermining the power of those states to regulate their own economic and social policies. Starting from the USA, military producers quickly joined the transnational race, and helped push forward both the cold war arms race and half a hundred lesser military markets in hot spots around the world.

Looked at from the vantage point of the USA, these companies found space to grow in the spare technological capacity of the vastly productive American economy. Thompson is right to stress how far the Military Industrial Complex monopolises Research and Development costs, especially Governmental R and D. More: it has also monopolized the third industrial revolution. President Reagan's fearful programme of "star wars" most surely has a very "rational" intention of assuring an American lead over Japan and Germany in these vital technologies. But precisely *what* will exercise this lead? The state structure which promotes the leading process will remain lowly profiled, and it will be a range of giant transnational corporations which will continue their aggrandizement, develop their capacities and maximise their profits. The word "profit" may frequently be used with vulgar disregard for realities: but those who try to dispense with it will lose a key concept for the analysis of militarism, even if we have entered a new "exterminist" age.

There is a further weakness in the view that the two superpowers "do not *have* but *are* military industrial complexes". It does not allow for degrees of relative autonomy of political processes. Is there *no* difference between the administrations of Carter and Reagan? In the lesser scale, among clients, are Thatcher and Macmillan the same thing? This view is not only over-simple, it is also over-pessimistic, because if rampant and unaccountable military formations have taken over their respective societies, the scope of oppositional forces must necessarily be sharply restricted. Thatcher, of course, also differs from her American mentor, in that she is little influenced by the needs of industrial capital, which has suffered its own holocaust at her hands. In Britain it seems that it is finance-capital which is calling the tune.

However, there could be no clearer demonstration of the autonomy of these state processes than the recent scandalous episode of the Falkland (Malvinas) war. Innumerable multinational interests were anxious to reach a settlement with Argentina which could painlessly transfer the Falkland Islands from British rule. A succession of meetings had proposed quite radical formulae by which this goal might be achieved. What pressure brought the British Foreign Office to seek such a change? There was no desire among the inhabitants of the Islands to change their allegiance. Indeed, after the Argentine occupation, there was bitter recrimination from the Islanders about the way they felt their interests had been neglected. No, it was that part of transnational industry which is interested in the development of offshore resources, especially oil, which sought a suitable political environment in which to begin such development. The resignation of Lord Carrington from the British Cabinet, immediately after the Argentines landed on the Islands, showed little instinct for self-criticism: indeed, wiseacres at the time said that Carrington had sacked Thatcher, contrary to the official report on the matter. Mrs. Thatcher's subsequent war, which defied the United Nations Resolution 502, exacerbated the political crisis for the United States throughout the Americas, and still renders difficult the management of major banking deficits at a moment when the world banking system is stretched almost beyond endurance, is widely held to have won her the 1983 General Election in Britain. No one can doubt Mrs. Thatcher's fidelity to capitalism: although it might be difficult to find significant capitalists who would have advised her to behave as she did.

The thrust to war cannot be denied, and if "barbarism" is an emotive word, imprecise in its meaning, it nonetheless evokes appropriate responses. "Exterminism", if it is simply a literary coinage is no worse a word. But as an analysis of the causality of the arms race, it is deficient, and needs to bring its feet back to the earth on which Luxemburg stood, if it is to seek real answers. What is the relationship between economic crisis and war; slump and arms race; monetarism, militarism and the multinational corporations? How do military formations fit into the real power structures which sustain and promote them?

E. P. Thomspon has given a notable impulse to the new movement for non-alignment, and few will doubt the practical significance of this. Luxemburg would have given him high marks: in the beginning was the deed. But the political theory of non-alignment still needs its exponents who will need to analyse not only the undoubtedly real phenomenon of hegemonism,[16] and, for instance, to explain conflicts between socialist states, but who will also seek to do far more than has yet been attempted to explore the relations between these matters and that desperate world crisis of capitalism in which all of us are now caught.

The peace movements need the help of Marxian scholars who are willing to celebrate the Marx centenary in this difficult but necessary labour.

Notes

1. *The Communist Manifesto*, Centenary edition, Lawrence and Widbart, 1948, pp.13-14.

2. *The Junius Pamphlet*, The Crisis in the German Social Democracy, Merlin Press, London, 1967.

3. Cf. Major General J. F. C. Fuller: *The Conduct of War*, Eyre and Spottiswoode, 1962, chapter 8.

4. Luxemburg: op cit., p.9.

5. Marcuse: *Eros and Civilization*, Routledge and Keagan Paul, p.4.

6. E. P. Thompson: *Notes on Exterminism, the Last Stage of Civilization*. In *Exterminism and Cold War*, Verso, 1982, pp.4-5. Later, Thomspon insists that he is *not* claiming that exterminism is a new and distinctive mode of production in the Marxian sense.

7. Ibid, p.3.

8. Bertrand Russell, *Which Way to Peace?*, 1936, p.16.

9. R. L. Silvard: World Military and Social Expenditures, 1982. Washington, p.22.

10. SIPRI, *The Arms Race and Arms Control*, 1983, London, pp. 155-167.

11. Thompson: op cit., p.22.

12. I have extended the argument in my foreword to Alva Myrdal, *The Dynamics of European Nuclear Disarmament*, Spokesman, 1981.

13. The USSR and the Arms Race in the "Exterminism" volume, pp.153 et seq.

14. Robert Kaiser, *Russia, the People and the Power*, Penguin Books, 1977, pp. 323-4.

15. Tuomi and Vayrynen: *Transnational Corporations, Armaments and Development*, Gower, 1982, pp.2-3.

16. This is the main weakness in the otherwise admirable text of the Medvedev brothers on Soviet involvement in the arms race.

A New Internationalism

Ken Coates

Published in New Socialist, *September 1985.* New Socialist *was the journal of the Labour Party and published voices from across the movement. Ken Coates served on its editorial advisory panel.*

No reader of *New Socialist* needs to be told that Britain is being laid waste by unemployment. The precipitate decline of manufacturing industry, temporarily masked by support from oil revenues, has made all thinking people aware of a deep structural crisis. No voices are nowadays heard suggesting that this will all resolve itself, that perhaps tomorrow a new longwave upturn will carry us all back to yesterday's levels of employment and economic activity. On the contrary, recovery presupposes a rupture with existing policies.

Not surprisingly, Labour Party activists are increasingly unanimous that the return of a Labour government must be given overriding priority, precisely in order to reverse the drift to what threatens to be irreversible decline. The truth is that such decline is part of an overall crisis, affecting many countries at once.

Previous international collapses of this kind have been resolved by desperate measures, usually involving war. This solution is no longer possible. War might quite possibly result from the intense competition and conflict which seethes beneath this crisis, but it will provoke no regeneration, because it will end in nuclear winter.

Never, certainly not in 1945 when it obtained its most overwhelming popular victory, has the Labour Party faced such a daunting set of prospects. What can British socialists do to promote recovery, restore employment, and regain the social initiative? The strange thing in 1985 is not that this question is discussed, but that the debate is so subdued.

After 1979, Labour was involved in a debate about an alternative economic strategy, which then offered some realistic choices (assuming that oil revenues could be directed to industrial recovery). But time has been running out, and even if the oil has not, its price has been seriously undermined in the continuing slump. Today, the prospect is dismal. Greater unemployment will be followed by still greater problems, while the wreckage continues unabated. We now have to ask ourselves, what is the scope for a national recovery?

The unhappy record of the Callaghan government no longer stands alone. In France, in spite of some important ameliorative measures, the trajectory of the Mitterrand government seems from this distance to be very similar to Labour's 1974-79 experience. In Spain, the Gonzalez team presides over staggering levels of unemployment, and begins to encounter strikes and protests on an ascending scale. The very least we can say about these European experiments, while hoping that they may yet rescue themselves, is that they show how very difficult it is for middle-sized nations to escape from the effects of structural crisis. When any medium-weight state goes for growth, it stimulates imports from other nations, and creates jobs for them. Shortly afterwards, it encounters problems with its balance of payments, and hostile visits from the bankers. Then it retrenches, deepening the slump at home and abroad. To break this jinx, the lesser states will have to act together. In large parts of the world which are crippled by the debt crisis, the same truth applies. But even the best governments are timid about such cooperation. How can they be encouraged to act? How can the peoples who are the victims of crisis join their forces to re-orient or remove governments which oppose joint recovery? It is this problem which must figure at the top of the socialist agenda for the next decade.

British and European trade unionists are increasingly aware of the uncontrolled power of multinational corporations. But we do not always link the questions which their power poses. Every recent Labour Party briefing on the economy has stressed the outflow of capital from Britain: nearly £50 billion during the Thatcher years from 1979-83, and over £15 billion a year now. There are more modest counterflows, amounting to £4 billion foreign investment in Britain in 1984. Both these statistics are usually seen as cash-flows, and the larger of them is rightly perceived as a deprivation of our ruined areas. That is a proper and a natural reaction: but it is even more important that they should also be seen as a shifting and concentration of *power*, involving still further transnational encroachments in Britain, in Europe, and further afield.

British capitalism is being abolished, not as Tony Crosland and others thought, by the advance of managerialism, but by the processes of internationalisation. Increasingly, British workers in what is left of the viable (to a frightening degree, transnational) economy in their own country stand in the same bargaining position that the British mineworkers or other trade unionists occupied in the early decades of the nineteenth century. Area and county associations of labour then linked up, only to find that the employers were a jump ahead and able to offset their local claims by calling in supplies or resources from other districts. The same logic that forced our British pioneers to take to the trains, and exploit the penny post, to begin to form their links at national level, now positively compels similar, functional association at international level. This becomes urgent, not only in such vital bodies as the European Trade Union Confederation, but in the creation of links between enterprise-level trade unions which can enable them to match and outpace their footloose employers.

The collapse of the old consensus in Britain was the result of the erosion of the "Keynesian World Order". The very Keynesian prescription which created post-war full employment also positively assisted the development of giant transnational corporations. Because these gradually acquired the power to override or ignore national economic regulations, they directly seeded the malaise which ultimately destroyed full employment. More and more trade has carried on "internally" between different national outposts of the same giant companies, so companies could duck out of taxes and harvest their profits in the most favourable patch. Governments lost almost all direct power to regulate economic activity by the major enterprises in their territories.

A Dutch auction of interest rates (and inflation) between different states resulted. Governments which had never openend the door to any constructive involvement by workers in the democratic management of industry, and which only imperfectly understood what was happening in the world of the multinationals, found themselves confronting the trade unions in order to limit inflation by restricting the once hitherto unchallenged union prerogative, of free collective-bargaining. Transnational corporations, the real culprits, remained completely unchallenged.

The Thatcher government's policies have put the transnationals in an even stronger position. Their untrammelled powers demand a radical response. If trade unions need to join hands and heads to meet them, how much more do the political organisations of labour? Already in 1983, the Labour Party fought the European elections alongside other European socialist parties on an agreed platform. The economic section of the combined manifesto was strongly influenced by the programme *Out of Crisis*, evolved by a group of European socialist economists and members of Labour and Socialist governments. This group was coordinated by Stuart Holland. The manifesto demanded (in Stuart Holland's phrases) an end to "Beggar my neighbour" deflation and the adoption of coordinated "Better my neighbour" expansionary policies, a package of proposals which based recovery on a move to joint policies of redistribution and restructuring. *Out of Crisis* was also committed to participatory involvement in planning.

There is room for argument about how such initiatives can be exercised within different countries, all with their own systems of industrial relations; but there is surprisingly general agreement that there will be small chance of recovery unless the initiative and inventiveness of working people can be brought directly into play.

The power of multinational companies has called up a variety of responses from trade unionists. The idea of planning agreements, widened out in *Out of Crisis*, was originally put forward in Britain in an effort to enlist trade union help in controlling their direction. Throughout the lifetime of the Wilson-Callaghan governments, however, no real planning agreements were ever concluded. Labour ministers, of right and left, also steadfastly stonewalled when they were asked to bring pressure for the implementation of an "alternative corporate plan", prepared by workers at Lucas Aerospace, for the conversion of their plants to socially-useful production. The Lucas plan caught the imagination of labour movement activists as did no other single socialist initiative of that time, and a new generation of Labour councillors drew inspiration from it. The Lucas workers' pathbreaking initiative became the foundation of a whole industrial strategy in local enterprise boards.

Lucas workers may have found their own Labour government to be deaf: but they attracted prodigious attention from trade unionists overseas. Mike Cooley, a most compelling spokesman of the stewards' combine committee, found himself preaching all over Europe, from Italy to Sweden. The shop stewards' committee was nominated for a Nobel Prize.

It is not an accident that Cooley soon found himself working with the Greater London Enterprise Board. Mass unemployment and the disciplinary forces of anti-union legislation were a powerful check on trade union rank-and-file initiative and on the movement for workers' control, which burgeoned from the 1960s to the late 1970s. Experiments in industrial democracy, squeezed out of factories, moved into the field of local government, where protection could be afforded, not only to cooperatives, but to other sometimes more challenging initiatives.

The development of alternative, and more "green", technologies became materially possible within this more sympathetic environment. It became thinkable to socialise the entrepreneurial function, and at the same time vastly to increase the scope for action by women, as well as by minority groups against whom discrimination is common. At this level, we find a potential growth point for ideas of European recovery. As local authorities seek to tackle unemployment and enter into a wide variety of job creation schemes, they begin to need international links which can facilitate mutual support.

Neither at the level of governments and party general secretaries, nor at the level of the town hall and the trade union combine committee, does European cooperation imply acceptance of the framework of the EEC. But it does imply a resolute rejection of the kind of nationalism voiced by Les Huckfield and some of his colleagues in the European Parliament. As the interpenetration of capital locks the continent into a great transnational voice, such voices sound more and more like those of the provincial diehards, who, a hundred years ago, saw no point in linking their local union to a national movement.

Ken Livingstone has offered wiser counsel. In a report to the Greater London Council (in May 1984) he argued that to the extent that each national economy in Europe is still tied to the rules of an external international financial regime, "independent macroeconomic management has been reduced in scope without [developing] the mechanisms for European macromanagement, [so] that Europe is, as a result, overcast by the shadow of the American economy just as it is overcast militarily by the shadow of the American arsenal". The need to escape from this dominion led him to insist on "a much stronger public, interventionary body in the EEC – a European Enterprise Board (EEB)".

Such a board would, he thought, replicate on a very much larger scale the experience gathered in London. It could afford a central role to trade unions and user groups in evolving sectoral strategies of genuine benefit to the working community. The argument for these kinds of structures is, of course, quite inimical to the original prospectus of the Treaty of Rome, and this gives rise to the need for either a comprehensive review of that Treaty, or for joint action outside its framework, in order to insist upon top priority for the restoration of full employment. But whether or not this happens, what is to prevent linkages between municipalities across Europe to build cooperation from the ground up? Is the Labour Party committed to this kind of strategy, or is it still anchored to the view that Britain must go it alone? It hardly seems plausible that Labour could carve out a truly non-nuclear defence policy, requiring the withdrawal of all American nuclear bases from these islands, and confront friend and opponent alike in western Europe at the same time. Why not declare war on China as well?

But this is not simply a matter of prudence, a necessary restriction of options for tactical reasons. The fact is that west European nations, just like Britain, no longer have adequate scope for effective autonomous economic action. Can Europe (all Europe, not simply the EEC) converge upon a common recovery strategy, and create the instruments with which to carry it through? The only practicable approach which offers itself for such a convergence would involve a completely new set of relationships with the third world, and with developing China. This would be a coalition for peace, as well as development and recovery. It can certainly be argued that whilst any oil money remains, there remains a continuously diminishing possibility of an independent British reform strategy. But what is clear is that the British disease is already spreading across Europe, and the scope for joint action against its effects is growing as steadily. Before our time runs out, the sensible thing to do is to use what leverage we have to create the alliances we need for survival.

If this argument is well-founded, then it follows that labour movements throughout Europe should be aiming at a joint representation committee in which rank-and-file trade unionists and socialists can find a common focus on their problems. Even if it takes time to establish such a forum, it is necessary to try, in order to create the kind of fulcrum from which to lever movement in the political institutions of the states which make up Europe.

In Britain, everyone understands that we need a Labour Party which is broadly inclusive of all the relevant strands of thought and organisation present among working people, and that we need such a party regardless of the shape which may be taken from time to time by local government structures, political constituencies, and economic institutions. A European Labour Forum is also needed, whether there is an EEC or not, or whether that community deploys itself to our advantage or against it. Only by seeking agreement on detailed policy, and arousing general discussion which can bring together all the divergent interests of European working people, can we begin to arrive at the possibility of new choices. A beginning has been made by the peace movements of Europe, which held their fourth general assembly in Amsterdam, the END Convention, in July. Representatives of all the major peace movements took part in a wide series of workshops, some of which have maintained continuous contacts since the first convention in Brussels in 1982. If the peace movements can organise this kind of discussion, why not Labour Parties and trade unions as well?

If we set ourselves the goal of creating a truly European labour movement before the end of the century, and of elaborating the policies which can unite such a movement, then we can mark out a series of national policies which lead in that direction. We can greatly expand our political activities for shorter working time as well as joint recovery measures, which will give practical solidarity to Danes, Spaniards and Germans who are fighting the same battles, and help to widen the linkages. Our towns can form material as well as political links, exploring all the practical possibilities of job creation and joint production, from Sweden down to Greece.

To advocate joint action does not mean waiting until all have agreed: it means doing what can be done, and reaching out for support. It means helping others and seeking help. It means a revolutionary change in "foreign" policy, moving to create a world in which there are no foreigners, only comrades.

A New Age of Trade Unionism

Ken Coates

Published in New Socialist*, October 1985.*

It is already very clear that 1985 has been a crucial year for the trade unions. The 1984 Trade Union Act, the culmination of a sustained programme of hostile legislation, began to take effect. Unemployment remained well over three million in the official statistics, and more than a million over that level in reality.

After a lacerating struggle, in which the mineworkers showed the kind of loyalty which is the stuff of Greek tragedy, the NUM was defeated. Arthur Scargill, who throughout the struggle showed remarkable courage, did everything possible to put a brave face on this, but on this occasion his argument was less than convincing. Fidel Castro, he explained, lost the battle for the Moncada barracks, and was forced into exile, while the Vietnamese seemed beaten after the failure of the Tet offensive. Both parties, however, went on to triumph, first in Havana and then in Saigon, which is now Ho Chi Minh City. Likewise, the miners had only lost round one.

There is, however, a simple reason why it is unlikely that London will be re-christened in a similar way to Saigon, much though some of us would quite approve of naming it after A J Cook or Nye Bevan: contrary to the implication of Arthur's analogies, the miners were fighting an industrial dispute, not a civil war. They were victims, not soldiers. They did not prepare to lie in ambush to shoot down opposing policemen, but were themselves shepherded into ambushes at Orgreave in order to be cudgelled by the police.

Strikes are essentially forms of passive resistance, and the British miners struck completely within the given constitutional framework. No councils of action or soviets were formed to challenge official power structures, and none were proposed. Indeed, the political objectives of the dispute could not have been more justified, or more restrained: to uphold the specific contract of the Plan for Coal and the general postwar industrial relations settlement in the mining industry.

For all these reasons, defeat in the coalfields was real, since there were no continuing perspectives within which conflict could be renewed with wider forces to bring ultimate victory. A guerrilla war succeeds when alternative power centres can be established firmly enough to survive reverses in particular battles, and it is for this reason that the initial battles are all limited surprise encounters, tentatively moving to establish such power. The miners' strike, by contrast, was an attempted all-out shunt, undertaken at such cost in endurance and moral courage as to be most difficult to repeat.

The only appropriate response for an NUM, now facing the worst that a vindictive management can impose in pit closures, arbitrary rationalisations, discrimination and outright victimisation, would be to develop a widespread defence of mining communities, unless, that is, it is seriously thought possible to avenge Moncada by finding a boatload of suitable trainees to begin their preparations for Orgreave's round two, somewhere in Mexico.

The miners' strike, it now seems plain, was the last of an old wave of struggles, not the first of the new. Compulsory strike ballots, conducted in the gloomy shade of lengthening dole queues, now mean that big strikes will be more difficult to organise, fewer and further between. The real danger of secondary legal actions has been purposefully imposed to ensure this. Whenever strikes do happen, they will be fought out more in the public conscience than on the narrow picket line.

The defeat of strike action proposals in the NUR, first on the London underground, and now later in the dispute over one-man operated trains, reinforces this judgment. Of course, the board of British Rail are behaving with peremptory disregard for normal negotiating practice. Robert Maxwell adds his own example to the new employer brutalism. Nobody should believe that life will be easy under the new age of industrial relations: it will be Thatcher, red in tooth and claw, stalking through the land. In the world of strikes, the new examples will be like those of the teachers, who will succeed to the extent that they can win support from parents and pupils, and tilt the wider political balances.

But the most important battles will have to take place on a different field: unless the unions turn to politics, in a firm and calculated way, they will risk not only temporary defeat, but sometimes disaggregation and even dissolution. The gap between promise and performance in the mobilisation of strikes is becoming too great to bridge with inspired rhetoric, which sounds the more arthritic and wheezy as we move on from one Congress to the next. Real radicalism will not preach general strikes that are not going to happen, but will mobilise mass demonstrations that do actually take place. It will lead activists back into the mass memberships, to campaign on issues to which ordinary members can respond. It will engage lobbies and petitions which can build confidence instead of cynicism. It will see that a few hundred thousand people in Hyde Park, calling for shorter working hours, or against poverty wages, are worth more than a few hundred resolutions wrought in fire and piety, and signifying nothing.

We can begin to see how a turn to political action becomes not only possible, but even inevitable, when we contrast the succession of industrial defeats of 1985 with the progression of other political victories.

The most encouraging of these has come in the chain of union ballots on the maintenance of political funds. Writing as one who was frankly pessimistic about the possible outcome of these votes, it is a very great pleasure to record how wrong I was. The first ten unions to vote on this vital question all recorded decisive majorities for the continuation of their political levies. Nearly two million people cast their votes in this cause, representing an average poll of 85.2 per cent in favour. The eleventh union to poll, ASLEF, actually recorded a larger proportional majority in a turn-out of 85 per cent.

There are several lessons to be drawn from this. First, the results reflect a very systematic process of campaigns. In these campaigns, national leaders have been able to mobilise with their activists at branch and regional levels, and among shop stewards, to argue for, and win over, substantial support from the mass memberships.

In some unions, the funds have received more proportional support than was accorded by their members to Labour candidates in the 1983 election. The majorities now recorded for them far outweigh those secured after the imposition of the 1913 Act, which first made such ballots mandatory.

This obviously reflects the achievement of a very real sense of unity, and is a closing of ranks in the literal sense. From 1979 until today, the Thatcher administration has brilliantly exploited every vestige of disagreement between the three levels of union organisation, playing off national leaders against activists, and seeking to cast mass memberships in the role of a "silent", conservative and, above all, passive majority. The game plan has been to lever a lid of conformity over the unions, using all the real fears which have been unleashed by slump and mass redundancies. The purpose of every new government measure during these years has been to build on the frustrations of activists in order to isolate them from the people they represent.

Second, because this process has been checked in the political fund ballots, we can now see how to carry forward our unity in a whole series of political campaigns for industrial objectives, and thus to counter actual and potential splits which governmental threats and inducements have encouraged.

It ought to be evident that action for legislative help for the low paid is equally urgent. Today, this surely demands the establishment of a statutory minimum hourly rate. And no trade unionist will doubt the need for legislative support for local authority job creation plans, public works on a vast scale, and democratic advance in the workplace.

But third, while all these issues lead us in the direction of politics which working people will see as reasonable, even "moderate" in their scope, they should not lead us away from politics which are equally radical. The present terrifying slump admits no possible solutions other than radical ones. There are two key areas for such radicalism. One imposes a new internationalism on our responses, and I wrote about this in last month's *New Socialist*. The other calls for a new departure in all our work, prioritising the growth of democratic initiatives to match needs to resources.

The miners would quite possibly have won their strike if their central demand had been the alleviation of fuel poverty by government enabling action. Ten million pensioners, and all the dependents of the unemployed, together with six million families living in substandard damp houses, would have brought a major public opinion shift towards the coalfields, if it had been generally understood that the strike was about applying coal stocks which were going to waste to meet needs which were crying aloud for help. Hypothermia now takes infant lives as well as killing pensioners, and monetarism offers no solution to this but paupers' funerals.

When British Rail set out to impose economies in manning, should not a part of the argument in response be to widen the question along the lines pioneered by the GLC and the City of Sheffield, to demand widened provision for free or cheap travel for those who are excluded from the present market?

A good example of this kind of initiative has been reported by Mike Cooley, one of the main inspirers of the Lucas workers' plan for alternative production, which remains a key signpost for any workable socialist strategy in the 1980s and 1990s. He reports that telecommunications workers in Australia, faced with technological unemployment, bargained for a two-level response. Part of their deal conferred personal protection and benefits on members of the workforce. But part of it consisted of the creation of space for a community programme of free use of the telephone network for social purposes, funded by the company in exchange for the concessions made by the unions. The workers were not split into "commercial" and "community" sections, but each year were deployed for some time in both areas. Social distribution thus became part of the overall response to technical change.

When he was drafting *Capital*, Karl Marx prepared some profoundly important notebooks, full of exciting insights: "The true economy is economy of labour time." It is easy to read this as an argument for personal leisure, and better horticulture by amateur gardeners. Surely it is partly that. But the Australian telephone system offers us a much richer perspective, of free social time, in which we can create for one another, together.

Labour's Political campaign should explore these ideas to their limits, and encourage working people to develop them fully in their political practice. The defeat of Thatcher and her works will only be assured when the labour movement refuses to permit waste any longer. The new politics, and the new unionism, will attack want in all its forms by directly seeking to join unmet needs to unused resources. Surely, all available means of action, through collective bargaining as well as the ballot box, can be called into service in such a cause?

Jack Jones and Ken Coates

Israel's Bomb
The First Victim

The Case of Mordechai Vanunu

Israel's Bomb

Ken Coates

Published in the book Israel's Bomb: The First Victim – The Case of Mordechai Vanunu *(Spokesman, 1988).*

The nuclear test which took place in the South Atlantic on 22nd September 1979 was monitored by a United States satellite. The explosion, which gave off a characteristic double flash, took place at a height of eight kilometres, which is commensurate with the performance of the GS Howitzer, which has been manufactured in South Africa since the United States supplied Pretoria with a range of modern artillery delivery systems. The Americans have also supplied the South Africans with 300,000 shell casings, adequate to deliver a two to three kiloton nuclear device.

It has been confirmed that forces of the South African fleet were present in the South Atlantic in the area of the explosion at the time that it took place. And further, it is credibly alleged that the 1979 explosion was a joint Israeli-South African achievement, as necessary to the Israelis for verifying their technology as it was to the South Africans for threatening their neighbours. That the United Nations were persuaded to record a verdict of "not proven" about this explosion tells us a good deal about the respect of some of its experts for the rules of evidence.

However, new evidence continually appears, and it would be instructive to reopen this enquiry in order to evaluate it. Since we now know that the allegations of Fuad Jabber, or the judgements, from a different perspective, of Robert E. Harkavy, were founded on realistic assumptions, it becomes necessary to evaluate the contemporary analyses of Israeli-South African cooperation, all over again.

Valuable evidence for such a new investigation has been presented by Jane Hunter in her most disturbing work on *Israeli Foreign Policy.*

> In 1965, after South Africa brought its Safari safeguarded reactor on line, Israeli scientists began advising South Africa on their Safari 2 research reactor. In 1968, Professor Ernst Bergmann, the 'father' of Israel's nuclear program, went to South Africa and spoke strongly in favour of bilateral co-operation on the development of nuclear technology.
>
> According to the authors of a novelized treatment of Israel's nuclear program – barred from publication by the Israeli censor – as early as 1966, South Africa had invited Israel to use its land or ocean space for a nuclear weapons test. Led at that time by Prime Minister Levi Eshkol, Israel declined the invitation. However, according to the Israeli authors, whose sources included Shimon Peres, an enthusiastic intimate of the Israeli nuclear program, and Knesset Member Eliyah Speizer, during his April 1976 visit to Israel Premier Vorster again extended the invitation to Israel to conduct a nuclear test.
>
> It is commonly held that Israel wanted a test venue far from the Middle East in order to uphold its longtime position that it would not be the first to introduce nuclear weapons into the region. This 'position', hinging on some arcane reading of the word 'introduce', is as meaningless as the endlessly heard term 'peace process'.
>
> The following year, a Soviet satellite picked up unmistakable signs of preparation for a nuclear test in the Kalahari Desert. Fearing that such a test 'might trigger an ominous escalation of the nuclear arms race,' the U.S., Britain, France and West Germany joined the USSR in pressuring South Africa to abort the test. As to the bomb that was to be tested, 'I know some intelligence people who are convinced with damn near certainty that it was an Israeli nuclear device', said a high-ranking Washington official.

At three o'clock in the morning on September 22, 1979, Israel and South Africa conducted a nuclear weapons test where the South Atlantic and Indian Oceans merge. A newly recalibrated U.S. Vela intelligence satellite recorded the characteristic double flash of light. It was a small blast, designed to leave very little evidence. The CIA told the National Security Council that a two or three kiloton bomb had been exploded in 'a joint South African-Israeli test'. A Navy official revealed that U.S. spy planes over the test area had been waved away by South African Navy ships and forced to land secretly in Australia. The CIA knew (and later told Congress) that South African ships were conducting secret manoeuvres at the exact site of the test. The South African military attaché in Washington made the first ever request to the U.S. National Technical Information Service for a computer search on detection of nuclear explosions and orbits of the Vela satellite.

Almost immediately the Carter Administration convened a special panel to conduct an investigation of the incident. The panel heard reports from the U.S. Naval Research Laboratory, the Defense Intelligence Agency, and the CIA; and representatives of the Los Alamos National Laboratory, the Department of Energy and the State Department presented evidence supporting the occurrence of a nuclear explosion. Their findings were summarily dismissed by the Carter White House, which after a delay of seven months declared:

> Although we cannot rule out the possibility that this (Vela) signal was of nuclear origin, the panel considers it more likely that the signal was one of the zoo events (reception of signals of unknown origin under anomalous circumstances), possibly a consequence of the impact of a small meteor on the satellite.

Moreover, as new information became available, it was simply ignored. In one critical instance, evidence of radiation observed in the thyroid glands of Australian sheep was discounted. The initial lack of this "smoking gun," traces of radiation, suggested to a Los Alamos scientist that the low-yield weapon tested had been a neutron bomb. However, the Carter panel had used the absence of radiation as a prime excuse in its cover-up.

Many who had been involved with the investigation were aghast and wondered why the Carter White House was 'equivocating'. Some within the government said that the Carter Administration was hiding behind the 'zoo' theory to avoid dealing with the political headaches that would accompany acknowledgement of the test. An affirmative report might have affected the ongoing negotiations over the creation of Zimbabwe in which South African co-operation was needed and upset the just negotiated Camp David accords between Israel and Egypt. Carter also had reasons to fear 'complications in gathering Jewish votes during the upcoming Democratic Party primary campaign against Sen. Edward Kennedy.'

But beyond that, as a State Department official explained, coming clean on the test 'would be a major turning point in our relations with South Africa and Israel if we determined conclusively that either had tested a nuclear bomb. It makes me terribly nervous just to think about it.' Of course by deciding to ignore reality the Carter administration – and following in its footsteps, the Reagan administration, which went on record May 21, 1985 as upholding the Carter 'verdict' – destroyed the already tattered credibility of the nonproliferation posture of the U.S. There was no challenge forthcoming from Congress. Quite the contrary: in 1981 Representatives Stephen Solarz and Jonathan Bingham withdrew legislation they had introduced calling for a cutoff of U.S. aid to nations manufacturing nuclear weapons after they learned from the State Department "that such a requirement might well trigger a finding by the Administration that Israel has manufactured a bomb." The U.S. government turned its back on the potential victims of Israeli and South African nuclear aggression and stuck its head in the sand like an ostrich.

Five years later, the Washington Office on Africa Educational Fund in cooperation with Congressman John Conyers (D-MI), the Congressional Black Caucus Foundation and the World Campaign Against Military and Nuclear Collaboration with South Africa issued a report on the 1979 nuclear weapons test. Based on documents obtained from the government under the Freedom of Information Act, the report detailed scientific evidence not taken into account by the Carter panel. It demonstrated conclusively that a cover-up had been perpetrated by the Carter Administration. Written by Howard University Professor Ronald Walters, the report warned that the cover-up, 'coupled with the Reagan Administration's subsequent allowance of an increase in nuclear aid to South Africa has serious implications for international peace and security.'

The sponsors of the report urged that the investigation be reopened under the auspices of the National Academy of Sciences and the National Academy of Engineers, and also called for a Congressional investigation and the release to the public of all pertinent information.

Of course whether enquiries are reopened in the USA, or the United Nations, or not, many African States are deeply uneasy about these events. Unsurprisingly, the conclusions which they have drawn reflect considerable alarm. A number of African countries have quite reasonably concluded that they are prospective candidates for nuclear bombardment by South Africa. No Government in the front-line states can possibly ignore this threat. Persistent cross-border military activity by the apartheid regime is a permanent fact of political life in the southern part of the African continent.

But it is not only in the front-line states that alarm bells have been ringing. As Oye Ogunbadejo informs us:

> Nigeria, for example, sees itself as ... a potential target. Lagos has consistently argued that any improvements in South Africa's military power and nuclear capability, with the assistance of the west, pose direct military threats to Nigeria, and make it an open target of long-range nuclear attack. Alhaji Shehu Shagari, as President, continued to emphasise the need for his country to catch up with South Africa in the nuclear field. For the time being, however, Nigeria's efforts are geared, essentially, towards energy purposes.

Yet, Ogunbadejo cites other prominent African spokesmen who are very impatient with the restrictions of nuclear capacity to the civilian sector.

Thus, Ali Mazrui is reported as a strong critic of the Non-Proliferation Treaty:

> From a third world point of view, I don't believe the Treaty is worth the paper it is written on. And if I were to become President of a third world country, I would not hesitate to withdraw from it. Imperialism in the nuclear age is the monopoly stage of nuclear technology.

Mazrui foresees an alliance of black South Africa with Nigeria and Zaire, which would develop its own African 'deterrent'.

> Africa under its triumvirate of diplomatic leaders partly endowed with nuclear credentials, will have begun to enter the main stream of global affairs. And the world as a whole, once it discovers the lunacy of its nuclear ways, will have learned an old lesson in a new context: the lesson that wild mushrooms are dangerous.

Of course, the attitude of the Government of Free South Africa cannot yet be determined. Fortunately, for many years, progressive people throughout the African continent have given their support to the goal of a nuclear-free zone in the whole region. Kwame Nkrumah froze all French assets because of the tests in the Sahara desert during 1961. At the same time, Nigeria severed its diplomatic contact with France. The advent of the Non-Proliferation Treaty was perhaps more keenly welcomed in Africa than in any other sector of the globe. Ogunbadejo believes that only a major initiative towards nuclear disarmament by the great powers can maintain this kind of wider global commitment.

> In the maintenance of future world order, the close co-operation and understanding between the superpowers and the other states with nuclear weapons is an essential precondition.

The advent of the Gorbachev-Reagan summits, and the conclusion of a Treaty to dismantle intermediate nuclear forces, welcome though it is, nonetheless arrives after the eleventh hour, when we consider the savage implications of the problems of proliferation. Conventional theories of deterrence are deeply flawed, and nowhere more than in their standard presumption of a bipolar model of nuclear confrontation. In a crude way, several thousand warheads may, when confronted by several thousand other warheads, determine a certain kind of behaviour. No such determination may be presumed, however, once proliferation has extended to the 'pariah' states. In the hot spots which include and surround these states, there is sufficient turbulence to encourage the insane idea that nuclear weapons can be useful as means of actual warfare. What elsewhere would be normal restraints of public opinion are here conspicuously absent.

We have more than a little evidence that neither domestic nor international law controls the potential responses of such governments.

In small things, the Israeli Government kidnaps its opponents, and visits exemplary repression upon them. In large things, it misleads the United Nations and extends the threat of nuclear destruction to two of the most dangerous areas in the contemporary world.

It is hardly surprising that good people who are facing such threats may flinch in their commitment to oppose all or any reliance on nuclear weapons. Thus, Ogunbadejo tells us:

> Edem Kodjo, the last substantive Secretary-General of the Organization of African Unity, caused quite a stir at the 19th summit during June 1983 in Addis Ababa, when he militantly urged African Governments to match 'South Africa's nuclear mights': 'it is the duty of member states which are able to resolutely embark on the nuclear path to do so.'

Nuclear proliferation is the tragic *reductio ad absurdem* of deterrence theory. That old cynic, Harold Macmillan, cogently expressed the problem:

> If all this capacity for destruction is spread around the world in the hands of all kinds of different characters, dictators, reactionaries, revolutionaries, madmen – then sooner or later, and certainly, I think by the end of the century, either by error or insanity, the great crime will be committed.

The Non-Proliferation Treaty, and the idea of nuclear-free zones, can neither of them continue unaffected by the nuclearization of the military forces of Israel and South Africa. If there is still time to maintain the civilized commitment of Africa and the Arab world to non-nuclear defence policies, it must be evident that that time is rapidly speeding away. Mordechai Vanunu has removed the last veil which had been concealing this ugly situation.

Now, in order to survive, the Non-Proliferation regime must discover how to disarm Israel and South Africa of their nuclear bludgeons. A failure to confront this intransigent issue may not at once create the field full of dragon's teeth which will eventually grow. Problems of resources and technology will ensure an uneven development of nuclear military potential. But here, we are talking about something more fundamental than budget allocations: at stake is the whole question of the political will for peace and disarmament, as well as the deep-rooted problem of social justice. If the rest of the world abandons the front-line states to South African intimidation, including nuclear intimidation, all Africa will conclude that Ali Mazrui is right. If everyone outside the Middle East remains deaf to the process which is now reopening behind locked doors in Jerusalem, then the call for an Arab bomb will become irresistible. We are members of one another, and it is at critical moments like the present that it becomes necessary to demonstrate this fact.

So widespread is the international movement for peace that the Third United Nations Special Session on Disarmament will see continued healthy pressures for the destruction of nuclear weapons, and the extension of ever wider nuclear-free territorial agreements. Yet, it seems to me, that all these events provide us with a powerful argument that disarmament can no longer be left to governments.

There are widespread debates about the need for reform of the United Nations system, and many new proposals are emerging from the different peace movements, as they experience the weaknesses and limitations of the inherited UN system. Even within the old system, however, many voices have been raised for the creation of a new information order, as a pre-condition for an enlightened and active world public opinion.

The confrontation between Israel and its neighbours, the plight of the Palestinian people, and the abscess of apartheid are major parts of a global crisis of militarism. This is worsening as a result of economic crisis, contraction and collapse. If the Stock Exchange crash leads through trade wars to the explosion of the world's debt bomb, then the present proliferation of nuclear weapons is a perfect formula for Armageddon. No-one can tell where conflict will spill over, once any of these sinister devices are detonated.

So urgent is this problem that nothing less than a worldwide popular movement is needed to meet it. It cannot be left to the immediate victims of these new nuclear threats to protest and appeal in isolation. "Send ye not", said our English poet John Donne, "to know for whom the bell tolls: it tolls for thee."

BERTRAND
RUSSELL
PEACE
FOUNDATION
END

Listening for Peace

Ken Coates

First published as END papers special 2, *1987. This detailed account of the European Nuclear Disarmament initiatives of the 1980s examines some of the disagreements that arose and how they might have been resolved.*

The coalition of peace movements which came into being in Europe at the beginning of this decade has, in July 1987 completed its sixth international gathering, at the European Nuclear Disarmament Convention in Coventry.

A lot of things have changed since the process leading to these meetings began in 1980, and some of the changes have vast implications.

It is therefore hardly surprising that a number of lines of argument have crystallized to the point where several distinct if overlapping alignments are visible within the movement, so that the earlier unstructured informality of the process has become more and more difficult to maintain. There are those who think that all disagreements are signs of weakness. Intolerance easily grows within such a perspective, because it is easy to stop arguing with people, and blame them instead. By contrast it seems to me that reasoned discussion is a far from divisive process, and in the present circumstances of the peace movement organized debate could become a healing action. But the precondition for this remedy is that all the arguments should be openly and clearly stated, and that all the different advocates be given every opportunity to express themselves.

The peace movement needs to be very careful of "either/or". Either we should talk to the grassroots, or we should talk to the politicians, some say. Either we should talk to the dissidents in the East, or we should talk to official peace movements, say others. Either we should address particular deployments of deathly weapons, or we should address the political environment in which the armourers flourish, is another view. Either we should embrace the given power structure or we should seek to overturn it, imply others again. These nice dichotomies will not work in the present age, because there is a nuclear lid over all of us. No purifying upheaval will sweep away evil at one swoop, without also sweeping us all to oblivion. Today, "He who would seek truth about must and about must go." Opposing the poisonous linkages of strategic systems, all we have on our side is the light of rational argument, and the linkages of humane social thought.

The most passionately contested either/or in the contemporary peace movements concerns whether or not to talk to "official" Soviet representatives, and we must begin by examining this question.

* * *

As Europe entered the 1980s, many of us had powerful reasons to believe that it was unlikely that we would complete the decade before we were swallowed up in war. Ponderous military structures were reinforcing themselves on both sides of a divided continent. The two great powers were elaborating more and more deadly, destructive and accurate weapons, and installing them with less and less regard for the possible consequences. At the end of April 1980, the Russell Foundation convened a press conference in the House of Commons, at which was launched the appeal for European Nuclear Disarmament. "Twice in this century" said this appeal "Europe has disgraced its claims to civilization, by engendering world war. This time we must repay our debts to the world by engendering peace". The deployment, over a wide arc of Europe, of a new generation of intermediate range nuclear missiles was the catalyst of public concern, which made our appeal interesting to many thousands of Europeans. In the logic of the time, escalation on one side provoked matching responses on the other. A kind of insane leapfrog ensued, as each power set in place its most devilish inventions and invited the other to improve upon them. In our appeal, we sought to bring Europeans together "to free the entire territory of Europe, from Poland to Portugal, from nuclear weapons, air and submarine bases, and from all institutions engaged in research into or manufacture of nuclear weapons. We ask the two superpowers to withdraw all nuclear weapons from European territory."

For several years, peace movements railed against the powers, and tried to prevent new deployments of nuclear weapons. One by one, the separate national battles were lost, and the missile bases were put down and fortified, from Greenham down to Comiso. But in October 1986, the Reykjavik summit created a sudden new flare of hope, a giant illumination which, for an instant, lit up an entire world. During that instant, the great power spokesmen seemed to be agreed that it was necessary to abolish nuclear weapons altogether, and to do it all within a time span of ten years. From the Soviet side, Mr. Gorbachev suggested that all strategic missiles could be destroyed within five years, leaving the remainder of the decade for the completion of the agenda. Just as suddenly as the world was bathed in this unreal light, night returned. We saw the two summiteers returning home, tight-lipped, because the United States refused to accept that its Star Wars project should be restrained to a purely experimental stage.

There have, of course, been major recent shifts in the policies of both great powers. Crises of different kinds afflict them both. Mankind could be excused for a certain resistance, caution, even cynicism about their statements. But we must also appreciate that there has been a consistent pattern of behaviour, building through the last years, which must invite us to suspend such cynicism. On the American side, there is a resolute commitment to the Strategic Defence Initiative, or President Reagan's "Star Wars", which already pre-empts an investment of many billions of dollars, in spite of the warnings of so many scientists that the whole project may be fruitless. The Soviet leadership does not believe that the American President is simply crazy, whatever his own countrymen may think. Soviet leaders must presumably discount the propaganda presentation of all this military research in space, and see only its manifestly aggressive potential. The allies of the United States perceive it with increasing clarity as an economic aggression, seeking to recover leadership in the domain of advanced communication technologies, and to offset, through military research, competitive threats from Japan and, to a lesser extent, Europe. Meantime, the aggressive potential of the American Government on a more mundane plane remains, as ever, promiscuous. The bombardment of Colonel Gaddafi, the sordid attempt to bring about a "liberation" of Nicaragua, the policing of the Persian Gulf, each provokes wider and more unpredictable risks, with fine disregard for the letter of international law, and an almost equal contempt for that of the American Constitution.

At the beginning of the decade, we might have been tempted to be equally censorious of the Soviet leadership. Today, this would be quite unjust. Since the 10th March 1985, Mikhail Gorbachev has carried the Soviet Union into an increasingly vigorous policy of disarmament, in which he has not hesitated to use unilateral initiatives in order to mobilise international opinion. In August, soon after his accession to the General Secretaryship, he declared a moratorium on nuclear testing, and invited the United States to follow suit. The Five Continent initiative (of Sweden, Greece, Argentina, Mexico, Tanzania and India) determined upon a comprehensive Test Ban Treaty as the most practicable method of controlling the nuclear danger and restricting proliferation. These neutral leaders found a uniquely generous response from Mr. Gorbachev. More: this response was maintained month after month, as the nuclear tests of the United States continued inexorably. Throughout 1986, the moratorium continued, even while the President remained obdurately deaf to all appeals to react in kind. At last, Gorbachev was persuaded to announce that if the Americans continued their tests into 1987, Soviet testing would have to resume. But for more than a year, a completely unilateral Soviet initiative had reinforced the appeal of non-aligned statesmen, and for the first time in a long while, raised the hopes of ordinary people right around the world.

The moratorium was not alone. It was followed by audacious proposals for total nuclear disarmament, launched in January 1986. These in turn were further developed at Reykjavik, as we have already seen.

Almost as impressive as these substantive proposals of the Gorbachev team has been the back-up in ancillary proposals. The Soviet Union is negotiating vigorously, with the aim of reaching agreement. All questions of inspection and control are now seen as perfectly capable of resolution. Solely as a result of the new Soviet policy on these matters, there are no alibis or excuses for failure. Peace movements should be aware of the evidence for this view.

Immediately after Reykjavik, we launched an appeal which was endorsed by most of the European peace movements. It read as follows:

> "The collapse of the Reykjavik summit meeting, now that the details of its exchanges are leaking out, can be seen to offer Europe a warning, but also to offer a hope.
>
> Europeans are not present at these great power negotiations, even though it is our security and our future which are being decided there. We have been deeply concerned about the presence of the intermediate range missiles which are stationed in Europe. Cruise and Pershing on one side, and SS20s on the other, render lethal the divide which cuts our continent in two. In Iceland a preliminary solution was found which could have enabled all such weapons to be dismantled. This solution must be implemented. It must not be lost in a linkage with other questions. Just because we are excluded from the conference rooms, the people of Europe must make their wishes felt on the streets and in the lobbies, to insist upon this first crucial step to wider disarmament. We appeal to the Soviet peoples for their support for this call.
>
> But at the same time, Europeans share the planet with all its other inhabitants, and cannot avoid the other issues which came to a head in

> Reykjavik. On the brink of an agreement to cut stockpiles of strategic weapons by half, the talks failed because of President Reagan's insistence on the testing and deployment of space weapons. Reasonable proposals to solve this problem are available, but they require a willingness on the American side to negotiate. This is, at the moment, not evident. Therefore, in all our demonstrations, we call upon the American people to join us in the effort to persuade their President to reconsider the whole disastrous 'Star Wars' commitment.
>
> By joining our forces in this way, we may heed the warnings of Reykjavik, and begin to realize its hopes."[1]

Two responses followed. Firstly, in the old-fashioned vein, Yuri Zhukov, then President of the Soviet Peace Committee, issued a stern rebuke to the Europeans. "Our proposals are not", he said, "a menu from which you can take your pick". They were an integrated package. In the circular in which he argued this, Mr. Zhukov was maintaining a vigorous relationship of agnostic, not to say abrasive, polemic, which had already been established almost at the beginning of the END process.[2]

But far more decisive was the response of Mr Gorbachev himself, who shortly afterwards firmly announced an end to the linkage between negotiations on intermediate nuclear forces (Cruise and Pershing missiles, and SS20s) on the one side, and the Strategic Defence Initiative on the other. Thus, INF negotiations could be resumed forthwith, and soon they were in full spate, with a high prospect of agreement. Once again, we could see the Soviets bargaining with panache, and a keen sense of urgency.

In December 1986, there was a peace conference in Athens, sponsored by the Greek peace movement KEADEA. I was sitting with Bruce Kent in one of the panels when the Vice-President of the Soviet Peace Committee, Mr. Vladimir Oryol, made a powerful contribution. "You ask us", he said to the assembled Western peace movements, "to make concession after concession". We had indeed asked for the delinkage. As the Americans continually triggered their tests, one after another, we had in fact asked the Soviets to maintain their moratorium none the less. Over and again, Soviet initiatives had answered the requests of the peace movements: but where was the answering response? This seemed to me to be a fair question, and I said so. Today, as I write, the INF talks are menaced by the totally indefensible claim that Pershing IA missiles in Federal Germany must be exempted from any agreement, on the entirely specious claim that they are "German". The warheads, which are all that matters about them, are American, and the position in international law is crystal clear. Should this issue not come to the very top of the peace movement agenda?

During 1987 the momentum of the Soviet initiatives has continued. Mr. Gorbachev made an incredibly advanced appeal to a vast international gathering in the Kremlin at the beginning of the year. In it, he has seized the high ground as has no other statesman since the end of the second world war. Andrei Sakharov, recently released from exile in Gorki, was among the audience to hear the General Secretary declare that the famous doctrine of Clausewitz, that "war is the continuation of politics by other means", no longer applies to world wars in an age which stands on the threshold of nuclear winter. More: it was clear in the text of the Soviet leader's speech that he had drawn from this appreciation precisely the same conclusions as had the Western peace movements during the opening years of the present fraught decade.

In May, the Soviet Peace Committee held its Fourth Information Session and Dialogue in Moscow. A wide cross-section of European peace movements were invited, and the discussion was extremely open, and friendly. I was most surprised to find that our old critic, Mr. Zhukov, was not present, and even more astonished to be asked to report on my own workshop in the plenary session. Openness was the order of the day. When their sessions were over-polite and insufficiently critical, various Soviet spokesmen took it on themselves to provoke more frank exchanges.

Changes in disarmament policy were being followed by changes in the policy of the Peace Committee: a restructuring indeed. The representative of the Campaign for Nuclear Disarmament in Britain has recounted her view of what happened at this important conference when Irina Krivova of the Moscow Trust Group was invited to participate in one of the sessions.[3]

What was even more important was the way in which younger members (and some who were not so young) of the Soviet Peace Committee were so anxious to insist that the Soviet Disarmament policy had really been influenced by the ideas of the Western peace movements.

The experts, as usual, are quarrelling about the meaning of Soviet events. But the Soviet leadership is very clear about them. They insist that the policies of disarmament abroad and democratization at home amount to a "revolution", and that they are indissolubly connected. Of course, neither policy will necessarily succeed. The present Soviet leadership will be opposed by powerful conservative forces abroad and at home. Disarmament is difficult, and we would today need to invent a peace movement even if none already existed. Domestic reform may prove to be almost equally difficult, since vested interests can so often neutralise the intentions of reforming legislation, and suffocate their promise in a fog of routine. The good comrade Schweik is alive, not only in Czechoslovakia. At every level of society, people have evolved their own ways of living with authority, and of circumventing its rigours. Even these popular mechanisms, to say nothing of the resistance of powerful functionaries, will conspire against reforms, unless there is wholesale political renewal.

And yet ... There is a renewal. Cultural life has exploded into extraordinary new developments. Every effort is made to encourage discussion and participation. Journalism has come alive. Experiment is in the air. The rejuvenation of Soviet society would, indeed, amount to a revolution, and Mr. Gorbachev's revolution might succeed. But we should face the pessimist argument. It might not. The only part of it we can influence is that part which concerns disarmament, and it is doubly in our interests to ensure that this does not fail: It cannot be right to stand on the sidelines and watch, when so much is at stake, for the Soviet peoples themselves, and the rest of humanity at large.

Can we not see, just for a moment, how things must seem to the courageous team which has set itself these audacious goals? Acres of print have been covered in the British press, explaining how the Labour Party may have lost votes because of its doctrines on disarmament. Yet the same commentators never pause for one moment to ask why Mr. Gorbachev's doctrines should by contrast, be universally popular, and what resistance he might arouse in the Soviet Union. If our press is blind to such questions, that is no reason why our peace movements should look away. We have now, from the Soviet Union, a whole series of generous and relevant initiatives. We need to understand them, and we should also, surely, try to help them. Concretely, this means that we should be concerned to help them obtain a friendly reception by public opinion, East and West alike.

Not every peace activist sees these events in the same light. Speaking in the Sixth Convention, Mient Jan Faber said that Gorbachev had brilliantly destabilized NATO with his disarmament policies, and it was the task of the peace movements to similarly destabilize the Warsaw Treaty Organization with their politics of detente from below. That is not what most of us have meant by "detente from below". It is perhaps imaginable, although not very likely, that if the peace movements bounce around a lot in Poland they might be able to encourage some demonstrations against the authorities there. Poles are not altogether reluctant to join such demonstrations. If this is simply an act of tomfoolery on our part, it will do little harm. But let us do Mient Jan the favour of taking him seriously. Supposing we really could destabilize Poland? What would this mean for the future of detente and disarmament? Is it not evident that an upheaval in Eastern Europe would be precisely the best way to undermine the Gorbachev revolution, both at home and abroad? What should the Soviet Government do if it was confronted by such turbulence? If it were to respond with repression not only would it be judged to be wrong by Western observers, but it might also fall in the domestic backlash. Even if it survived, its reforming policies could well be jeopardised. Or should the Soviet authorities sit by, and allow events to take their course? How, then, would their backwoodsmen respond? In point of fact, Western movements cannot appreciably influence events in Eastern Europe for good, or for evil. All that we can do is try to establish common perspectives, and a sense of solidarity and mutual support. But all the most creative forces in Eastern Europe will be passionately concerned that Gorbachev should succeed, and very unhappy to think that Western peace movements might be indifferent to their hopes and expectations.

It was the founding charter of END that our processes should be open to all who supported them, and no-one would wish to change this. Today, we have new supporters, some of them in very high places. Is it such a problem to learn to talk with them? Is it quite impossible to listen'?

As I sat in the chair at the Coventry focus meeting, with the lively young Russian delegates who formed the panel in the Cathedral, I tried to call a cross-section of the peace movements to ask their questions. Most were hostile. The Russians did not duck, or weave, in trying to respond. Sometimes they disagreed among themselves. They were deeply impressive, not because of their advocacy, which was fluent, but precisely because of the uncertainty and fear which they from time to time expressed. It was our own doubts, and our own fears, which we could hear in these responses. What worried me was this: how slow we are, in Western Europe, to appreciate what is happening. Now, at last, we stand on common ground with a decisive section of Soviet opinion. Must we wait until it is too late before we begin to see that dialogue and joint action go together, and that we are members of one another?

* * *

Our next 'either/or' concerns politicians. On this matter we have heard a great deal from the representative of the London-based END group, Lynn Jones. Now she has published a summary of the view she has been canvassing during recent months (END *Journal*, 28/29, Summer 1987). She says it is "anathema to many of us to turn the Convention into a forum for debate between politicians. They have enough space anyway and enough sense of their own power. We at the grassroots are still struggling to be heard". She goes on to talk of "completely corrupt political discussion". "We can" she says "no longer rely on an alliance with socialist or social democratic parties to achieve our goals, if only because they seem to have become politically redundant. We have to create an effective political opposition with or without them."

In passing, we should note that Lynn Jones is also very discontented with the "grassroots". She speaks of the routinism of the Campaign for Nuclear Disarmament, whose recent demonstration, she thinks, echoed slogans which "would have fitted any year in the past eight". But the slogans of the Campaign for Nuclear Disarmament were not determined by professional politicians, whether "social democratic" or otherwise. They arose from the understanding of CND's own grassroots leadership, and reflected the state of thinking within the organization. To the extent that Lynn Jones is right, she is diagnosing a general condition, which has similar effects in both what she calls the "political" and "grassroots" sections of the movement. Day by day, indeed, it is more and more difficult without prior knowledge to say which of these constituents is which, or to lay down intelligent criteria for dividing them. It is true that socialist parties have lost elections in Northern Europe. Outside Scandinavia, Greece and Spain, they no longer speak from positions of power. In Italy, the communists have also lost ground. Whatever harm is done by the erosion of leftwing support in Europe's heartlands and in Britain, it surely has one little advantage in that it brings the losers closer to all the other powerless forces in society. Should this not make easier the opening of dialogue? What is the real reproach against the socialist and communist parties? If they are judged to be guilty only of lacking power does this imply that the "grassroots" should be seeking power themselves? Or are the peace activists instead, as used to be consensually argued, seeking to change the relationships in society, and annul various harmful meanings in the concept of power itself? If they answer that they are in fact seeking power, then we must observe that they remain far further from it than the oppositional constitutional parties. If they agree that operational concepts of power are seriously flawed, then is the very moment when such power has escaped the diverse forces of the left, the optimum time to *stop* talking with them? Surely it is more likely to be an optimum time for them to listen?

The Conventions of the European Nuclear Disarmament movement were created as forums, and those of us who designed and established the process intended that every point of view should have open access. Very deliberately, we resolved not to agree resolutions or seek binding mandates. In what respect, then, is this discussion inhibited, if space is allowed for all contenders?

Lynn Jones offers an account of the history of this END process: but it is gravely defective since there are large parts of it which she does not know. She begins with a moving quotation from Edward Thompson's pamphlet, *Protest and Survive*, which she read on a train to York, early in 1980. This pamphlet was published by the Russell Foundation, and it was not an accident that Edward Thompson asked us to undertake the work.

In fact, we had been seeking a basis upon which to associate a European peace movement ever since 1974, when we convened a seminar at Bradford under the title *The Just Society*. This seminar consisted almost entirely of recognised political forces. Present were: representatives of Willy Brandt and Bruno Kreisky; Tony Benn, Michael Meacher, Stuart Holland and Audrey Wise from the British Labour Party; Lucio Lombardo Radice from the Central Committee of the Italian Communists; Hans Janitschek, Secretary of the Socialist International, Michel Raptis, one-time secretary of the Fourth International; and, from the East, Eduard Goldstuecker and Zhores Medvedev. The conference met under the presidency of Professor Edwards, the Vice-Chancellor of Bradford University, to consider a paper from Roy Medvedev, and to develop responses to it. Professor Andras Hegedus, from Hungary, sent a paper, but was unable to obtain travel documents in order to be present with us. Edward Thompson took part in this seminar, although he had already left when Goldstuecker made the suggestion that the impasse in relations between East and West Europe, and the adverse conditions of work suffered by independent socialist thinkers in the East, were intricately related and that only a new and comprehensive European peace movement could open any possibility for a real change for the better.

From that moment on, we began to explore every contact which might help to generate such a movement. Very serious help was later to be given by all the participants in the Bradford symposium to the launch of END. I and others returned to this theme again and again, at international conferences of one kind and another. For example, on the 1st December 1978, I gave a paper at a conference organized by the Italian Socialist Party, which concluded:

> "We must face the overwhelming fact of the world's balance of terror, in which our Western economic crisis is liable, as so often before, to provoke renewed speed-up in an already dizzy arms race. The effect of this, were it to develop unhindered by popular protest, would be to rigidify the Eastern bureaucracies, and brake the widening social pressure for reform. This would inhibit necessary change both in the East and West. For those who seek a marriage between socialism and liberty, the first task is, beyond doubt, the pursuit of wider international unity, overcoming old divisions, and challenging both the mass unemployment which capitalism has inflicted on our peoples and the threats of

> rearmament which it once again begins to imply. If socialists and eurocommunists could move in this direction, they would gain more than increased autonomy and popular response. They might begin to create a political situation in which the choices were no longer structured around labels attached to dead heroes or villains, but crystallised around the living issues which we need to face."

I spoke in the same sense at a succession of meetings in Yugoslavia, France, England and Scandinavia. But until 1979 the proposal remained abstract, and without immediate targets. At the end of that year, the decision to deploy Cruise and Pershing missiles across a wide arc of Western Europe drew Edward Thompson into public protest. In a magnificent series of articles, he denounced this new twist in the European nuclear spiral. He also began to lobby privately, in order to develop a new campaign. At the very end of 1979, he wrote to Tony Benn, to ask for his help in mobilizing civil disobedience against the projected new nuclear bases. He was kind enough to send me copies of his letters, because he remembered the meeting between the three of us back in 1974. Tony Benn had met Edward Thompson for the first time at Bradford: since then he had been very much engaged with Frank Allaun in committing the Labour Party to resuming anti-nuclear demonstrations, and in fact the demonstration which took place under the Party's banner in the Spring of 1980 was the first sizeable indication of the rebirth of the movement for nuclear disarmament in Britain. But Benn did not at the time believe that he could meet Edward's precise request. It was at this point that I rang Edward to propose, instead of a purely national response, we should seek to create a European answer. The formula which had escaped us hitherto was absolutely simple: we should seek to create a nuclear-free zone in all of Europe. Edward enthusiastically accepted this idea, and prepared a draft for such an appeal at the same time that he wrote an article for the *Guardian* along the lines which we had discussed.

I rehearse this background because the entire initiative was taken by people with political commitments. Before I made the original proposal for END to Edward, I had discussed it with Stuart Holland and Ralph Miliband. On Stuart's suggestion, we approached Mary Kaldor and Dan Smith: both of whom had been advising the Labour Party on defence questions.

Having negotiated certain important changes in Edward's draft, I then circulated it for discussion and amendment. Significant alterations were made before we convened a series of consultative meetings in London. At an early stage it was agreed, on a proposal by Arthur Scargill, that the END appeal should be open to signatures from Britain, and that a separate endorsement should be sought from European signatories. What the Europeans endorsed was the statement:

> "We have received with sympathy the proposal of the Bertrand Russell Peace Foundation for an all European campaign to free the soil and territorial waters of all European states from nuclear weapons.
>
> In our view, this proposal merits urgent attention, and we support its object. While consultation must take place within each country, to take into account the particular conditions of each nation's life, we urge that this be pressed forward immediately, with a view to the encouragement of such an all European movement.
>
> To facilitate this work we should welcome a European meeting to explore the problems involved in creating a nuclear-free zone, to discuss a variety of intermediary proposals which are already being suggested as possible steps towards the objective, and help in the development of a major popular campaign for peace and disarmament.
>
> We think such a meeting should be convened as soon as the organizational and financial problems can be resolved."

Unlike the END Appeal itself, which was a collective effort based on much discussion, this short statement was by two hands: it began precisely in the words of E. P. Thompson, which were adopted by the Foundation as he wrote them, adding only the last two paragraphs.

The appeal was launched at a press conference in the House of Commons on the 28th April 1980. The speakers at the press conference included Zhores Medvedev, Edward Thompson, Mary Kaldor, Bruce Kent and myself: but there was also a strong force of politicians: Tony Benn, Eric Heffer, Robin Cook, and Stuart Holland. The list of signatories which we announced to the press was, I recall, heavily populated by well-known political leaders, including former Prime Ministers and Foreign Ministers, the International Secretaries of the Dutch and Austrian Socialist Parties, the Leader of the Dutch Radical Party in the Senate, the National Secretary of the Unified Socialist Party of France, Members of Parliament from many European countries, and all the original participants in the Bradford seminar, except Eduard Goldstuecker who was unable to be present at the birth of his brainchild.

Celebrating the press conference, Edward Thompson published an article which made the genesis of the appeal abundantly clear. It began as follows:

> "When I was given hospitality on this page three months ago, the notion of an all-European campaign to clear nuclear weapons and bases from the whole continent – from the Urals to the Atlantic, or from Poland to Portugal – was only a glint in the eye of the Russell Peace Foundation. Today the Foundation will release its first, preliminary, report upon the campaign, and will outline its opening stages. The support has been profoundly encouraging, and each day the post brings in new adherents."

In all these days there was very little talk about the relative merits of "political" and "grassroots" members of the peace movement. This, I suppose, probably reflects the fact that our lawn was a bit bald. Grass rooted itself later. Having lifelong anarchist proclivities, I am always glad when the grass grows well: but it would be a total distortion of the truth to see the END process as a spontaneous show generated by telepathy and intuition. I do not think that many initiatives have been born with longer gestations or more careful discussion and thought and at no time were these processes confined in a ghetto. They benefited constantly from the advice of far-sighted politicians, trade union leaders and churchmen and other men and women active in public life, no less than from the courageous exertions of people who held no recognized office.

The files of correspondence concerning the launch of the appeal are thick with letters to and from European statesmen. Willy Brandt urged us to make contact with Olof Palme, and Palme introduced us to Alva Myrdal, with whom a long and affectionate exchange ensued. From Palme we received a copy of the speech which he had delivered to the Socialist International Conference in Helsinki, back in 1978. We immediately published this in the *Bulletin of Work in Progress*, which the Foundation established to service the infant END movement:

> "Europe is no special zone where peace can be taken for granted. In actual fact it is at the centre of the arms race. Granted, the general assumption seems to be that any potential military conflict between the superpowers is going to start some place other than Europe. But even if that were to be the case, we would have to count on one or the other party – in an effort to gain supremacy – trying to open a front on our continent, as well. As Alva Myrdal has recently pointed out, a war can simply be transported here, even though actual causes for war do not exist. Here there is a ready theatre of war. Here there have been great military forces for a long time. Here there are programmed weapons all ready for action ... Today more than ever there is, in my opinion, every reason to go on working for a nuclear-free zone. *The ultimate objective of these efforts should be a nuclear-free Europe* (my italics). The geographical area closest at

> hand would naturally be Northern and Central Europe. If these areas could be freed from the nuclear weapons stationed there today, the risk of total annihilation in case of a military conflict would be reduced."

None of the English adherents of END expressed these arguments with greater clarity, and all of us were two years behind the Swedish Prime Minister in arriving at them. Palme was not alone among the spokesmen of the Socialist International. Walter Hacker from Austria and Kalevi Sorsa from Finland were no less committed. From the Euro-Communists came Lucio Lombardo Radice from Italy, one of the old Bradford team: these were people who carried forward the argument of the END process in its earliest days. The first Greek signatory was Andreas Papandreou. I collected his support during a visit to Madrid, where I went to meet Manuel Azcarate and others to set up a conference under the sponsorship of two political research institutes, associated with the Spanish Socialist and Communist Parties respectively. When this conference was later held, one of its stars was Luciana Castellina of the Italian PdUP, an independent Communist group. In Madrid, then, we met one of the major architects of the growing END process, whose initiatives in the European Parliament were to prove absolutely vital. Nobody is more of a "grassroot" than Luciana, who has had her head broken at Comiso by the Italian police, and has been present from the beginning in every major initiative of the Italian peace movement, including innumerable demonstrations. For her sins, she sits in the Assembly at Strasbourg, and tries there to use her influence for disarmament.

If Luciana Castellina crossed the bridge from the political establishment to "independence" and grass-rootery, there has been a large queue of people forming to traverse it in the opposite direction. The new intake into the British Parliament includes several welcome faces from CND demonstrations, most notably that of Joan Ruddock. In Germany, one of the most persuasive and dynamic organizers of the Berlin Convention was Joe Leinen, now a Minister in the social democratic administration of his province. Not all peace activists arrive on the socialist benches, of course. In addition to the Greens numerous far left and centre groupings have also adopted well-known peace campaigners on their political lists. More: we should observe that to cross the bridge the other way, one does not necessarily need to enter a Parliament. What are we to say of that most disciplined of organizations, the IKV, whose increasingly political commitment has for a long time impacted, not only on Dutch politics, for better or worse?

The argument about the relationship between spontaneous activism and organized political pressure is not new. It began before the Rome consultation which launched the Conventions, in the winter of 1981. A number of members of the British END organization were opposed to this meeting, and while the reasons which they gave varied considerably, one constant theme of the opposition was that such Conventions as were proposed might open the peace movement to subversive influences from politicians. There were then, and there are now, two unanswerable responses to this complaint. First, only if the access to political forces is restricted can any "takeover" be thought possible. In a context in which there is a plurality of political parties, contending for influence, competition will ensure that any manipulation or electoral trickery by one political representative will quickly be denounced by another. Since the cardinal fact about the END Conventions has always been their openness, this safeguard has always been fully operational. I remember several famous spats, between, for instance, Spanish Socialists and Communists, or German Greens and the SPD. Insofar as we have been able to keep an open door, they have all been resolved in a remarkable degree of amity.

But second, how would the critics of the Convention-idea propose to substitute for its loss? In the earliest days, attempts were made to organize international pop festivals and similar cultural events. Undoubtedly such initiatives are useful: but they provide no antidote to manipulation. Indeed, they are more vulnerable to "management" than any process involving dialogue and debate. If a spokesman of the peace movement is gently lowered to the microphone on a purple cloud at the climax of some great musical event, that spokesman exercises greater personal power and influence than any number of contending politicians. If there were a lot of such pop festivals (which, alas, there are not) there would need to be more conventions, not fewer.

Another widely canvassed alternative in the earliest days was that a filter should be established through which only activists would pass. Such activists would then maintain the purity of the dialogue. Here it is necessary to offer just one or two reminders of the actual history of the argument. As we have seen, the notion of a nuclear-free Europe did not emerge as an inspiration on the Common at Greenham, but was a political proposal by the Prime Minister of Sweden. The main theorist of such disarmament measures was Alva Myrdal, who had served as a Minister in the Swedish Government, and mobilized tremendous diplomatic pressures at the United Nations. The results of this prodigious work became plain in the first Special Session on Disarmament, and largely influenced the Nobel Committee when they made Alva a Peace Laureate.

When the Russell Foundation belatedly proposed supportive action to peace movements and other activists across Europe, we were acting within the framework of a careful discussion with political forces across a wide European spectrum.

When Lynn Jones tells us that politicians "have enough space anyway", and when she denounces "completely corrupt political discussion", she is doubly wrong. If the political parties of Europe already had a satisfactory forum for the discussion of disarmament questions, they would not have taken so great an interest in the establishment of the END Conventions as an appropriate platform. Is it to be thought that there is some special magnetism in the peace movements, some unique quality which draws these lesser political mortals into orbit? Any participant in the work of the Liaison Committee is bound to doubt this judgement. Some of the representatives of political parties are reticent, and perhaps unduly reluctant to press their points of view. But their deference, where it exists, stems more from courtesy than the recognition of superior qualities of grassroot reasoning. The truth is that one of the major attractions of END for Europe's political parties is precisely the facility it affords to enable parties with widely divergent traditions, ideologies and affinities to talk freely with one another, and to be broadly associated in a common endeavour.

What other network is so comprehensive? Engaged in the END dialogue, we find Socialists and Greens, Communists and Catholics, radicals of many persuasions and all the varieties of peace activists. Of course, some of these forces do have existing international machinery through which they may be able to relate to one another. The Socialists and Communists are members of broad families of parties, which can elaborate common policies on whatever issues find them in agreement. But the families have had their feuds: the seventy-year old political split between the main forces of the left has meant that division has been more evident than unity during some of the crucial moments of the twentieth century.

Now, on the platform of END, socialist and communist parties find themselves in harmonious association, for the first time in half a century. And this is not simply a marriage of the old lefts: END is as green as it is red, and as ecumenical in confessional terms as it is pluralistic in political ones. To tell us that this rare forum is but one of the many places in which politicians hold sway, is not a very brilliant perception, to put it mildly. It avoids the question, why are these politicians foregathering with the rest of us? For what purposes are they listening to one another, (and the rest of us) and joining their forces? And with whom are they linking arms, as the process develops?

It would be very nice if Lynn Jones were right. If all the democratic voices of Europe could find a common forum to defend civil rights and freedom of expression, to struggle for economic recovery with humane and full employment rights for all, and to create the fabric of a fully democratic European culture, then we might all be very happy to adjourn END into this more general framework. But such a framework does not exist. If anything, END is only the first step towards it. No-one can predict how long the present peace movement will take to accomplish its work, or how soon all our agendas may be changed for us. But because Lynn Jones is wrong about the existence of ample space for discussion of the political issues, we are bound to see the END Conventions as an important, if perhaps temporary move in the right direction. What we might expect from the radicals who are so impatient with constitutional processes in all our different countries is that they should be truly radical. When we search beneath the nuclear carapace, we find Europe crippled by a dysfunctional political structure. Nation states represent the main embodiment of our separate democracies, but they are no longer adequate controllers of economic organization and development. All around us the arbitrary powers of great multinational corporations grow continually, with scarcely any effective restraint. The emergence of a European democratic culture is a precondition for the formation of consensual political institutions. The most striking thing about divided Europe is the paucity of its interactions, and the inordinate difficulty which attaches to any attempt at spontaneous and unstructured intercourse. We might expect true radicals to see in END a pilot project for a democratic future. Such a future will be made by people who do not all see themselves as "politicians", but making it is evidently a political labour.

We must face the facts. Associating a large body of people for a political objective is politics. Whether such politics are to be approved or not depends partly on the chosen objective, and partly on the methods by which it is pursued. But there is no innate moral superiority whatsoever in the choice of this or that mode of action as such. Of course, we may invoke such principles if we seek to choose between a peace demonstrator whose politics do not include voting in elections, and her neighbour who is a ward secretary campaigning for electoral representation. One of them, it may be agreed, is probably right, and one of them is probably wrong: but only strictly political criteria would allow us to decide, each in our own way, which was which.

Any campaign against all "politicians" is chemically pure demagogy, in short. Criticism may be valid and important when it is directed against this politician for that reason: but any opposition to all politicians is either ignorant or unclean, since "all" politicians include peace politicians of every stripe, from militant anarchists through to the highest of high church dignitaries.

* * *

Now, let us turn to the third either/or, concerning Eastern independents and the power-structure.

The primary objective of the European Nuclear Disarmament Conventions is now, and always has been "to explore the problems involved in creating a nuclear-free zone, to discuss a variety of intermediary proposals ... and to help in the development of a major popular campaign for peace and disarmament". This was the declaration (to which we have already referred), which was endorsed by the several thousand signatories of the "Russell Appeal". Those who signed this short statement were, of course, expressing their support for the more general END Appeal which has become the basis of affiliation to the Liaison Committee which prepares the European Conventions. This reaffirms the goal: "We must act together to free the entire territory of Europe, from Poland to Portugal, from nuclear weapons, air and submarine bases, and from all institutions engaged in research into or manufacture of nuclear weapons". In pursuit of this objective "we must defend and extend the right of all citizens, East or West, to take part in this common movement and to engage in every kind of exchange". The appeal elaborates upon the meaning of this kind of exchange as follows:

> "We envisage a European-wide campaign, in which every kind of exchange takes place; in which representatives of different nations and opinions confer and co-ordinate their activities; and in which less formal exchanges between universities, churches, women's organizatons, trade unions, youth organizations, professional groups and individuals, take place with the object of promoting a common object: to free all of Europe from nuclear weapons."

The very first Convention concentrated most of its effort on promoting space for such "lateral groups". Some have, indeed, survived and developed: notably the group of trade unions, which has received very consistent support from the Transport and General Workers' Union and the Italian CGIL. Many lateral groups quickly became independent of the Convention process, and have developed their own momentum. This is a fact which should be celebrated, since it was always hoped that this could happen.

In Lynn Jones' article, there is an extended, and largely mistaken, account of the impact of all this on Eastern Europe. She begins by charging the Western peace movements with failure to "take note of ... the Polish trade union Solidarnosc". About this, she is quite wrong. In September 1980, the Bertrand Russell Peace Foundation named a commission to visit Poland in order to study the settlement of the strikes of July to September, and to discuss peace and detente. Like the TUC delegation, which had been scheduled for the same time, this commission was denied visas. Bob Cryer MP, Dan Smith (Vice-chairman of CND) and Tony Topham made up the members of the proposed team, and the documentation which they collected was published by the Institute for Workers' Control in its Bulletin at the end of 1980. A pamphlet was off-printed and circulated widely.[4] Various other Britons were more successful in entering Poland, and one END supporter in particular stayed for several months. We maintained a constant liaison with such visitors, and gave help where we could. Extensive enquiries showed that there was absolutely no interest in European Nuclear Disarmament among the Polish independent trade unionists. Most took the view that they did not wish to provoke the Russians by questioning military alignments and matters of foreign policy. At that time, a small minority were of the opinion that strong armaments in the West might intimidate the Russians into making greater concessions in Poland. Subsequently, events enlarged this grouping somewhat. They did not, however, prove it right. Today, the contrary is plainly seen to be true.

But some Polish signatories did rally to the END Appeal, even if the Union was indifferent. We should remember that it was from Poland that Adam Rapacki launched his famous plan in 1957, seeking the establishment of a nuclear-free zone in Central Europe. This plan had been modified in November 1958, to take account of objections which had been aroused by the first version. Prime Minister Gomulka returned to this issue more than once, with further modifications. Many of the more enlightened Polish Communists saw their political space as needing new initiatives for detente, and were very happy to support proposals for disarmament.

There were also some individual signatories of the END Appeal, mostly from the Universities. The most persistent supporter of the Appeal in Poland did not come from Solidarnosc, and maintained a resolute independence of all political forces which Lynn Jones might bring herself to admire, which was only equalled by his independence of those she detests. He is Josef Halbersztadt, who opened a prolonged correspondence with various END personalities, back in 1980, and subsequently became a valued member of the END Liaison Committee.[5]

The formation of the Polish organization, Freedom and Peace, happened long after these events. In my opinion, this organization does not really fit into the European peace movement, although some of its members probably do. What it has in common with other peace movements is its support for conscientious objectors. However, it diverges from the other movements in that it seems to make the disarmament of other countries conditional on a change in the political regime in Poland. Some of its statements imply that the West should only disarm after Poland has become an "independent and democratic" state. From the point of view of the Convention process, which is and should remain open, there is of course no reason why Freedom and Peace members should not participate, and say what they think and why they think it. It is interesting to probe their views. But in my personal opinion, it was absolutely wrong to invite this organization to provide a speaker in the closing plenum at Coventry, since he certainly did not represent the consensus of the European peace movements, and indeed had very little to do with the overall objective of European Nuclear Disarmament. More important, perhaps, is the fact that quite clearly, he in no way represented the opinions of other independent persons in Eastern Europe, many of whom have quite different perspectives on both disarmament and change within their own societies. In this zone of our continent, END supporters are certainly no less pluralistic than their Western colleagues. If some are intransigents, others, far more numerous, are "loyal oppositionists". Others again, more numerous still, are quite simply public-spirited citizens who identify with the aims of their own governments no less than they seek disarmament and a more relaxed international environment.

There is no time to labour through the long catalogue of East-West connections to which Lynn Jones makes fleeting allusions. The first contact between the "Swords and Ploughshares" activists in East Germany and the END process outside Germany was made by myself and Michael Meacher, on Good Friday 1983. We had gone to meet with Robert Havemann, a very distinguished politician, who had unreasonably been given the soubriquet of "dissident". Havemann was an independent Communist who consistently maintained that the German Democratic Republic was by far the most civilized state that had ever existed on German territory. His disagreements with its Government meant that he was often inconvenienced, and sometimes ill-treated. He could have emigrated to the West at any time he liked, because he was a close friend of the Head of State, whose life he had saved when both men had been imprisoned by the Nazis. Like Socrates, Havemann kept his own law. He stayed at home. To our great distress, he died just as we arrived in East Berlin. His death was a great loss to the peace movement, and politician though he undoubtedly was, it was keenly felt by Pastor Eppelmann and his associates in the East German independent peace group. It was Michael Meacher and I who spent several hours at Eppelmann's house drinking endless supplies of tea, and learning about the development of the Swords and Ploughshares movement within the Protestant Church. We brought out all the main documents of this movement from East Berlin, and published them.

If the Berlin Convention in 1983 was naturally concerned about the East German activists, it was also very much involved with the Hungarians. Not only was Gyorgy Konrad a speaker in Berlin, but the Hungarian Group for Dialogue petitioned the Convention to ask it to open more normal relations with the Hungarian Peace Committee. At the same time, the Hungarian Peace Committee sent a conciliatory and reasonable letter to the Convention organizers, as a result of which it appeared that the project for a three-way dialogue between Western peace movements and official and unofficial Eastern spokesmen might, at last, become feasible.

And just this happened, at the Perugia Convention in 1984. Both Hungarian groups were represented, and Andras Hegedus and Ferenc Koszegi, on behalf of the Dialogue Group, spoke at a joint press conference with the Hungarian Peace Committee at the end of the session. This notable breakthrough aroused no positive vibrations among that small faction of English END supporters most closely associated with our critics. Rather, it was for them an indication that Hegedus and Koszegi were unreliable allies. Lynn Jones describes the demonstration which took place in Perugia at the opening session, when a column of people wearing red blindfolds joined hands across the platform in an orderly protest against the refusal of travel documents to the East German independents. This demonstration was not, as Lynn Jones says, "condemned because it insulted the official Eastern bloc participants". Liaison Committee members who participated in the protest were reproached for quite different reasons. All the negotiations with Eastern bloc countries had been conducted in a completely consensual manner. No dissent had been registered in the meetings of the Committee. The talks had strictly followed the lines suggested in the two Hungarian appeals to the Berlin Convention. For a minority of members of the Liaison Committee to protest in public against its decisions was to imply quite wrongly, that their expressed opinions had been disregarded. Therefore the "insult", if insult there was, was to their own colleagues, not to any group of visitors. Modestly, Lynn Jones omits all reference to her own part in these proceedings. After the opening plenary, the Liaison Committee unanimously appealed for an end to such demonstrations, in order to allow discussions to take place in a reasonable environment. Lynn Jones led a mock-feminist mutiny, allegedly in order to secure adequate placing for women on the final platform of the Convention, at the closing plenary. Surprisingly, once it had been agreed to meet this request, the women in question used their access to the plenum to bring off yet another demonstration. Duplicity, these women established, is blind to gender. A handful of demonstrators thus ran away with all the Perugia headlines, leaving all the work and tireless campaigning of the peace movements, and all their carefully prepared discussions, for the footnotes. The members of the Liaison Committee did not then cry "foul", and nor do they now. If peace movements could be discouraged by unfair reports in the press, they would long ago have given up. But this kind of stunt does not really change anything, it is not persuasive, and therefore it is bound to be thought of as unhelpful.

Of course, only one Eastern European country had met the requests of the peace movements to facilitate both official and unofficial participation in the Convention. When one country had begun this step, and might reasonably have expected some thanks for so doing, indiscriminate demonstrations offered, instead, a blanket condemnation, giving support to the cold war mythology that all the states of Eastern Europe are politically indistinguishable.

At Amsterdam, in spite of a somewhat unbalanced concentration on this particular question, the 1985 Convention completely failed to resolve the problem of East-West dialogue. True, some emigres attended, from a variety of organizations. But the official organizations mainly stayed away. So did most of the "independents", not always involuntarily. Part of the reason for this was than an experiment was made in decentralised "sponsorship" of particular East-West exchanges. Some people thought that this was mistaken. But a more important mistake was made in the preparation for Amsterdam. At a Madrid meeting of the Liaison Committee, a representative of the German Socialists made it clear that, whilst he completely agreed with the invitation of independent groupings from the East to participate in the Convention process, it would be one-sided in the extreme to ignore all discussion of detente and ostpolitik, and of the need to improve relations between states, in an END Convention. I intervened in the discussion after this statement, and drew attention to it: a forum should include all significant viewpoints on the question, I argued, and should not suppress so salient a view as that of the SPD. Unfortunately, no arrangements were made to offer an adequate platform to the arguments of the SPD and its co-thinkers, with the result that is now completely familiar to every participant in the END process. Amsterdam was a festival of detente from below, but no tangible progress was made from idea to reality.

The following year, at the Convention in Evry, near Paris, East-West questions were temporarily shelved, to allow time for reconsideration. The main advance made during that year was that relations with the German peace movements improved, and that the Initiative for International Peace and Security (IFIAS) agreed to re-join the process in an active capacity on the understanding that the agenda for the Coventry meeting would include detente from above as well as below.

Let us be clear what this corrective account is arguing. It is not arguing that one approach should suffocate another. It is merely insisting that in a forum, all relevant views should be given space. This is a measured commitment, and one which makes possible a continuation of dialogue. But to suppress all discussion of a major issue, or all contributions from a particular school of thought, is to invite disruption and fragmentation in the peace movement.

Of course, this simple commitment can be misrepresented or misunderstood. Lynn Jones 'quotes' what I said in a recent Liaison Committee as follows: "We want to embrace the changes at the top, Ken Coates of the Bertrand Russell Peace Foundation argued. It is a process that could be stopped if it is not supported. We are not a league of oppositions." What I actually said is recorded in the minutes of the Liaison Committee: "There were two schools of thought on Eastern Europe. There is a disagreement between them on the emphasis that should be placed on 'detente' and 'detente from below'. We had to recognize that the situation in the East was changing rapidly both 'at the top' and 'below'. Many of us welcome Gorbachev's initiatives. But these might be reversed if they do not meet with success. Never forget that the Prague Spring was initiated from above. We need to discuss the issue calmly amongst ourselves, and then perhaps debate it in the open plenary of the Convention."

It remains true that this debate, if only we organize it fairly, will do more good than harm. Untoward opinions may be distressing, but they will not go away as a result of exclusions, proscriptions, or bad behaviour. What we need to do in preparing for the Stockholm Convention, is to arrange a platform from which all the important arguments can receive a proper hearing. This means we must positively work to bring together the politicians and the grassroots, the East and the West, the officials and the unofficials, and everyone who thinks they have something to offer to help us develop the movement on this, the most vital question of our age.

* * *

There remain the really big either/ors. Should we continue our emphasis on opposing particular weapon-systems, or should we shift more attention to the political underpinnings of militarism, and the economic circumstances in which it flourishes? And should we seek to overturn the existing power-structures, or can they be modified "from within"? It seems to me that the great merit of an inclusive forum is that it allows such daunting issues to be carefully discussed, and thought through. My own answers to these questions I have tried to set down in other writings, especially in the book called *The Most Dangerous Decade*. But for the purpose of this argument, my answers are not what is relevant. I hope they are sufficiently tentative without losing their bite, but I am bound to admit that they may be wrong, or perhaps only partly right. The only experience I feel keenly enough to be firmly dogmatic about is this: often, I have observed, good people have been mistaken, sometimes about small things, and sometimes about great ones. This leads me to doubt whether we should seek infallible leaders, or gurus of any kind. That is the spirit in which many of us have found it valuable to listen to others. Is it not evident that peace movements, which seek to generate a new culture of common humanity, will only succeed in involving the mainstream of their societies if they can first establish the growth-points of that culture among themselves? And is it not equally plain that to retreat from the exchange of opinion in our Conventions would be to retreat from facing that agreed task itself?

To paraphrase a poet whose work I have abused before: "We must listen to one another or die".

If only our diverse movements can co-operate, together, we have a universe to learn, and, in that sense, win. Divided, we, and the world we are defending, are all-too-likely to fall.

Notes

1. This appeal was signed by:

Austria: Gerhard Jordan (ARGE UFI); *Belgium*: Alfons Boesmans MEP; Andrew Bogaert (President, VAKA); Robert de Douai (Vice-President, CNAPD); Robert de Gendt (President, OCV); Jaak Vandemeulebroucke MEP; *Czechoslovakia*: Zdena Tominova; *Denmark*: E.H. Christiansen MEP; Dagmar Fagerholt (No to Nuclear Weapons); Niels Gregersen (No to Nuclear Weapons); Judith Winther (No to Nuclear Weapons); France: Sylvie Mantrant (CODENE); Claude Bourdet; *Germany*: Jo Leinen(Minister of Environment, Saarbrucken); Eva Quistorp (Women for Peace); Gert Weisskirchen MP; *Greece*: The Orthodox Bishop Kissamou; Selinou Erenaeos (President of the Orthodox Academy); Michalis Stathopoulos (Rector of Athens University); General G. Koumanakos (Vice President, KEADEA);Michael Peristerakis (Vice-President IPB); Demetrius Konstas (Rector of Athens Pantios School Political Sciences); General Konstantin Konstantinidis; Panagiotis Gasgas

(Vice Mayor of Athens City); Christofer Argiropoulos (President of AKE); Eva Kotamanidou (Actress); Vasso Katraki (Engraver, Venice Bienalle Prize Winner); Kostas Filinis MEP; Kostas Kritsinis (Ex Governor of North Greece); Demetrius Kakavelakis (Author, General Secretary of the International Peace Committee, Crete); Manolis Glezos (President of the United Democratic Left - EDA); G. Romeos MEP; Andreas Lendakis (Mayor of Imitos City); *Italy*: Luciana Castellina MEP; Jiri Pelikan MEP; *Netherlands*: Maarten van Traa (Dutch Labour Party); Jan ter Laak (Pax Christi); Alex de Zwart (Gruppa Doveriga); Mient Jan Faber (IKV); Walter Bohle (Dutch Labour Party); *Poland*: Jan Minchevitz (Polish Freedom and Peace); *Spain*: Manuel Bonmarti.(International Secretary, UGT); Marchi no Camacho (General Secretary, Comisiones Obreras); Antonio Gala (Playwright, former President Platform Civica para la Salipa OTAN); Manuel Garnaho (UGT); Enrique Gomariz (Editor, Tempo Paz); Gerardo Iglesias (Communist Party Leader, President United Left Coalition); Luis Otero (formerly Army Major, Spokesman Democratic Military Union); Jose Antonio Martin Pallan (Lawyer, President Human Rights Association); Marisa Rodriguez (Secretary, FEPRI); Francisca Sequillo (Senator, President MPDL); Professor Ramon Tamames (Economist, MP United Left); Professor Juan Jose R. Ugarte (Theologian); *Sweden*: Gunnar Lassinantti (Swedish Labour Movement Peace Forum); *United Kingdom*: Richard Balfe MEP; Bob Cryer MEP; Glyn Ford MEP; Win Griffiths MEP; Alf Lomas MEP; Michael McGowan MEP; David Morris MEP; Stanley Newens MEP; Carole Tongue MEP; Sidney Bidwell MP; Robin Cook MP; Eric Heffer MP; Stuart Holland MP; E. Layden MP; Martin Flannery MP; Bob Clay MP; Richard Caborn MP; Roland Boyes MP; Robin Corbett MP; Michael Meacher MP; William McKelvey MP; .Stan Orme MP; Ron Brown MP; Tony Banks MP; David Blunkett (Leader, Sheffield City Council); CND; Ken Coates (BRPF); Peter Crampton (Chair, END); Ken Fleet (BRPF); Mary Kaldor (END Journal); Margaret Morton (General Secretary, Scottish CND); Paul Rogers; Steve Rose (Russell Committee against Chemical Weapons); Tony Topham; Lord Jenkins of Putney; Professor E. Edwards; Lord Hugh Scanlon; Zhores Medvedev; Ron Todd, General Secretary, T&GWU; Raymond Williams; Victor de Waal; Professor Teodor Shanin; Istavn Meszaros; Leslie Christie, Gen. Sec. Society of Civil and Public Servants; Julie Christie; Edna Smee; Steven Lukes; Bishop John V. Taylor; Susannah York; *Yugoslavia*: Miios Djukic, Vice-President, Yugoslav League for Peace, Independence and Equality of Peoples; Borut Zupan, Yugoslav League for Peace, Independence and Equality of Peoples.

2. See 'The Zhukov File', pages 13-19, END *Bulletin of work in progress* No. 12: spokesmanbooks.org/product/european-nuclear-disarmament-bulletin-of-work-in-progress-no-12-1983/

3. See the report by Jane Mayes in END *Journal* Summer 1987, page 6.

It would be difficult to find a more blatant bias than this report: "The rapporteur from the 'humanitarian' session, chosen like the other rapporteurs for safety rather than freshness (I have been a friend of the Soviet Union for thirty years ...), hardly alluded to the occasion." In fact, the reporter in question was Carol Pendell, of the Women's International League for Peace and Freedom in the United States. She did not claim long years of philo-Soviet commitment. Her speech did refer to the participation of the Trust Group member, in a perfectly adequate way. It was a lively and at times moving speech, and quite unworthy of the kind of put-down accorded to it in the END *Journal*. The first of the reporters chosen came from Scientists for Nuclear Disarmament in Canada, and the second was Professor Goran von Bonsdorff, the President of the Finnish Peace Union. Professor Bonsdorff was among the first signatories of the END Appeal in Finland. He has an international reputation as a scholar and as a defender of civil and human rights. It is not probable that Jane Mayes had the faintest idea who was speaking in the plenum, since she might have been reluctant to express herself so unkindly about someone who is a loyal friend of all the causes with which END and CND have been associated.

I was the offending fifth reporter. Although it never crossed my mind to make the claim in Moscow, I must confess to "having been a friend of the Soviet Union for thirty years". In fact, my sins go back longer, to 1942, when as a child I began to follow the progress of battle on the Soviet front. But I have also been a member of Bertrand Russell's team for 23 years. He was an opponent of arbitrary repression, bureaucratic misbehaviour of all kinds, and similar abuses, so that during all the years of his strong friendship with Khrushchev he never ceased to make representations on behalf of people who were out of favour with authority. Khrushchev, of course, liberated whole legions of political prisoners, and no subsequent Soviet Government ever incarcerated even the merest fraction of their numbers. He always replied most kindly to Russell's letters, so that all our founder's interventions were private until Khrushchev fell. The new leadership did not respond to such appeals, which, alas, became somewhat more frequent. By the end of the sixties, Russell began to go public on them. When he died, the rest of us were of very minor consequence as public figures, so we had to resort to collective representations. So it came about that the Soviet Government received, at my instigation, petitions on behalf of various political detainees and all sorts of other representations. My post was intercepted so many times that the British Post Office paid over £500 in compensation for registered letters which were "lost". My files on these issues contain dozens of cases, one or two of which have not yet been resolved. I now believe that they soon will be. In short, I have commonly been regarded as something of a nuisance by large numbers of other friends of the Soviet Union, including, I suppose, some citizens of that country.

That I was received in Moscow in a warm and cordial way, leave alone afforded the rostrum at an important international meeting, might have been thought to have been telling Jane Mayes something. Unfortunately, she was in no mood to listen. Instead, I became, like the other panellists, for her, "safe", mere apologists, indeed, life-long apologists, whose opinions could be, indeed should be, ignored. We had all "crossed over to the other side". This mentality, if it were maintained, would mean that "dialogue" could never move beyond confrontation. If Jane knows of our backgrounds, her report is not very fair. If she does not know; it is at least ill-informed.

My opinion of this is not important. But the opinion of CND is important. Does it really wish its representatives to react in this kind of way? Was it the intention of CND, in accepting the Soviet invitations, to greet all new gift-horses with hefty kicks in the teeth? I doubt this very much. What I have noticed is that this has not at all been the way that Sakharov has responded to the same phenomena.

The Soviet and West European political institutions are different, and will remain different even when the current reform programme in the Soviet Union is far advanced. Both communism and liberalism make big claims for human rights and liberties, and both have often fallen short of their prospectuses. For this reason, Jane Mayes is not wrong when she asks awkward questions. It is, however, quite wrong to ignore the evidence of change, especially when that evidence is as strong as it is in the Soviet Union today.

4. This pamphlet was written by Tony Topham, and explored the long history of international solidarity with the Polish people.

5. In a remarkable concession, the Polish official Peace Committee invited Mr. Halbersztadt to join their delegation to the END Convention in Coventry. As a member of the Liaison Committee, we might expect that there would be some concern for his right to travel on the part of his colleagues. But the British Government refused visas to the Polish Peace Committee delegation, so that Halbersztadt was unable to be in Coventry. No protests were made about this exclusion by the English END Committee, and I had to interrupt the Press Conference at the Convention in order to draw attention to it, since this information was not given by CND's international organizer.

International Cooperation on the Left

Ken Coates

SOCIALISM IN THE PRESENT-DAY WORLD SOCIALISM IN THE PRESENT-DAY WORLD SOCIALISM IN THE PRESENT

SOCIALISM IN THE WORLD

elmar altvater
national state, regional relations and the capitalist world market
fuad muhić
national equality and the policy of nonalignment
michel beaud
la nation, l'économie nationale dans le système national mondial hiérarchisé (SNMH)
zoran trputec
the scientific-technological revolution and the nation
peter stier
scientific and technical progress and national self-determination of developing countries

67 '88

UDC YU ISSN 0350-8234

From Socialism in the World, *Number 67, 1988.*

"To win peace, we have to win more than peace." This thought was the theme of the English scholar, Raymond Williams, in his contribution to the debate about the arrival of Cruise and Pershing missiles in Western Europe. The fear of war, and the folly of the run away arms race, have combined to unite a very inclusive peace movement, in many nations, and from every part of the political spectrum. But to address the underlying issue posed by Raymond Williams, it will be necessary for those forces which favour reform and social justice to find a new basis for joint action and mutual help.

It is a commonplace that the world has entered a deep crisis. Mass unemployment runs at some ninety million, while a further three-hundred million people are working precariously in underemployed occupations. The population explosion ensures that the workforce is increasing very rapidly, and will grow from its present level of 2.2 billion to at least 2.8 billion by the end of the century. World-wide, then, we must create six-hundred million jobs for the newly arriving workforce, and nearly four-hundred million for those who are already out of work or inadequately employed. Ninety percent of this shortfall of one billion jobs is the under-developed South, which is locked in an appalling debt, which eats up every possibility of productive investment for many years to come. It is in this context that we must look at the evil efflorescence of military budgets, which take something between five and ten percent of the whole world's income and at least a quarter of all manufacturing production. Worse still, they spoil the future, by distorting research efforts everywhere.

Karl Marx might have been excused for

thinking that such a situation would be charter for the creation of world-wide socialism. But the ill-effects of this crisis have not left the socialist countries unscathed. Some suffer directly, as part of the world debt trauma. Others are more indirectly affected by the pressures of military competition, which push them into imitating the wasteful expenditures of the capitalist world, often from inferior economic bases. In the capitalist countries, the socialist forces, still separately organized in socialist and communist parties, have held their own far better than they did in the last long wave of unemployment and slump. Then, we saw the rise of fascism and the extinction of trade unions and working class political movements in whole areas of Europe.

Up to now, parliamentary democracy has survived in post-war Western Europe, and in some countries harassed socialist governments try to manage the crisis. For the most part, the socialist and communist parties there are on the defensive, and afflicted by problems that are sometimes serious. A succession of labour governments in different countries have found that the scope of the national economy to insulate itself from world pressures has been totally inadequate to beat off the crisis. Reforming governments have embarked on policies of economic redistribution and recovery in one country after another, only to find that such policies have bought about adverse trade balances and intervention from the international bankers. It seems to many that the Western European nation state is no longer a large enough entity to determine effective alternative economic policies.

It has been a savage paradox that world-wide, socialism has evolved in the direction of greater national autonomy, while capitalism has been steadily more cosmopolitan in its organization. Today, it is the giant transnational corporations which call the shots, not only in their direct dealings with national governments, but still more in their normal internal operations as they necessarily shift funds from one market to the next and manipulate their transfers in order to maintain their overall returns. Already, before the OPEC crisis hit Britain and the United States, foreign production by their multinationals was respectively four times and more-than-double their total visible export trade. Such foreign production undermined their export performance, and with it the exchange rates of the pound and the dollar. In 1967 it had been necessary to devalue sterling, and the readjustment of the dollar followed in 1971. Thus collapsed the international system of Bretton Woods. This collapse effectively neutralized Keynesian policies of management, and confiscated the main tool of social reformist government, whether of the left or centre-right.

To recover the capacity for effective management of their economies, international co-operation is essential to all but the super-states. A realistic proposal which would allow several socialist or social democratic governments in Western Europe to co-operate in a wider recovery programme was drawn up under the leadership of Stuart Holland in 1983. With an international team of socialist economists, he proposed a detailed programme called *Out of Crisis*. This sought to show how even a small number of countries could join forces to reflate, restructure and redistribute resources, in order to seek a combined solution to stagnation and decline. The thinking behind this document was further developed and extended in the programme of the Socialist International, published in 1985 under the title *Global Challenge*, and sponsored by Michael Manley and Willy Brandt.

The proposals of *Global Challenge* were approved at an international congress of the Socialist International, grouping 77 different parties around the world. The Chinese Communist Party sent observers to this meeting. None the less, the parties of the Socialist International have not been able to implement their proposals in a sustained way, because they have not been able to persuade a sufficient number of electors in the key countries of its feasibility.

While the transnational operations were concentrating ever greater power, the international communist movement was embarking upon a process of polycentrism and national devolution. Initially there is no doubt that this was a necessary and positive development. During the postwar years, first the dispute between Stalin and Yugoslavia, and later the Sino-Soviet conflict were only the most dramatic episodes in a process of national self-assertion, during which all the most important parties evolved distinctively autonomous policies. Because there were numerous moral pressures restraining and inhibiting this autonomy in the beginning, practical co-operation has perhaps been more difficult for these movements than it has for the parties of the Socialist International, which never possessed any centralized power to speak of. The fact remains that independent as they are, and should be, such parties now desperately need to find relevant forms of sustained co-operation not only between themselves but also with their socialist brothers. For the major working class movements of Western Europe, this becomes a particularly urgent priority, since, as has always happened in every deep slump, the institutions of working class democracy are beginning to come under attack. Trade unions are being weakened, and democratic agencies undermined.

It is this point that the process of restructuring and democratic reform begins in the Soviet Union. Had it been possible for this process to have begun decades ago, we may be sure that the forces of communism would not have disaggregated so considerably, and that that the continuing harmful division between socialists and communists would have been largely overcome. None of this is to detract from the tremendous consequences that the new reforms in the Soviet Union could have. They could inspire a veritable renaissance of world socialism, not as everyone reported to Moscow for their instructions, but as everyone began to relate, in free choice, to a hopeful new potential in the world.

It is arguable that inadequate democracy was a major component in the erosion of international organization among both communists and socialists. Everything now depends on whether renewal democracy is correlated with the development of a new internationalism. If it is, then we should begin at once to open every possibility of dialogue between socialists, communists and independent radicals such as the Greens. The beginning of recovery is international support and confidence. Openness can dissolve sectarian and negative international divisions just as it can liberate internal forces for development.

The new Soviet leadership inherits considerable problems at home, and prodigious threats from abroad. Gorbachev has begun to confront these with great courage and resolution. Most eyes have been concentrated on the relations between the Soviet Union and the United States, and the hope that perhaps the arms race might be diminished. In this field, the Soviet Union now occupies the high ground. But détente is necessary for all the world, not only for the two greatest powers. As socialists, we are bound to pay attention also to the need to overcome the divisions between the Soviet Union and People's China, which divisions are counterproductive for socialists everywhere. I think this is a problem for all socialists, and it is not the only one. Nobody will suggest that all the seventy year old divisions between socialist and communist parties will simply melt away, given goodwill. Even the divisions between communists, which are of much more recent duration, will not all be easy to overcome. But surely it is becoming practical to suggest that we should all start talking to one another, sooner rather than later? Yugoslavia was in the forefront in encouraging such conversations, with the establishment of the forum at Cavtat. Are there no takers to widen and deepen the circle? Surely we must aim to seat the whole socialist family round one harmonious table, before the year 2000, if only because world capitalism may wreck our planet if we do not.

Why the European Parliament should meet the Supreme Soviet

Ken Coates

Published in European Labour Forum, *Summer 1990. Ken Coates was elected to the European Parliament in 1989. He launched* European Labour Forum *journal to aid and encourage debate on issues facing Europe and the wider world.*

Every new day creates unforeseen choices for Europe. In both its Eastern and Western halves, our continent is becoming familiar with a new dimension of crisis. We are informed that when the Chinese write this word, they combine two other ideographs. "Crisis", thus, contains in itself the concepts of "danger", but also that of "opportunity".

Understanding the danger, this complex combination explains why I proposed, six months ago, to try to make an opportunity. My suggestion was that the two largest emerging democracies of East and West should arrange a suitable meeting. Separately, they were doing similar things. The European Parliament was seeking to prepare a democratic foundation for political union, at the same time that the Supreme Soviet considered how to lay out the groundwork for political pluralism and the rule of law. Each of us, I thought, had something to say to the other. We could help one another. Together, we might build more surely than we could apart. Even if they rejected the notion of "common home", surely, I thought, colleagues might see advantage in ensuring that the structure we were seeking to erect could be safer if it were at least semi-detached! And if we talked, might we not see how to improve the architecture? In My Father's House there are many mansions …

A mark of the speed of change is that the frank expression of disbelief which often came across the faces of those who heard this proposal when first I made it, is now seldom seen. In the beginning perhaps half of my Western interlocutors thought I was crazy. Now, that number is well down. Of course, in truth, the hope for genuine

European unity may really be crazy, but if it is, then we must at least observe that the world is going with it. In short order, first Poland, then Hungary, then the German Democratic Republic and Bulgaria, then Czechoslovakia and, latest, Romania; all embarked on the search for new political frameworks. Are they to be forever separate?

Some of the people who sought to dissuade us from any joint Parliamentary exchange with the Soviets were arguing, only a month or two ago, that the European Parliament should only meet with fully pluralist legislatures, and that Article Six of the Soviet Constitution precludes and the development of any such openness. But now Article Six is on the way out. No one can be certain of continuity in any political process, as present events certainly argue. But how much further evidence is required before we open our eyes to what is happening? We have one sign after another, following so fast that one has to run to see them all: what new doubts can be invented to justify repudiation of what all of us know to be true? The present Soviet administration is trying to introduce major democratic reforms. It may be frustrated in the effort, but that effort is real. If we could help it, would we not be insane to refrain?

Another argument in Strasbourg was, initially, that perhaps it might be inconvenient to our Soviet partners to join in such a collaboration as that proposed. Then Mr Scheverdnadze visited us, and said he would be willing to be present at a joint meeting. I visited Mr Zagladin, shortly aftetwards, and he offered a careful four-point programme of stages for its realisation. On my return I briefed Mr Vinci, the European Parliament's Secretary-General, on this conversation. He received the information with great interest, and was obviously intrigued by it. How is it possible still to argue that the project is too difficult, too uncertain, too expensive?

The original proposal suggested that preparations be undertaken by joint Committee sessions, pairing off the appropriate bodies of both Parliaments. If the preparatory work took two years, perhaps each joint Committee would meet twice, once in Brussels and once in Moscow. If appropriate, smaller subgroups might deal with specific problems. Some agreements, for ratification in joint plenum, would be easy to reach: exchanges of documents, information, trainees, for instance. Others could be more difficult.

But inter-committee collaboration is a functional exercise, and the Committees of both Parliaments are well-used to methodical and efficient work. It would not be beyond their powers to determine what could appropriately be tabled on their joint agenda. Some Committees have more to learn from one another than others. Some are already involved in overtures, one to another. None of this framework of activity involves superhuman feats of organisation, funding, or control.

A joint plenary might be slightly more difficult. However, using our powers of improvisation, it could be arranged at Strasbourg, or in any one of a dozen European cities. Whilst the costs would not be negligible, they would certainly be rapidly outweighed by the benefits.

What, in fact, could be done by joint East-West action, to resolve present problems?

The first phase of crisis, in Eastern Europe and the USSR, involves the political collapse of authoritarian systems, and the difficult search for democratic renewal. It has provoked, and is partially reinforced by, national tensions and economic imbalances. At another level, indebtedness aggravates social distress to a point which drives national differences beyond democratic resolution, into xenophobia. Without economic co-operation on a large scale, we risk the disaggregation of societies whose economies are falling down.

A deeper crisis is all too likely to arrive. The global disproportions between rich and poor nations have developed an unbelievable pattern of debt. The United States, which, after the Second World War, was powerful enough to initiate the Marshall Plan for European Recovery, and to impose the dollar as the international currency, is, today, the world's largest debtor nation. The potent Japanese economy operates on a global scale, but has not generated political institutions which can think globally, or any other than the defensive plan. More precisely, Japanese investors can go anywhere to close a barrier or make a space: but overall economic policy is reactive, not initiative. In the European Community there could, perhaps, arise a group of statesmen with the vision and the skill to convene a new Bretton Woods conference, to tackle the problems involved in creating a new international economic order, a new world currency, and effective measures to unravel the bonds of debt.

Would this not be easier with the help of the Soviet Union?

Superimposed on any Western economic crisis will be the problems of disarmament and development. If economic activity is not reoriented, disarmament will contribute to the circle of decline and contraction. If world trade is about to enter a phase of stringent compression, we may well be standing on the brink of trade wars. Less propitious conditions for major democratic reforms could scarcely be envisaged. The common sense answer speaks of converting military investments to civilian purposes. But then, common sense finds the notion of economic crisis difficult to comprehend ...

It may be that current falls in commodity prices are only a "blip". It may be that pessimism about the Western economies is unfounded. In such a case, the arguments for joint efforts towards democracy, East and West, would stand or fall solely on their political merit. Is it not sensible, when one is embarking on a road of reform, to go along together? In which ways, by what devices, might we help one another? Are there any reasons which would justify ignoring each other's efforts, or even, undermining them? Should we listen to such reasons for *raisons d'état*, or discount them as immoral?

Perhaps, though, the economic wolf is really at our doors. If he is, co-operation takes on a special urgency.

The new global framework is unlikely to function if it is directed against a particular interest, to benefit a section of mankind. If we found how to redistribute resources in order to expand circulation, encourage sustainable development, focus resources to undo environmental damage, and open a total war on poverty, would this not also benefit the richest nations?

This seems to me to be the agenda of the "common home". Others might have a broader vision. Not the least of the virtues of the proposal for a joint meeting between the European Parliament and the Supreme Soviet, lies in the fact that it stimulates people to enquire, what might this agenda be?

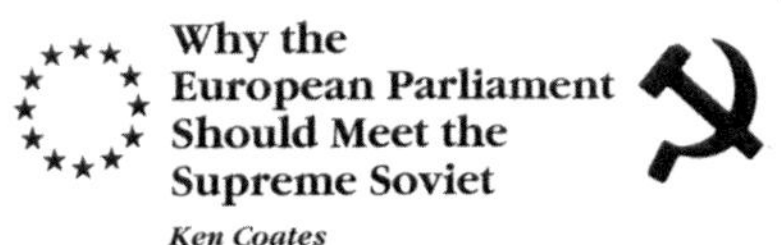

Why the European Parliament Should Meet the Supreme Soviet

Ken Coates

Every new day creates unforeseen choices for Europe. In both its Eastern and Western halves, our continent is becoming familiar with a new dimension of crisis. We are informed that when the Chinese write this word, they combine two other ideographs. "Crisis", thus, contains in itself the concept of "danger", but also that of "opportunity".

Understanding the danger, this complex combination explains why I proposed, six months ago, to try to make an opportunity. My suggestion was that the two largest emerging democracies of East and West should arrange a suitable meeting. Separately, they were doing similar things. The European Parliament was seeking to prepare a democratic foundation for political union, at the same time that the Supreme Soviet considered how to lay out the groundwork for political pluralism and the rule of law. Each of us, I thought, had something to say to the other. We could help one another. Together, we might build more surely than we could apart. Even if they rejected the notion of "common home", surely, I thought, colleagues might see advantage in ensuring that the structure we were seeking to erect could be safer if it were at least semi-detached! And if we talked, might we not see how to improve the architecture? In My Father's House there are many mansions . . .

A mark of the speed of change is that the frank expression of disbelief which often came across the faces of those who heard this proposal when first I made it, is now seldom seen. In the beginning perhaps half of my Western interlocutors thought I was crazy. Now, that number is well down. Of course, in truth, the hope for genuine European unity may really be crazy, but if it is, then we must at least observe that the world is going with it. In short order, first Poland, then Hungary, then the German Democratic Republic and Bulgaria, then Czechoslovakia and, latest, Romania; all embarked on the search for new political frameworks. Are they to be forever separate?

Some of the people who sought to dissuade us from any joint Parliamentary exchange with the Soviets were arguing, only a month or two ago, that the European Parliament should only meet with fully pluralist legislatures, and that Article Six of the Soviet Constitution precludes the development of any such openness. But now Article Six is on its way out. No one can be certain of continuity in any political process, as present events certainly argue. But how much further evidence is required before we open our eyes to what is happening? We have one sign after another, following so fast that one has to run to see them all: what new doubts can be invented to justify repudiation of what all of us know to be true? The present Soviet administration is trying to introduce major democratic reforms. It may be frustrated in the effort, but that effort is real. If we could help it, would we not be insane to refrain?

Another argument in Strasbourg was, initially, that perhaps it might be inconvenient to our Soviet partners to join in such a collaboration as that proposed. Then Mr Scheverdnadze visited us, and said he would be willing to be present at a joint meeting. I visited Mr Zagladin, shortly afterwards, and he offered a careful four-point programme of stages for its realisation. On my return I briefed Mr Vinci, the European Parliament's Secretary-General, on this conversation. He received the information with great interest, and was obviously intrigued by it. How is it possible still to argue that the project is too difficult, too uncertain, too expensive?

The original proposal suggested that preparations be undertaken by joint Committee sessions, pairing off the appropriate bodies of both Parliaments. If the preparatory work took two years, perhaps each joint Committee would meet twice, once in Brussels and once in Moscow. If appropriate, smaller subgroups might deal with specific problems. Some agreements, for ratification in joint plenum, would be easy to reach: exchanges of documents, information, trainees, for instance. Others could be more difficult.

But inter-committee collaboration is a functional exercise, and the Committees of both Parliaments are well-used to methodical and efficient work. It would not be beyond their powers to determine what could appropriately be tabled on their joint agenda. Some Committees have more to learn from one another than others. Some are already involved in overtures, one to another. None of this framework of activity involves superhuman fears of organisation, funding, or control.

A joint plenary might be slightly more difficult. However, using our powers of improvisation, it could be arranged at Strasbourg, or in any one of a dozen European cities. Whilst the costs would not be negligible, they would certainly be rapidly outweighed by the benefits.

What, in fact, could be done by joint East-West action, to resolve present problems?

The first phase of crisis, in Eastern Europe and the USSR, involves the political collapse of authoritarian systems, and the difficult search for democratic renewal. It has provoked, and is partially reinforced by, national tensions and economic imbalances. At another level, indebtedness

ELF
European
Labour
Forum
SOCIALIST GROUP, EUROPEAN PARLIAMENT
NUMBER 1, SUMMER 1990
Michael Barratt Brown: One World
Ken Coates MEP: Meeting the Russians
Glyn Ford MEP: Racism and Fascism
Stephen Bodington & Gyorgy Szell:
X Goes to Work
John Hughes: 35 . . . 35 . . . 35?
Contributors include:
Peter Crampton MEP, Royden Harrison, Denis
MacShane, Ian White MEP, Ulrich Maurer,
Gerd Walter MEP, Heidemarie Wieczorek-Zeul MdB

The Right to Work

Ken Coates

First published in European Labour Forum, *Summer 1996. The Full Employment Appeal attracted wide support from parliamentarians – including Tony Benn, with whom Ken Coates had a long political relationship – trades unionists, churches and public figures. Two 'Full Employment Conventions' were held at the European Parliament in Brussels.*

There are fifteen states which officially belong to the European Union. But the Appeal which we are canvassing ... seeks to express our solidarity with the population of a sixteenth state: the state of mass unemployment. Something like twenty million people are registered as living in this state today. More than seven million of them have been unemployed for over one year. A large proportion of them are young, and many young people have never had a job. If we counted the older people who would like to work, the numbers would be even greater. Millions of people have been compelled to retire early.

The population in mass unemployment is, of course, distributed all over the area of Europe. But it is also concentrated in particular places. In some regions, as many as half the young people have never been able to find a job. In many other regions, one in five of the young people have been unable to get paid work.

Unemployment shows us a society that is profoundly sick. Since 1948, the United Nations has promoted a Universal Declaration of Human Rights. This says:

> 'Everyone has the right to work, to free choice of employment, to just and favourable conditions of work, and to protection against unemployment.'

More than twenty million Europeans lack any such right, in some of the richest societies in the modern world. These societies tell us that they have a crisis in their welfare systems, because so many unemployed people need to be maintained. But all these societies are three times as rich as they were when the welfare systems were perfected, at the end of the Second World War. Poor and workless people could be forgiven if they did not notice this great growth of prosperity.

It is not only Europeans who are unemployed. In large parts of Africa, the economic system has been destroyed by debt and external intervention by such agencies as the International Monetary Fund. Africa would love to be able to purchase European goods, but her people have been impoverished and their poverty reaches out to depress conditions elsewhere in the world. The same dismal story is true in many parts of the third world.

The result is a complete collapse of human priorities. If society is to be organised to ensure the happiness of the great majority of people, then the right to work becomes a fundamental right. Human dignity depends on it.

It is not only the unemployed who suffer when masses are out of work. Those who retain their jobs enter a time of fear, misery, and frantic competition. Wages are depressed, and rights at work are trampled underfoot. The rot which is unemployment is profoundly damaging all our societies and it is for this reason that some of us in the European Parliament have decided to try to link arms, across frontiers, and across the division of Party and religion, to campaign for a return to full employment. Without such a return, social conditions will continue to worsen, and social morale will be destroyed.

We accept that significant changes will be necessary to ensure that human needs assume their rightful priority. We accept that there are many different views about how this can be accomplished. It is clear that large sums of money must be spent in order to generate employment, not only, as has been proposed, in improving the European infrastruture and modernising social amenities in nation states, regions, and localities, but also in recuperating the natural environment, and restoring the fabric of our inner city areas.

Vast increases in productivity in manufacturing industry have meant that large production can be maintained by a small workforce. But productivity in the social and caring social services needs to be measured in a completely different way. If we are making widgets, then it is productive if many widgets can be made by few persons. But if we are conducting schools, hospitals, or social services, then each employee works better and more intensively with fewer pupils, patients, or clients. This means we must transfer resources if we are to improve the standards of public services.

At the same time, society cannot sustain the punishingly long working hours which are imposed on part of the population, while others are unable to obtain any kind of paid work at all. Working hours that were suitable in the age of the internal combustion engine or the dynamo are completely unacceptable in the age of the micro-computer and robotics.

But up to now, mass unemployment has grown in the face of the disunity of its victims. Many of us seek a return to full employment. It is not wrong that we should come from different origins, and it is not wrong that we represent a wide diversity of opinions. But only if we can celebrate that diversity in unity, will we gather the strength to prevent the continued destruction of people in the remorseless and continuous crisis of employment.

* * *

A group of members of the European Parliament have met to draft the following Appeal. We belong to different political parties, but we have agreed to work together in order to help focus the growing European concern about unemployment. We seek to encourage forms of action conducive to new modes of full employment, and we want this issue to be put at the top of the political agenda. We believe that national governments and the European Union should undertake massive investment programmes in the public and private sectors to create employment. We favour a big expansion of employment in voluntary bodies and the social care sectors. We believe that society must find ways of using high levels of corporate profits to fund this kind of work and create new jobs.

There is some evidence that over-rigid adherence to the Maastricht criteria on monetary union can aggravate unemployment unless it is offset by joint and combined action at the European level, including the reductions in working time that are necessary.

Other proposals are invited, and can be developed as this initiative takes shape. We think it is necessary to bring together lay people and experts in Europe-wide meetings and seminars which can exchange their experiences about local and national efforts to overcome unemployment.

Will you help us? You can begin by signing the endorsement below and returning it to us ...

Full Employment: A European Appeal

In Europe today we live in a rich world. Yet our societies are deeply flawed. Millions of our fellow citizens seek paid work and cannot find it: many more than the 20 million officially unemployed. Many women, and many older men have given up the search. In some regions, among our young people, one in five cannot find paid work. In regions of high unemployment, up to half the young people are without employment. More than half of the unemployed have been without employment for over a year, and half of these even for two years or more. Ever more women and men are being excluded from any hope of earning their living by actively contributing to their societies' wealth. The welfare state is cut back, unable to cope with continuous unemployment. In some countries this misery has lasted for fifteen years.

We should call this exclusion from society by its right name: it is a disaster which is destroying peoples' lives, dissolving the social fabric in which we live and depend on one another, undermining the very foundations of democratic politics. It calls for urgent relief.

Creative work for each individual, personal participation in the production of wealth, and corresponding remuneration, are no less basic human needs than are the needs for food, clothing, and shelter. Unemployment generates insecurity and despair. Sickness frequently visits those who are unemployed, so that people may find their health undermined at the same time that they face poverty and social isolation.

Unemployment does not just happen. It is man made. Full employment can surely be achieved again, even if it is not the same kind of full employment we knew during the long post-war period in most Western European countries. Instead of guaranteeing a 'family wage' to the male wage earners, leaving other necessary work to be done by women as unpaid work, full employment will now be about guaranteeing access to properly paid work to every independent member of society, thus furthering the redistribution of unpaid work in a fair and better way. And rather than relying on a continuous expansion of every kind of material production, full employment will now have to be based on careful stewardship of natural resources and decent environmental conditions. Since Western European societies are at least three times richer than they were at the birth of postwar welfare politics, we could, in fact, afford to achieve such a new kind of full employment – by supporting an ecologically sustainable recovery, by redistributing paid (and unpaid) work, as well as through private incomes and public goods.

Everywhere there is a need for public provision of shared services. No-one doubts the usefulness, for example, of our caring services, or preventative health work, or of education and training. Why should we not also co-operate in restoring run-down areas, in recuperation of the natural environment, in improving housing security and energy efficiency, in developing sheltered housing for old people, or in offering better child care support, and sport and leisure centres for the young? Is there not equal benefit in support for small and medium enterprises, or for sustainable agriculture? Yet vital services are allowed to decline and decay in a destructive spiral. Public expenditure is reduced, instead of reducing public waste and tax fraud. At the same time, new technologies and methods of organisation are used to lay off ever more people, instead of offering them a role in a better network of public provision, and creating more, better qualified and better paid jobs.

Capital movements, all kinds of speculation and even production itself, are now more than ever arranged on an international, global scale. National governments have been set against each other, and trade unions and the working people of each country have been dragged into an economic war for competitive advantage. The arguments supporting this harmful process are misleading: in general, the rate of profitability in Western Europe is far above the global average, and even in countries which are at the forefront of world competition there are real alternatives to the kind of monetaristic policies currently being imposed.

The European Commission and Council of Ministers have launched various plans and proposal over the last few years to create large numbers of jobs all across the Union. But from the launch of the Delors White Paper to the Conclusions of the Essen Summit, in spite of a modest economic recovery in the meantime, the number of people in work has not risen. Throughout Western Europe, the numbers employed remain at least 16 million below what they were in 1990. At the same time, improvements in the number of women finding jobs in parts of the economy are marred by the insecurities of part-time work, and by severely exploitative low pay, while there has been a marked fall in male full-time jobs. The pattern of working time is still organised according to traditional roles for men and women, without adequately recognising the profound changes that have already taken place. Continued large increases in productivity mean that working hours overall can, and should be cut, without the reduction of the resources allocated to pay. At the same time, new fiscal policies could help safeguard earnings and income levels. Indeed, we now face the danger that unemployment and poor jobs will increase, as governments cut back their spending to meet their very restrictive interpretation of the terms of the Maastricht Treaty for a single currency.

Now, in many countries, we face a combination of social cuts with the removal of social protection in the labour market. A new misery threatens: the descent into poverty of those who have been long excluded, and of those others who now endure painfully low wages, saps the confidence and strength of their neighbours, and brings fear and insecurity to large part of Europe.

This European crisis is replicated throughout the world, and we seek allies in every continent to work out employment policies based on co-operation rather than raw competition.

There is no case for a fortress economy, either at the level of Europe, or at the level of a nation, a region, or a family. Some have tried: the rich in some countries fortify their suburbs, carry guns and teach their children to shoot. This will not work. The only way forward is to act together, each for all, striking a 'new deal' from below, between the poor and the better-off, using the instruments of public policy to advance common interests capable of stabilising broad popular alliances. At local, regional, national and European levels, we need joint and common action to create and to safeguard sufficiently well-paid jobs, and to re-distribute working time.

We have to persuade a broad majority of the people that it is better to finance socially useful and ecologically sustainable work than to subsidise unemployment. We want to press for a common European economic strategy to reduce unemployment, exclusion, and poverty on the way towards a new era of full employment. This choice involves a wide variety of public and private programmes, including a European level of borrowing and funding, and sustained efforts to reduce working time, share work, and make possible a rich programme of lifelong learning, while at the same time safeguarding the income levels of the working population.

New technologies and new management systems need fewer workers to produce more goods and services. Labour is, in fact, saved this way. We need, however, to use this saved labour in a new sharing of paid and unpaid labour, reducing the gap between those who are overworked, and those who are excluded from society's work, as well as using some of the additional earning for funding the creation of jobs in the environment, education, and the caring services. Voluntary bodies, churches and trade unions have already begun to study the effect of sabbatical leave for parents, the provision of training and schooling in working time, and other relevant methods of sharing work, as well as creating humane and satisfying forms of work to replace much labour that is boring and repetitive drudgery.

This Appeal seeks to encourage all forms of action and all modes of employment which will end the disaster of unemployment. Its signatories will seek ways to come together to exchange ideas, examine experiences, and co-ordinate their work. We shall seek to encourage relevant action in the political field, so that employment takes its place at the top of the agenda. We shall also do whatever we can to influence our neighbours and communities to refuse a Europe of exclusion and mass unemployment. Europe must include all its citizens, and afford to each the space in which to develop his or her capacity for happiness and social solidarity.

The
Universal Declaration
of
Human Rights

Fifty Years On

Ken Coates MEP

The Universal Declaration of Human Rights

Fifty Years On

Ken Coates

This pamphlet began as a paper given to the New European Left Forum in Athens on December 10th, 1998, the fiftieth anniversary of the signing of the Universal Declaration. Ken Coates served as President of the Sub-committee on Human Rights of the European Parliament. In 1991, he presented a report – Human Rights in the World *– to the Parliament.*

It was exactly fifty years ago, on December 10th 1948, that the United Nations General Assembly voted in favour of the Universal Declaration of Human Rights. Forty-eight member-states voted for the Declaration, and eight abstained. These included the USSR and five of its allies, as well as the Republic of South Africa and Saudi Arabia.

> The preamble of the Declaration states that the recognition 'of the inherent dignity and of the equal and inalienable rights of all members of the human family is the foundation of freedom, justice and peace in the world'.

It goes on to insist that

> 'If man is not to be compelled to have recourse, as a last resort, to rebellion against tyranny and oppression, that human rights should be protected by the rule of law'.

The thirty Articles which follow evoke other classic statements, going back to the original United States Declaration of Independence of 1776, and the Revolutionary Declaration of the Rights of Man and Citizen of 1789.

> 'All human beings are born free and equal in dignity and rights. They are endowed with reason and conscience and should act towards one another in a spirit of brotherhood' says Article 1.
>
> 'Everyone has the right to life, liberty and security of person' says Article 3.
>
> 'All are equal before the law' says Article 7.

A whole string of personal rights are then set out, although some of them were not to be implemented for almost half a century by some of the signatories.

Beyond doubt, the universal implementation of this Declaration would be a landmark moment in the evolution of modern civilisation. Most of the Articles agreed in 1948 bear the stamp of the horrendous experience of the Second World War, where personal rights were systematically infringed: but they also carry the imprint of the economic adversities leading up to that war, when mass unemployment reduced whole populations to misery, and denied hope to an entire generation. Thus there arose, in many countries at the same time, powerful movements for guaranteed social security, full employment and minimum economic rights.

These movements were sufficiently influential to mark the thinking of those who drafted the Universal Declaration. They were not, however, sufficient to secure its implementation. When he was asked what he thought of Western Civilisation, Mahatma Ghandi replied: 'It would be a good idea'.

Twenty-five years were to pass before there was any significant shift of ground affecting human rights. It was after defeat in the Vietnam War that the American administration began to change its focus, and became increasingly interested in presenting an image of concern for human rights and morality. This concern was strongly expressed by President Carter, who launched what was claimed to be a full-scale crusade for human rights. By 1977, former Presidential Adviser, Arthur Schlesinger, wrote

> 'In effect, human rights is replacing self-determination as the guiding value in American foreign policy.'

As Noam Chomsky was quick to point out, the United States' earlier concern for self-determination had previously been very much more strongly honoured in the breach than the observance: 'The record of American intervention to prevent self-determination, independence and – crucially – social change, in Indo-China, Guatemala, the Dominican Republic, Chile and elsewhere' provides 'a tribute to the effectiveness of the propaganda system' in that there has scarcely been a moment in United States history without one intervention or another, clandestine or overt, being mounted against governments of which the United States Government disapproved.

But nonetheless, even if it was partial and intermittent, the human rights crusade found an echo with American public opinion, and probably strengthened liberal sentiments. It also helped to destabilise Communist regimes where human rights were systematically violated, and it may, to some extent, have contributed to positive developments in Latin America where United States' interventions had buttressed a whole string of unsavoury dictatorships. Needless to say, covert American interventions continue, and the results of earlier interventions still undermine human rights over a wide area. One only has to think of the atrocities in Indonesia, to know at once that there is an immense amount of duplicity in all this official propaganda. But even mendacious propaganda imposes costs on the propagandist, and when a super state picks upon the banner of human rights, this action will actually encourage some defence of human rights, even at the same time as it justifies widespread cynicism.

Duplicity apart, the United States decision to run with its crusade for human rights raises other problems for human rights activists. Celebrating the fortieth anniversary of the Universal Declaration, the American administration (Richard S. Williamson, Assistant Secretary in the US Department of State) said:

> 'We view human rights as limitations upon the power of the state. Based on the principles set forth in the Bill of Rights of the US Constitution, our view of human rights is centred on defences from the state accorded every individual and protected by an independent judiciary. These rights are timeless, unaltered, not subject to the intellectual or political fashions of the day.'

But the state is not the only power in the modern world, and by no means the only oppressor. States have been ceding power and influence to multinational corporations, but even more they have been yielding up claims to power, withdrawing from economic intervention in favour of the aggravated indetermination of market forces. Always, but more than ever now, rights can be easier to defend against some states than they are against other secular powers.

Human rights, as established in the American Constitution and in the French Declaration of the Rights of Man, included the right to hold property. Was this, as Schlesinger thought ten years ago, timeless, invariable, unchanging? Of course not. The definition of property has been constantly changed throughout the history of modern times. The rights which such ownership carry are still subject to continual modification. Planning laws, for instance, have greatly restricted the power to 'do as we will with our own'. Taxation can in principle erode or even annul such rights. But the fundamental objection of socialists to this 'right' remain what they always were: as Marx put it when commenting on a famous historical dispute, as peasants were deprived of the right to gather firewood or wild strawberries on formerly common land:

> 'Property can be monopolised, and if it can be monopolised, then it will be monopolised.'

The concentration of property deprives non-property owners of the 'right' to hold property. A long history of dispossession marks the formation of all modern societies. Per contra, numerous expedients have been devised from time to time with the intention of opening up the question of ownership, and widening property rights to all. But globally, these expedients have been a dismal failure. The United Nations Development Programme, in its Annual Human Development Reports, has shown continuous polarisation in property holding.

> 'In 1960 the 20% of the world's people who live in the richest countries had 30 times the income of the poorest 20% by 1995 82, times as much income.'

The 225 richest people in the world have a combined wealth of over one trillion dollars, which is equal to the annual income of the poorest 47% of the world's people. (That is to say, 2.5 billion individuals). If we look at the Cross Domestic Project of the least developed countries, we find that the combined GDP of 48 countries is less than the wealth of the three richest people in the world. Fifteen billionaires have assets greater than the total national income of Africa south of the Sahara. Thirty-two people own more than the annual income of all the people of South Asia. Eighty-four rich people have holdings greater than the GDP of China, a nation with 1.2 billion citizens.

The UNDP estimates that the cost of maintaining universal basic education, health care for all, reproductive health care for all women, and adequate food and safe water for all, would be 40 billion dollars a year, or less than 4% of the combined value of the holdings of the 225 richest people. We can be sure of one thing: this polarisation will continue, come hell or high water, come whatever crisis may fall upon us. This year's UNDP Report was starker than last years, and next year's will be starker than that for this year. Why not raise a 4% tax on precisely these 225 people, and simply meet the outstanding needs identified by the UN? In our present polity, the right to property for some has suffocated all the other rights of many.

It is therefore clear that the 'right of property' as outlined in the classic liberal statements of human rights, is unsustainable. But it was not for nothing that Hegel told us that 'property is the first reality of freedom'. For this aphorism to be as true today as it was when Hegel wrote it, we should have to have evolved completely different forms of property, into access for all, or commonwealth.

Personal property in land did guarantee considerable freedom to American citizens whilst there was an abundance of land. This guarantee did not extend to Indians: and it would be truer to say that the rights of settlers were founded on ultimate wrongs done to indigenous peoples. But human societies of small farmers and small producers could once live with the freedom guaranteed by small property holdings. However, the modern world which has given us 225 billionaires, bestriding the contemporary economy as all-dominating colossi, cannot begin to found universal freedom on modern corporate property rights, which have become a badge of all our unfreedom, of our lack of individual or shared control over the economic environment, and of the mal-distribution of work and resources which amounts to deepening misery in both the third world and the first.

Let us look at what the Universal Declaration of Rights was willing to tell us long ago in 1948 about the right to work, which a modern philosopher might more reasonably characterise as the first reality of freedom. It is instructive to examine Article 23 and 24:

> 'Art. 23
>
> (i) Everyone has the right to work, to free choice of employment, to just and favourable conditions of work and to protection against unemployment.
>
> (ii) Everyone, without any discrimination, has the right to equal pay for equal work.
>
> (iii) Everyone who works has the right to just and favourable remuneration, ensuring for himself and his family an existence worthy of human dignity, and supplemented if necessary, by other means of social protection.
>
> (iv) Everyone has the right to form and to join trade unions for the protection of his interests.
>
> Art. 24
>
> Everyone has the right to rest and leisure, including reasonable limitation of working hours and periodic holidays with pay.'

It is noticeable that the Declaration speaks of 'the right to work', not 'full employment' which is the chosen name for this desired state in such contemporary publications as the preamble of the Treaty establishing the World Trade Organisation. 'Full employment' defines a situation in which everyone is employed, and therefore assumes a particular economic relationship as fundamental to the provision of work.

But it is not inevitable that work should always be organised by 'employers'. In a co-operative or free society, in which 'the free development of each is the condition for the free 'development of all', it can be envisaged that men and women might co-operate in work in relations of equality, allowing only such authority therein as may be freely given, and freely withdrawn.

This was the subject of a famous dispute in Britain between Sidney and Beatrice Webb, and the trade union movement which they described in one of their earliest classic works. They had defined a trade union as a continuous association of working people designed to regulate conditions of their employment. Some trade union members expostulated that part of their objective was to get rid of employers, so that production might be self-regulated by those engaged in it. The Webbs were sufficiently democratic in their thinking to take note of this objection, and they subsequently revised their opening definition, in order to meet it. But the Universal Declaration speaks of an older and more democratic objective, when it insists upon 'the right to work'.

Another international organisation, the International Labour Office, published a comprehensively damning report, World Employment, defending the goal of full employment. It has been widely argued that modern technology has brought about a new epoch of 'jobless growth'. Other social thinkers have introduced us to the idea of 'the end of work'.

The ILO has given careful scrutiny to these arguments, and offered substantial evidence that there is no such causal phenomenon as jobless growth. It has also shown that there is no evidence whatever that an increase in the amount of useful work is an unattainable objective. Yet there can be growth while employment fails to grow, but the rise of unemployment, insists the ILO

> 'has been caused by a decline in economic growth rates rather than the onset of jobless growth'.

Naturally, this analysis does not address the very material question of what kind of growth? But sustainable growth is likely to generate more jobs than would result from conventional forms of growth.

More: it has been widely argued that stability of employment has collapsed, and that everyone is changing jobs at increasingly frequent intervals. The ILO shows us that this view is also unfounded. Those presently employed have been in their jobs, on average, between six and twelve years, dependent on the country in which they are working: and this figure has not been declining.

Nor is unemployment correlated with technological advance: the number of working hours in Canada, Japan and the USA rose sharply over the last three decades, notwithstanding the high, or very high levels of technological innovation in those countries. Aggregate working hours did go down in Germany, France and the UK, but very slowly. One could continue: but the essential ILO finding is that full employment results from a policy commitment, and that without such a commitment, the unrestrained working of the market will continue to cost jobs and waste lives.

It makes little sense to celebrate the state of human rights in a context of mass unemployment. The unemployed have few rights, and these are being eroded daily, as the cost of subsistence for unemployed people bears in on national treasuries. Benefits are cut, and unemployed people are forced into ever deeper misery. But the existence of vast masses of unemployed persons also undermines the standards of those who are working. More vulnerable groups of workers feel this immediately in constraints on wages. The consequent erosion of trade union influences means that rights at work come under consistent hostile pressure. The last British Government survey of overtime hours showed that eighty million hours of overtime were being worked in the United Kingdom every week. Of course, this would constitute two million jobs with a 40 hour week. But even more shocking than this is the fact that almost half the overtime worked was completely unpaid. The workers involved dare not ask for compensation, for fear that the request might remove them from the workforce.

The impact of unemployment on communities is dismal. As hope dies, so people find themselves beset by a growing drug culture, and threatened by rising crime and alienation. These phenomena find a reflection in increased illness, depression and even suicide.

It is a depressing fact that we need to face, that unrivalled possibilities of technical progress are, in our world, combined with growing distress, and the rejection of increasing masses of people, who try to subsist in poverty and unemployment. This record gives us little to celebrate on the 50th anniversary of the Universal Declaration, even though this document does us a service in that it reflects the hopes of our parents, and allows us to measure the distance by which we fall behind those hopes.

A new Declaration would have to insist that the actual state of human rights may be understood by examining the extent of poverty and unemployment, as well as the numbers of political prisoners. The right to life itself is in jeopardy for many millions of our fellow human beings, in the grip of extreme poverty. And their right to a fulfilling social existence scarcely exists for the unemployed and those who are excluded in the mis-called 'advanced' societies.

Launch Conference: Brussel
31 January/1 February 200
in the European Parliament

Peace and Human Rights Are Overdue

Ken Coates

On January 31st and February 1st 2002, there gathered the inaugural meeting of the European Network for Peace and Human Rights. Some 300 people from more than thirty countries met at the European Parliament and agreed to advance their joint efforts for disarmament, peace and human rights. Ken Coates delivered this speech to the opening session. Published in The Spokesman 74: A better world is possible.

Why we need a European Network for Peace and Human Rights

Since we agreed to work towards the convening of this Conference, the whole world has been shaken to its foundations, first by the atrocities in the United States on September 11th and then by the American response, which was to proclaim a 'war against terrorism', and to launch the first instalment of that war in Afghanistan.

Critics at the time argued that terrorism ought properly to be understood as a criminal offence, and that a declaration of 'war' against an enemy which was often shadowy and ill-defined, involved not only logistical but also logical problems which would cause serious difficulties as the project unwound.

The subsequent bombardment of Afghanistan has of course created a large number of civilian casualties. By the end of 2001, as many or more innocent civilians had been killed in Afghanistan by high altitude bombardment as perished in the Twin Towers in New York in the September attacks. But more sinister still was the constant official whispering about subsequent targets.

Since terrorism is so difficult to pin-point with precision, it can be identified here, there and everywhere. Its pursuit has led Allied Governments to impose serious restrictions on conventional civil liberties, and to exert intimidatory pressures on a wide variety of other authorities. The slow collapse of colonialism took place amidst great turmoil, and in some countries, this turmoil generated genuine terrorism. Israel, for example, was born after a prolonged terrorist struggle against the British occupation of Palestine. Many other countries took shape in a cauldron of rebellion and war. Their political culture can be expected to reflect that fact.

Be that as it may, there have today been credible threats of United States military action of different kinds against Somalia, Yemen, Iraq, Sudan, the Philippines and possibly Syria. There have been dark murmurings about the need for better behaviour on the part of Iran.

Previous 'terrorist wars' have now been reclassified in the hope of cementing the American alliance which is embroiled in the conflict in Afghanistan. The war in Chechnya for instance, now seems to be understood in the United States as at least partly a terrorist offensive, involving Bin Laden supporters in the struggle to overthrow Russian rule. Chechen activities in Georgia and other allied territories have already been restrained as a result.

Conflict in the Islamic world has been heightened from the Philippines and Indonesia all the way cross to the Mahgreb. New wars may well be gestating over the whole immense region.

All this fits uncomfortably snugly with the doctrine of Full Spectrum Dominance, which was announced by the United States military during the earlier years. The ending of the Cold War clearly left the United States in possession of the military field, as by far the most potent power in the world. The National Command Authorities in the United States had no wish to cede this position, which they found highly desirable.

'For the joint force of the future', they announced in their Joint Vision 2020, published in June 2000, 'this goal will be achieved through full spectrum dominance - the ability of US forces, operating unilaterally or in combination with multinational and interagency partners, to defeat any adversary and control any situation across the full range of military operations'.

Continued dominance depends upon continued superiority not only in the area of military technology overall, but in particular upon military 'information superiority'. The American military vision 'is firmly grounded in the view that the US military must be a joint force capable of full spectrum dominance. Its basis is four-fold: the global interests of the United States and the continuing existence of a wide range of potential threats to those interests; the centrality of information technology to the evolution of not only our own military, but also the capabilities of other actors around the globe; the premium a continuing broad range of military operations will place on the successful integration of multinational and interagency partners and the interoperability of processes, organisations, and systems; and our reliance on the joint force as the foundation of future US military operations ... The label full spectrum dominance implies that US forces are able to conduct prompt, sustained, and synchronised operations ... in all domains - space, sea, land, air and information.'

Awareness of this enables us to appreciate the significance of 'missile defence', a completely misnamed operation for the military invasion of space. It became more and more evident that the threatened repudiation of the Anti-Ballistic Missile Treaty was not in aid of the prevention of missile attacks on the United States, but was designed to facilitate the development of American military technology in space, involving huge new experiments in laser techniques, the refinement of space-based information gathering, and of the capacity to destroy 'enemy' satellites which might be gathering their own intelligence. Star Wars were to facilitate a whole new step beyond nuclear technology, towards the ultimate destructive capacity. This would be the necessary sanction to enforce global dominance.

We have already pointed out the direct application of such doctrines in the terrestrial field by Zbigniew Brzezinski, who identified the domination of Eurasia as the necessary first step to global dominion. When Alexander conquered the Persians, he learned that their kings kept amphorae of water from the Nile and from the Danube, as evidence of their mastery of the world. Brzezinski favours no such timidity or half-measures.

> 'For the United States, Eurasian geostrategy involves the purposeful management of geostrategically dynamic states and the careful handling of geopolitically catalytic states, in keeping with the twin interests of America in the short-term preservation of its unique global power and in the long-run transformation of it into increasingly institutionalised global co-operation. To put it in a terminology that hearkens back to the more brutal age of ancient empires, the three grand imperatives of imperial geostrategy are to prevent collusion and maintain security dependence among the vassals, to keep tributaries pliant and protected, and to keep the barbarians from coming together.'[*The Grand Chessboard*]

Extrapolating from this theme, Brzezinski tells us that against his schema

> 'The most dangerous scenario would be a grand coalition of China, Russia, and perhaps Iran, an antihegemonic coalition united not by ideology but by complementary grievances.'

The strategic plans of the American forces have been refined in a very ingenious framework, which is deep-going. Colonel John A. Warden III of the US Air Force, summed up much of this thinking in his paper 'The Enemy as a System'. This represents a thorough-going revision of the thinking of Clausewitz and Napoleon, and begins with a severely rational examination of how to achieve the objectives of the United States.

'At the strategic level', says Colonel Warden, 'we attain our objectives by causing such changes to one or more parts of the enemy's physical system that the enemy decides to adopt our objectives, or we make it physically impossible for him to oppose us. The latter we call strategic paralysis. Which parts of the enemy system we attack ... will depend on what our objectives are, how much the enemy wants to resist us, how capable he is, and how much effort we are physically, morally, and politically capable of exercising.'

But what is the enemy 'system'? Warden offers a simplified model of five rings. At the centre is the leadership or brain. In the next circle are the organic essentials, food, energy, and so on. Thirdly, there is the infrastructure, of vital connections and skeletal essentials: roads, airfields, factories, transmission lines. The fourth ring is the population which is sustained by these essentials, and is necessary to sustain them. Lastly, and in fact least important for many purposes, is the circle of the fighting mechanism.

The purpose of modem war is not to confront arms, or kill soldiers. If this process could be avoided altogether, that would be fine by the controllers of modem war, provided only that they could exercise their will over enough of the other rings to bend the enemy leadership to their own purposes.

Colonel Warden explains these categories with a series of intricate diagrams. But such diagrams are not necessary for us to realise that within this model, American Generals do not give a fig whether the tanks destroyed by their rockets are made of metal or plywood, as were many of the decoys deployed in Yugoslavia. What they care about is the destruction of the system, if not by the liquidation of its leadership, then by cumulative damage to the essentials which sustain it.

'We must not start our thinking on war with the tools of war - with the air planes, tanks, ships and those who crew them. These tools are important and have their place, but they cannot be our starting point, nor can we allow ourselves to see them as the essentials of war. Fighting is not the essence of war, nor even a desirable part of it. The real essence is doing what is necessary to make the enemy accept our objectives as his objectives.'

Of course, such doctrines have a life of their own, and can develop mutations of various kinds. But while understanding this, the peace movements need to take stock of the implications of this thinking to our own conventional wisdom.

It used to be presumed that there exists a law of war, and that the Geneva Conventions could operate as a restraint on military misbehaviour. But the pursuit of the destruction of the enemy 'as a system' places a great deal of this thinking in serious doubt. How can the Geneva Conventions governing the protection of children, and therefore of women, stand up to high altitude bombing as a methodical principle in such destruction? How can the exigencies of war against terrorism be squared with the Geneva Conventions on the Protection of Prisoners of War, when the interrogation of prisoners is no longer restricted, and when they can be chained up, subjected to sensory deprivation, and incarcerated in unthinkable conditions, two continents away from the place of their detention?

With dominance in play, how can smaller states preserve their integrity and autonomy? How do the institutions of the UN, which once laid claim to the role of protector of the weak, escape from untold influences and pressures, in an overall context of domination? How can the international institutions be protected from the poisoning of their wellsprings by the pervasive exercise and threats of power? And how can non-governmental organisations uphold peace with human rights when both come under recurrent threat.

In short, all the architecture of peace, which was our inheritance from the Second World War, including the establishment of the United Nations, and the Universal Declaration of Human Rights, is now undermined. The principles upon which our parents built the UN framework are no longer unchallenged, and that framework is therefore endangered. Peace movements have to make a rigorous appraisal of these new circumstances, in order to insist upon their own sustaining principles. Not dominance, but democracy, is the key to a humane world order. It is easy in such turbulent times to lose the thread, and to mistake the style for the substance. But peace and human rights are the ultimate foundations on which the postwar settlement was designed, and we need to make sure that these foundations are defended and secured. Their effective defence is likely to require their comprehensive reform, a veritable re-foundation. Our task, therefore, is not only to stop the war, but to lay the basis for a Peace which embodies human fulfilment. The other name of that Peace is Democracy.

One first step to facing this task must surely be to improve our own liaisons with one another, where possible to co-ordinate our efforts, and always to keep each other informed. Already there is a strong will in Europe to join our forces in a renewed network for human rights and peace.

But Europe is neither a fortress nor an island. Not the least of our duties must be the effort to reach out to the wider world with a message of Peace. First, we should seek dialogue with those who share our views in the United States. Perhaps we should explore the setting up of a Peace delegation to tour some important American cities and talk with those who are interested in meeting us. Second, the time is already ripe for a serious exchange of views between peace and human rights movements in Europe and West Asia. War threatens to swallow many territories in that region, and it is urgent that we should inform one another about its problems, while seeking to establish the understanding that another world is possible.

Peace and Human Rights have been possible for a long time, but now we face a true crisis, which says very loudly that they are overdue.

Trident

Ken Coates

First published in 2008 as the Editorial to Trident – Nuclear Proliferation the British Way (The Spokesman 98).

Back in 1984, at a time when the British Labour Party policy favoured European Nuclear Disarmament, Gordon Brown declared that the Trident programme was 'unacceptably expensive, economically wasteful and militarily unsound'. In those far off days the Labour Party favoured the simultaneous dissolution of the North Atlantic Treaty and the Warsaw Pact.

Gingerly feeling its way, the Kinnock leadership gradually accomplished the retreat from unilateralism, at the very time that true multilateralism had become a possibility. The Warsaw Treaty demobilised itself and went home. Its East European members severed their connections with the Soviet Union, which itself disintegrated, losing the Baltic States, parts of the Caucasus, and considerable influence in Central Asia. For Russia, these areas became part of the 'near abroad' which gave rise to the need for complex diplomacy and a considerable effort to influence other alignments. As Russia generated privatisation, oligarchs, and confusion on a grand scale, all the paradigms of deterrence were evacuated of whatever meaning they might once have held.

But in Britain, the Trident programme went on and on. Britain's only system of nuclear armaments had been furnished by the United States, which provided the ballistic missiles direct, and also the blueprints of the submarines themselves as well as of the warheads, together with a not inconsiderable volume of technical assistance in their construction. The missiles themselves are pure-bred red-blooded American armaments in every detail. Fifty-eight of them are leased on rotation by the British Government and deployed on four Vanguard submarines. They apparently also figure in the calculations of the Americans themselves about their overall deployment. Various fail-safe mechanisms prevent stray missiles from launching themselves against anywhere in the world where the Americans do not wish them to go.

Of course, the main fail-safe device is an embarrassingly subordinate and totally compliant British Government. This has long since lost any pretensions to independence and sees its defence policy as necessarily anchored in every detail to the needs of Washington.

The United States entered the new millennium with a rigid commitment to 'full spectrum dominance' in all military matters. Top dog: that was where the U.S. of A. was at. This managed to shrink other commitments almost to the point of invisibility. True, the Nuclear Non-Proliferation Treaty survived, but since the world's megapower was determined to interpret this entirely selectively, it was unlikely to create problems. It would be useful in restricting the nuclear options of rogue or dubious States, but it could be instantly set aside in the case of putative allies. It never caused the slightest problems for Israel, perhaps the most serious proliferator in the most dangerous zone of the world, and it created only momentary difficulties for India and Pakistan.

But over time America's wars have sapped American hegemony. Timid signs of life have even been observed in the United Nations. It is no longer axiomatic that world diplomacy must follow the script written in the State Department.

What, in this context, happens to the doctrine of deterrence? This doctrine was clearly much cited in relations between East and West, in the days before the implosion of the Soviet Union. Did it ever apply in other regions, such as the Middle East? It is difficult to disentangle appearances from realities in this region. The Bush/Blair alliance strayed into the battlefield in order to suppress weapons of mass destruction that did not exist in Iraq. That made the task of suppression all the easier.

The same intelligence services which got things so dramatically wrong in that country have intermittently played up the dangers of nuclear weapons in Iran. But these too, it appears, are fictitious. According to most conventional doctrines of deterrence, the Iranians need nuclear weapons in order to inhibit possible attacks by Israel, which has already demonstrated not only its willingness, but also its competence, to assume the role of nuclear policeman by attacking and destroying the Osirak reactor in Iraq in 1981.

If Israel's responses were confined to belligerent rhetoric, it might be pardonable to dismiss the Israeli threat to neighbouring States. But there is a rather large record of painful military adventures which breeds fierce agnosticism on this score.

The Iranians are also hemmed about by other nuclear neighbours in India and Pakistan. In Western folklore India is a 'good' nation which cannot nourish militaristic expectations. That is as may be. But not many people will stand up to proclaim similarly benign interpretations of Pakistani policy, and there may indeed be doubt about whether the proprietors of the Pakistani deterrent will remain securely in place for very long. Senator Obama has let it be known that if the Pakistani bomb falls into the wrong hands, he would favour military action to 'recover control'. Were there any truth at all in the deterrence theory, the bomb in Pakistan would surely constitute a big enough threat, and a large enough uncertainty, to justify the speediest possible counter-deployment. But instead, and mercifully for all of us, the official Iranian reaction is to renounce any intentions of pursuing nuclear armaments. Not only does Iran repudiate the bomb, but her supreme leader pronounced a fatwa against it.

There is only one rational antidote to all those free range bombs, in the hands of all those temperamental and unstable leaders: and it is indeed the renunciation of nuclear weapons and the establishment of a nuclear-free zone in the entire Middle Eastern region. Difficult though this may be to achieve, its advantage over the alternative of frenzied preparation for nuclear mayhem all around the zone, is perfectly obvious to all but the proprietors of full spectrum dominance and military orthodoxy.

All of this argues that perhaps the most useful weapon in the UN armoury might be the Non-Proliferation Treaty, and the doctrine of nuclear-free zones. But the British Government, whose international doctrine is thick with pieties about the United Nations, is totally indifferent to this key institution.

We already drew attention to this (*Spokesman 92*), in John Ainslie's forensic discussion of the nuclear dependency of Britain on the United States, and the implications of the decision to renew the Trident programme. Significant parts of the British military are deeply concerned about this decision, because it would pre-empt vast expenditures which would be likely to wipe out, for purely ideological reasons, spending on vital military equipment which they lack in their present wars. Officially, the nuclear weapons programme is supposed to cost between two and three per cent of the Defence Budget, or between seven hundred million pounds and one billion pounds every year. But the decision to renew the British deterrent entails enhancements to the specification of Trident which would undoubtedly constitute a breach of the Non-Proliferation Treaty, and the commissioning of new submarines which can carry them. So costly will this equipment prove that it has already put in jeopardy the programme of building the necessary new aircraft carriers to carry British forces into new wars for the greater glory of the American Empire. Perhaps we can manage without the aircraft carriers: but why on earth can we not also manage without the renewed deterrent?

Of course, renewed diplomatic goads and provocations might be souring relations with Russia to the point where various kinds of official unpleasantness are thinkable. There are days when it seems likely that the oligarchs have bought the Foreign Office as if it were a common or garden football club. But an all out nuclear war …? The need to be able to destroy what is left of Russia, after they have wiped out the British mainland? Where has prudence gone in these calculations?

Now the *Sunday Herald* has produced evidence which shows that all the planning presumptions upon which British weapons' designers have been working are in meltdown, because the American designers appear to have unilaterally set aside the formal exchange of letters between President Bush and Prime Minister Blair on the modalities of missile renewal. In December 2006, Prime Minister Blair wrote formally to President Bush:

> 'The United Kingdom wishes to ensure that any successor to the D5 system is compatible with, or is capable of being made compatible with, the launch system for the D5 missile, which we will in the meantime be installing in our new submarines …'

Bush responded by inviting Britain to take part in the D5 replacement programme, or to discuss the extension of the planned life of the missiles.

> 'In this respect any successor to the D5 system should be compatible with, or be capable of being made compatible with, the launch system for the D5 missiles.'

But the *Sunday Herald* (22nd December 2007) presents evidence that American designers have asked for tenders for a test-bed for future underwater launched nuclear missiles, which implies the breakdown of the formal exchanges between Bush and Blair. The tenders specify a missile diameter of up to one hundred and twenty inches, while the diameter of Trident's outgoing D5 missile tubes is eighty-seven inches. The intention in preparing the new submarines was to begin by arming them with existing Trident missiles, only later replacing them with the new missiles currently being designed by the United States. The projected new American test-bed must not only be able to support missiles which are much larger than the present Trident ones, but also much heavier. The new missiles will be up to 200,000lbs, as opposed to the present missiles which weigh 130,000lbs.

The British military planners envisage maintaining the new submarines until at least 2055. But how the new submarines can be designed to cope with a missile whose dimensions remain fluid will be, as Ainslie was reported as saying in the *Herald*, 'a nightmare'.

Perhaps a bigger nightmare is the destruction of the Non-Proliferation Treaty, which all these new military decisions are calculated to accomplish. Was the NPT founded on illusions? Well, Gordon Brown is playing no small part in dissolving those illusions. What will we then have left but the continuous proliferation that we can already see in development?

Never was there a greater need for a rebirth of the peace movement, and a new campaign for nuclear disarmament.

Democracy – Growing or Dying?

Ken Coates

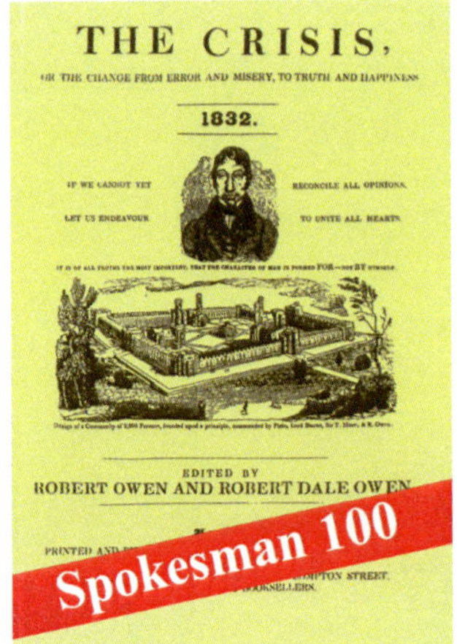

First published in 2008 as the Editorial to Democracy – Growing or Dying? (The Spokesman 100)

This is the hundredth number of *The Spokesman*, so we are expected to have a birthday party. Nostalgia is in order at such events, and we have accordingly devoted quite a large part of this number to reproducing articles and features which involved us, with many of our readers, in a variety of campaigns to change things for the better. Sometimes these have succeeded, if only, say the sceptics, in provoking our old antagonists to find new ways to make them worse again. Sometimes they have failed, only to stiffen our resolve to try again, when times may be more propitious for their success.

There are, of course, a number of key concerns which have continuously preoccupied us. There has been no possibility of forgetting, even temporarily, the desperate urgency of the struggle for peace and disarmament. It has been quite possible, but very regrettable, to forget the struggle for the widening and deepening of democracy, and this possibility has been amply brought into evidence by the progress of sundry statesmen, not to say less elevated tribunes of the people, some of whom have opted for popular emancipation, one at a time, me first.

This kind of apostasy does discourage people, if only temporarily. If hope springs eternal, so too does the aspiration for effective power over the terms and conditions of our own lives.

Politicians commonly tell us that the major social struggles are about power. 'We need' they say, 'power to prevent the next war, or to save the environment from destruction, or to protect people from exploitation and domination.' That is one way of putting it, but there are dangers wrapped up in it. Power does not come sanitised, pre-packed only for good causes. Time and again there is contrary evidence. What we really need is the annulment of power, so that none can make wars, burn the atmosphere, or lower the people into misery. Yet if we are to avoid the charge of piety, toothless anarchism, empty promises, then we have to concede that the first step to a higher freedom requires that we learn the necessary arts to stop the various evil-doers who breed for us all these wars, depredations and oppressions. But if such steps are truly to lead upwards, then the higher freedom itself must always remain in mind.

Fittingly, we have chosen a number of contributions by our founder upon which to thread the thoughts of our contributors on these matters. Bertrand Russell reviewed one of our books, Max Beer's *History of British Socialism*, when it first appeared shortly after the First World War. He highlighted Beer's acute perception that the English establishment could vainly attempt to school their people in the rites of caution and conservatism, but 'in periods of general upheavals … the English are apt to throw their mental ballast overboard and take the lead in revolutionary thought and action. In such a period we are living now'. After a long and depressing lull in their energies, it could be that we may be about to see their strong renewal very soon.

Russell's appreciation of the roots of English socialism is exemplified in the article we have reproduced by John Hughes and Charles Atkinson. This was initially commissioned for a book to celebrate Russell's centenary, and was published by Spokesman in 1972.

Three other contributions which we have selected from among many celebrate the movement for industrial democracy. In one of them, Karl William Kapp draws attention to the sharp growth in pollution which has resulted from rapid industrial development. Kapp's profound scholarship recalls the natural, as well as social spoliation chronicled by Marx and Engels which accompanied extensive air and water pollution, and gave rise to an early, and profound concern by trade unions to encourage environmental protection. When we published Kapp's article in *The Spokesman*, we were able to use it as a key text for a conference on Socialism and the Environment, in which we brought together a number of specialists including F. E. Le Gros Clark and Lord Boyd Orr, and activists such as Colin Stoneman, Malcolm Caldwell and John Lambert, who agreed to continue their work by establishing the Socialist Environmental and Resources Association, which carries on to this day.

Quite different but every bit as audacious is the contribution from Mike Cooley, which starts from the same premises, but, based on the author's profound experience of trade unionism in a high-tech industry, goes on to explore the prospects for long-term development of new techniques to benefit the natural and social environment. This great labour was stimulated by the fear of retrenchment in the Aerospace industry, when Tony Benn invited the shop stewards at Lucas Aerospace to put forward proposals for alternative uses which could harness the skill and creativity of a workforce whose talents would otherwise be jettisoned on the scrapheap of already widespread unemployment.

Cooley's team of shop stewards deliberately designed their research to cause 'respondents to think of products not merely for their exchange value but for their use value'.

They collected a large number of proposals for new products, and grouped them into six major ranges containing technical details, economic calculations and even engineering drawings. They sought a mix of products, some of which would be profitable under market criteria and some of which might not necessarily be profitable 'but would be highly socially useful'. After encouraging this enormous effort by trade unionists, Tony Benn was unable to see it through to fruition because he was redeployed by Harold Wilson in a cabinet reshuffle following the referendum on British membership of the European Community. Benn's demotion took him off to exile in the Department of Energy, and gave the subjects of the Department of Industry into the care of Eric Varley, whose appetite for industrial democracy had already diminished somewhat since he tasted the fruits of office.

The Spokesman never abandoned its interest and concern for democratic reform, especially in the areas of industrial autocracy and dictatorship. But we also maintained a continuous interest in the question of peace and disarmament, on which we have chosen two of our articles to celebrate the launch and development of the campaign for European Nuclear Disarmament. We launched this campaign alongside Edward Thompson, Dan Smith, Mary Kaldor and nuclear disarmament veterans such as Peggy Duff and Bruce Kent.

It was agreed that the Russell Foundation should canvass European support for this appeal, with the aim of convening a representative European Conference or Convention. After vigorous preparations the first such Convention met in Brussels in 1982, and it was agreed to follow it with a second such Convention in Berlin the following year. Retrospectively we can see that this marked the high-water mark of the END campaign.

It brought together strong representation from all the peace movements and pacifist groupings, together with most of the main European left and centre left political parties. The German Social Democrats and Greens were powerfully represented, as were the Italian Communists, the Labour Party and a cross-section of Scandinavians. We received strong support from Alva

Myrdal, the pioneering Minister for Disarmament in Sweden.

All this gave rise to profound misgivings in the Soviet Peace Committee which did not relish the success of another peace movement which was non-aligned. We have reproduced some of the salient papers which reflect this controversy. In those far off days the Labour Party in Britain agreed for the simultaneous dissolution of the North Atlantic Treaty Organisation and the Warsaw Pact. The Warsaw Pact dissolved itself many years ago, but the North Atlantic Treaty still seeks to expand itself eastwards to the great distress of all those against whom it is directed. Even if it reached as far as Vladivostok we sometimes get the impression that it would need new outlaws to mobilise against. President Eisenhower was right to warn us against the Military Industrial Complex, of which Nato is the living embodiment. If we continue to generate another hundred numbers of this journal, while we have breath left, we shall resist these embodiments of militarism, and continue to devote our energies to laying the foundations of the peaceful commonwealth which will come into existence with the abolition of war.

* * *

Eppur si muove

Of course the struggle continues. Labouring to produce 100 numbers of *The Spokesman* has taught us that none of our institutions can be taken for granted. The advance of democracy, in particular, needs to be maintained vigorously, or it will go into retreat. Years ago, Eric Hobsbawm wrote a famous article: 'The Forward March of Labour Halted'. But he did not accurately diagnose what caused the arrest. Actually, the trade unions continued to grow long after Hobsbawm thought that they were becalmed. The growth of trade union membership represented a growth in the negative power of Labour. It could block measures which offended it, but found the initiation of positive change far more difficult. That is why the 1970s began with a resounding debate about industrial democracy, leading to the Bullock Report and proposals for reform. These were all negated by a Parliament jealous of its powers, and above all anxious not to use them. Had the unions been able to initiate positive changes, British history might have been completely different. But the defeat of this impulse led directly to Mrs Thatcher, mass unemployment, and the wholesale reduction of trade union influence. It also led to an abrogation of many traditional democratic checks and balances.

Today, a new crisis is on us, and there may be a new birth of trade union disquiet. Can this mutate into positive change? If it does not, the future may be dire.

Selected Titles by Ken Coates

Available from www.spokesmanbooks.org

St Ann's: Poverty, deprivation and morale in a Nottingham Community
With Richard Silburn, first published in 1967, re-published by Spokesman, 2007

Poverty: the forgotten Englishmen
With Richard Silburn, first published in 1970, re-published by Spokesman, 2007

Workers' Control: Readings and Witnesses
With Tony Topham, first published in 1968, re-published by Spokesman, 2005

Beyond Wage Slavery
Spokesman, 1977

The Right to Useful Work
Ken Coates, Editor, first published in 1978

Work-ins, Sit-ins and Industrial Democracy
Spokesman, 1981

The Making of the Labour Movement: The Formation of the TGWU
Written with Tony Topham. Spokesman, 1994

Workers' Control: Another World is Possible
Spokesman, 2003

Heresies: Resist Much, Obey Little
Spokesman, 1982

Empire No More! ... the Lion and Wolf Shall Cease
Spokesman, 2004

The Most Dangerous Decade: World Militarism and the New Non-Aligned Movement
Spokesman, 1984

Think Globally, Act Locally: The United Nations and the Peace Movements
Spokesman, 1988

The Social Democrats: Those who went and those who stayed
Spokesman, 1983

Common Ownership: Clause Four and the Labour Party
Spokesman, 1995

The Blair Revelation: Deliverence for whom?
With Michael Barratt Brown, Spokesman, 1996

An extensive bibliography of Ken Coates' work is available on request.

Ken Coates Archives

Ken Coates's extensive political and parliamentary archives are housed at Manuscripts and Special Collections, University of Nottingham together with the archives of the Institute for Workers' Control.

www.nottingham.ac.uk/manuscriptsandspecialcollections